Watercolor Your Way to Peace

Painting Lessons for Nervous System Regulation, Energy Release, and Intuitive Creativity

STEPHANIE RYAN

rockynook

Watercolor Your Way to Peace: Painting Lessons for Nervous System Regulation,
Energy Release, and Intuitive Creativity
Stephanie Ryan

Editor: Kelly Reed
Project manager: Lisa Brazieal
Marketing Manager: Koryn Olage
Copyeditor: Linda Laflamme
Interior layout: Maureen Forys
Cover design: Frances Baca
Cover image: Stephanie Ryan

ISBN: 979-8-88814-491-6
1st Edition (1st printing, 2026)

Rocky Nook Inc.
1010 B Street, Suite 350
San Rafael, CA 94901
USA
www.rockynook.com
info@rockynook.com
(415) 747-8756

Represented in the E.U. by:
Rheinwerk Verlag GmbH
Rheinwerkallee 4
53227 Bonn
Germany
service@rheinwerk-verlag.de

Distributed in the UK and Europe by Publishers Group UK
Distributed in the U.S. and all other territories by Publishers Group West

This book is printed on acid-free paper.
Printed in China.

Contents

PART ONE

Building a Gentle Foundation

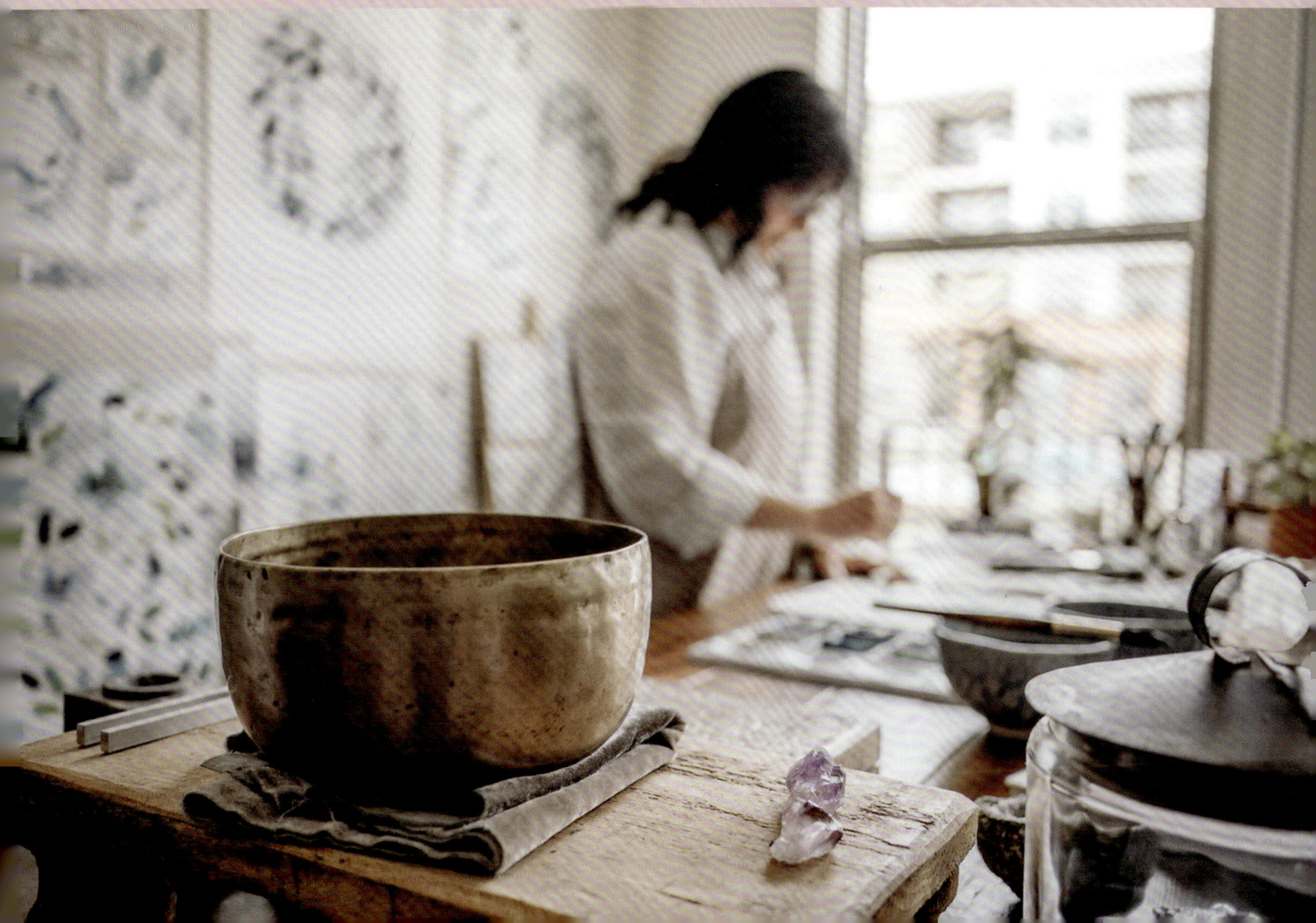

An Invitation

This book isn't really about becoming a better artist or even becoming an artist at all (though, if that happens for you, how amazing). Its true purpose is to guide you, intuitively and practically, through simple, supportive watercolor rituals that will help you to slow down, calm your nervous system, and come back into a relationship with yourself.

You don't need art experience. In fact, you don't need to know what you're doing at all! All you need is a willingness to show up, pick up a paintbrush, and move a little color around on the page in these intentional ways.

I'm Stephanie Ryan, your guide, and I'm *really* glad you're here.

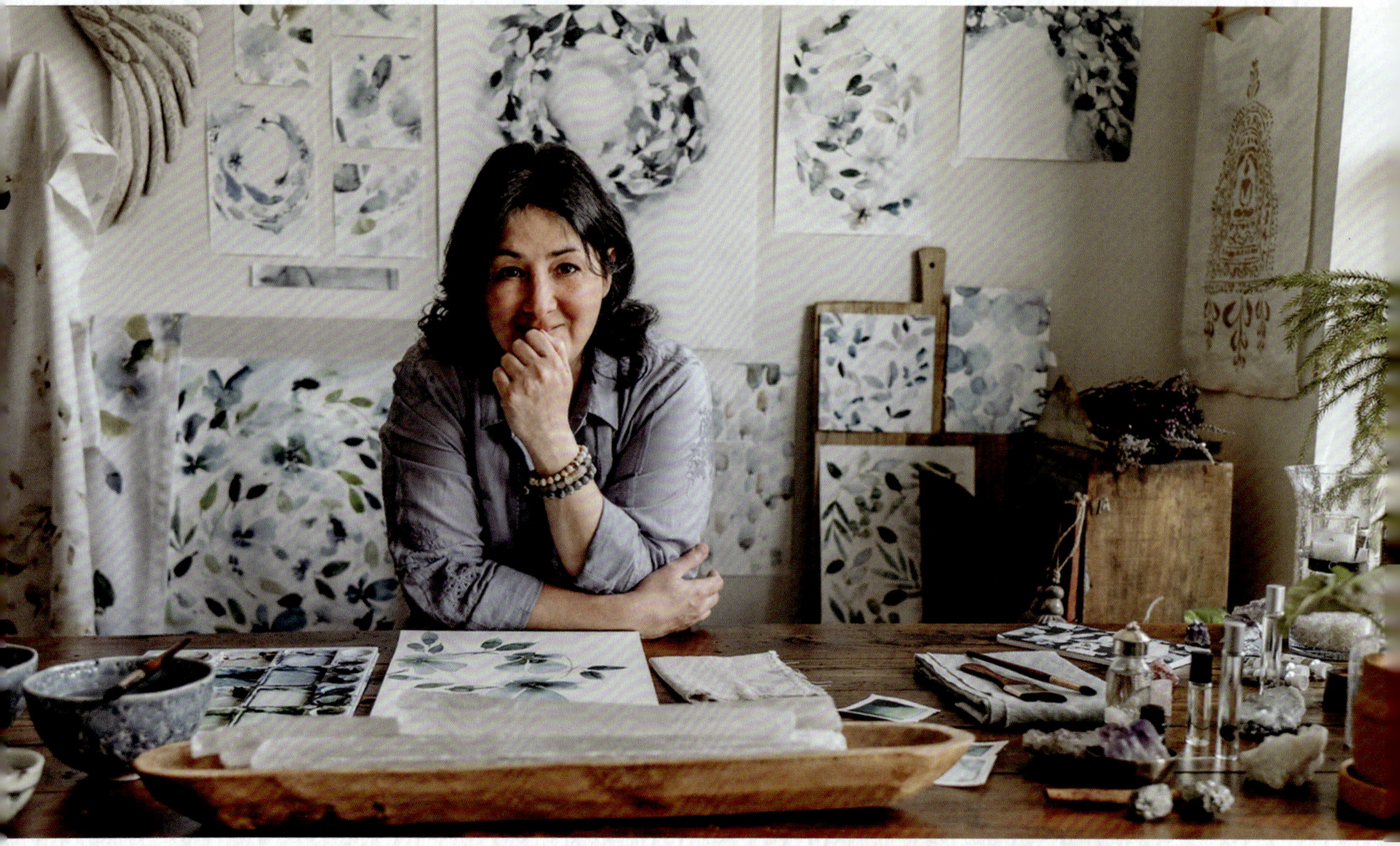

A Note About this Book

For a long time, I was tired in a way I didn't yet have language for. I was not just physically tired, but tired in my nervous system and in my body, in a deeper place that I couldn't quite name.

What I didn't know was that I was dealing with chronic anxiety. Back then, I had never even heard the term "nervous system dysregulation." I thought of myself as a pretty calm, laid-back person, so anxiety didn't really seem to apply—and yet, something didn't feel right.

When I began working with a therapist, I started learning more about what the nervous system was and how much it was shaping the way I experienced life. I started to understand that my body had been under long periods of stress and got stuck in survival mode, even though nothing looked obviously wrong. Around that same time, I began thinking about my art differently.

Painting had always been a place where I felt a little more grounded and a little more present. Somewhere along the way, I found myself wondering what might happen if I intentionally paired my watercolor painting with the same gentle regulation tools I was learning for myself about the nervous system.

My intention was not to create perfect paintings or push myself creatively. It was simply to create a sacred, ritual space around my painting practice, one that would be supportive to the mental, emotional, and physical healing I was already doing elsewhere.

This changed everything.

I began experimenting with simple watercolor exercises that I could practice alongside the nervous system tools I was learning as a way to gently support my own healing. Over time, those personal experiments grew into a consistent practice, which grew into my watercolor teaching, and now, they've grown into this book.

This is why the lessons inside these pages are intentionally simple and repetitive. It's also why they use lots of water, slow movement, and predictable patterns. When painting your way into safety and calm, it's important to place more emphasis on how you *feel* while you paint rather than the result of what you create.

If you're carrying stress, anxiety, or exhaustion, I want you to know you're not alone. Your nervous system has been doing its best to protect you. Somewhere along the way, it forgot what it was like to return to safety.

This book is my offering to you: a set of simple rituals you can return to again and again to support your nervous system and find safety within yourself.

My Story

When I was twenty-nine, I was fine one day and chronically ill the next, without warning and without a clear explanation. My body simply stopped working the way it always had, and I found myself suddenly in pain.

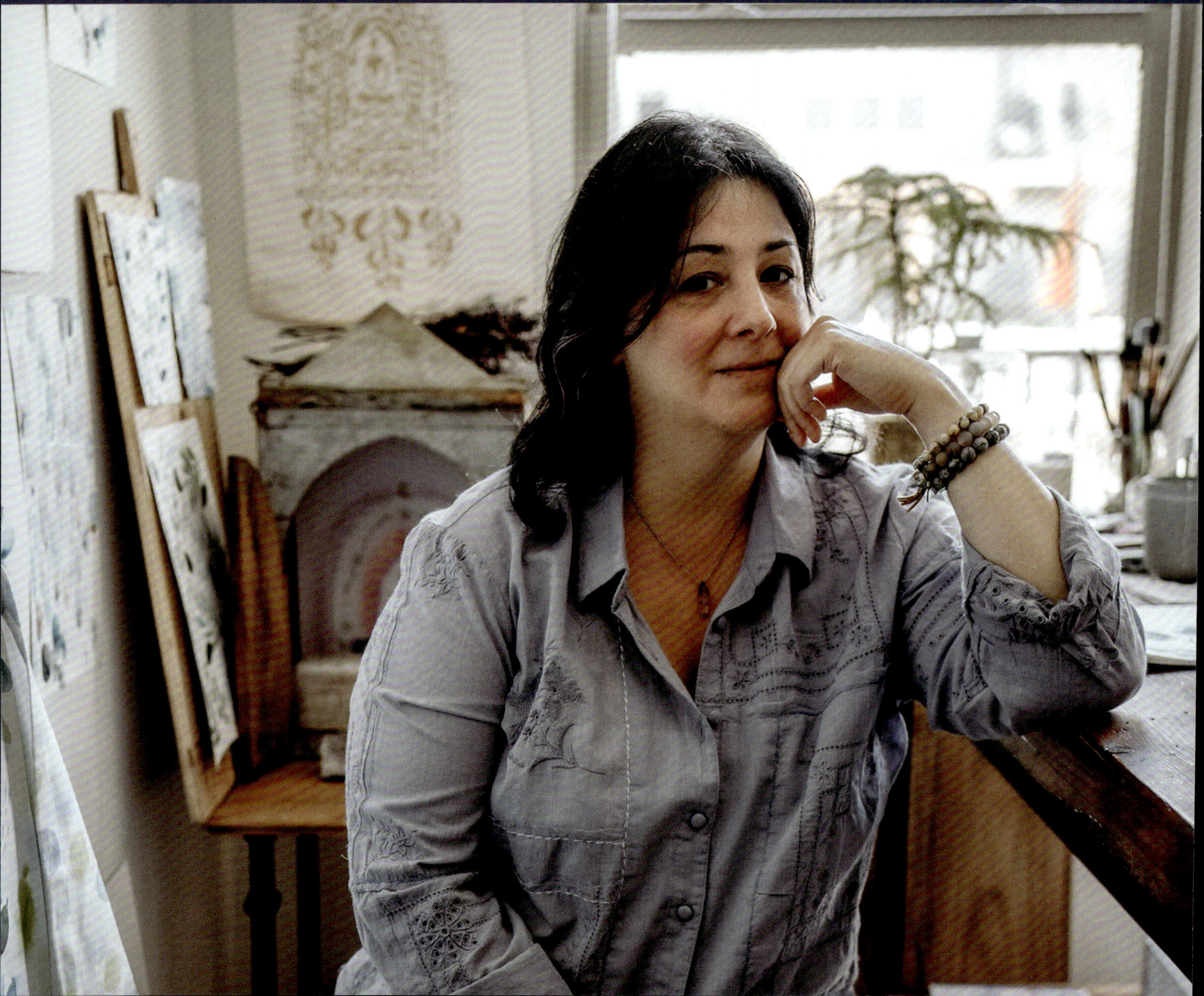

1

I was exhausted all the time and struggling with a kind of brain fog that made it hard to think clearly. At the time, I had no idea my life was about to take a sharp turn or that it would force me onto a healing path that would shape everything that came after.

For a long time, I lived with the same question: "What is *wrong* with me?" I made appointments to every kind of practitioner I could find: medical doctors, functional medicine doctors, psychologists, and energy healers. I desperately tried protocols, supplements, therapies, and treatments, always intensely hoping the next thing would finally be the answer!

Sometimes I would feel a little better, sometimes I would feel worse. But most of the time, nothing truly changed in any kind of way that lasted.

It would take eleven years before I finally received a diagnosis: I had Lyme disease. By then, I was already deeply tired from searching for answers, but I decided to move forward with the treatment anyway. For the next three months, I was in a clinic, five days a week, four hours at a time, with antibiotics running through a PICC line in my arm. That PICC line left a scar I still carry as a reminder of that chapter of my life. But when the treatment ended, I didn't feel better.

In time, my symptoms settled to a level I could *somewhat* manage, but life for me had become a daily exercise in endurance. I woke up every morning feeling like I had been hit by a bus: My body carried so much hurt, my energy was severely limited, and my mind was in a constant fog. Yet, somehow, I kept going.

In that first decade of illness, life still happened. I got married, went back to art school, began work as a designer, moved several times, and, eventually, went through a divorce as well. On the outside, I like to imagine it looked like I was functioning, but on the inside, I was silently struggling.

There were many moments when I felt completely lost. There were also many small sparks of hope that kept me going. One of those sparks arrived in the most unexpected way.

Painting in Bed

During this difficult season, I carried a secret dream of becoming a self-employed artist, even though I didn't know what kind of artist I wanted to be. At the time, I was mostly doing graphic artwork on a computer and rarely painting. By the time I got home from work each night, I was usually too exhausted to even consider pulling out my art supplies.

Then one evening, I was lying in bed, feeling overwhelmed by all the ideas and longings swirling inside me. I wanted *so badly* to paint but had zero energy to get up and go into another room. And then, I heard the very soft whisper of my inner voice say, "paint in bed."

I immediately thought this was a ridiculous idea. But as I considered it, I realized that watercolor actually could work. It was simple and gentle and doable from a bed in a way nothing else was.

Somehow, this gave me the smallest push to heave myself up from bed and shuffle around my art studio, grabbing my small set of watercolors, some paper, a few brushes, and a cup of water. I placed my water on my nightstand, spread out the rest of the supplies in front of me, and started painting watercolor flowers right there in bed.

I felt something shift almost immediately!

I explored and played and was completely absorbed in what I was doing. For the first time in a very long time, I didn't notice how tired I felt. That first night changed my whole future.

Soon after, I bought one of those little rolling carts that can slide over a bed and began to create a tiny studio around myself. From this little spot, painting became my regular practice. I had no plan and no need to do it for anyone else, just simply for me. Painting became the place I could rest, the place where I forgot about symptoms for a while, and the place where I felt a small sense of freedom open up inside my body. I didn't know it then, but I had just begun using art as a form of self-regulation. I was about to begin to truly heal.

Finding My Way as an Artist

As I kept painting in my bed, something inside me started to wake up. Yes, I was making beautiful flowers, but I was also developing a style and starting to recognize my own voice in my work. I began imagining what it might look like to actually build a life around art instead of squeezing it into the edges of an already exhausting day.

I had known about art licensing for years through the design world and had always loved the idea of creating artwork that could live on products like greeting cards, calendars, fabric, dinnerware, and home décor. What I didn't have before was the energy, clarity, or consistency to truly go after those kinds of projects. Painting in bed changed that.

It was a sentimental day when I moved from painting in bed to painting in my art room. A true testament to art working like medicine. Little by little, I began practicing more, developing small collections, and building a body of work that felt cohesive. I started believing that maybe, *maybe,* I could really do this!

A series of synchronistic events then occurred. I landed some freelance contracts, which gave me the financial bridge I needed to leave my full-time job. From there, I poured myself into building my portfolio, refining my style, and learning everything I could about licensing. I eventually found an agent and officially started my art business.

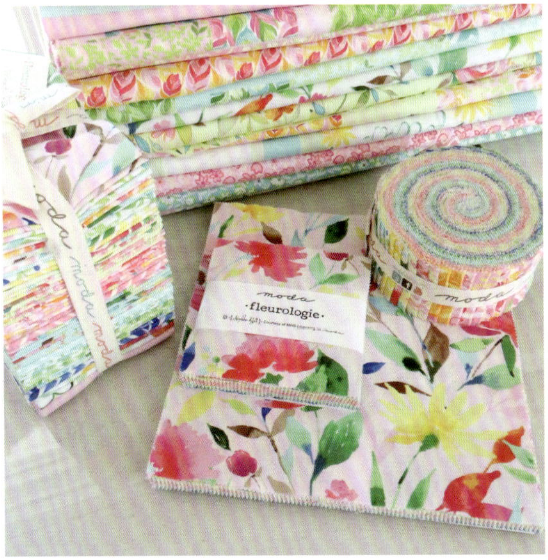
moda
·fleurologie·

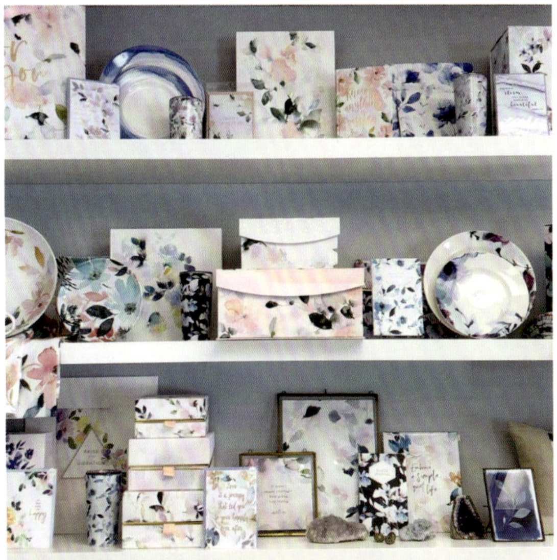

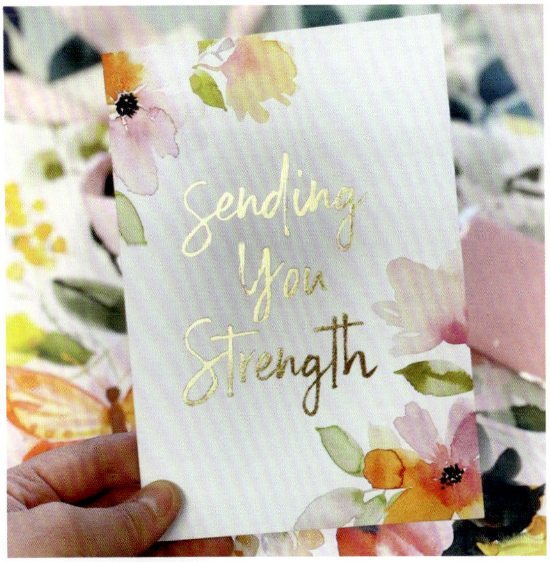
Sending You Strength

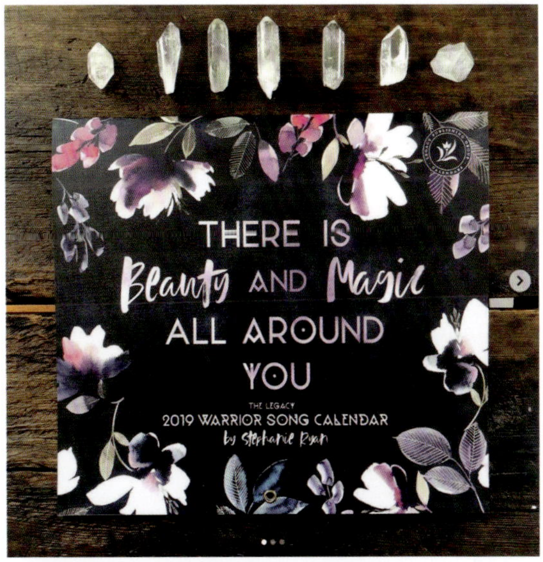
THERE IS
Beauty AND Magic
ALL AROUND
YOU
THE LEGACY
2019 WARRIOR SONG CALENDAR
by Stephanie Ryan

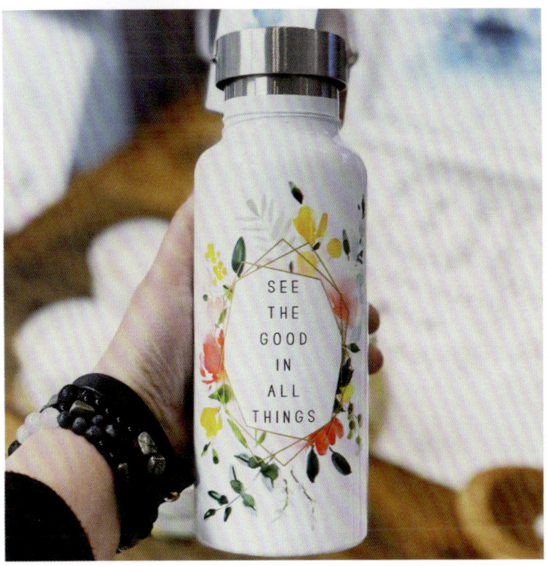
SEE THE GOOD IN ALL THINGS

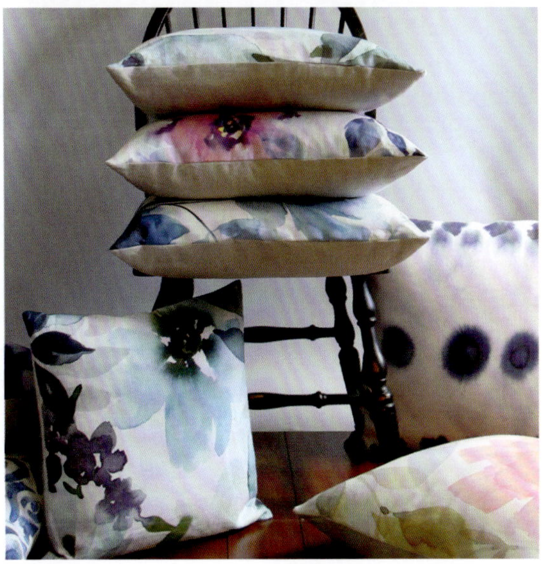

Over time, to my pleasure, my artwork began appearing on greeting cards, calendars, dinnerware, shower curtains, wall art, fabric, and many other products. It has been seen in HomeGoods, Target, Kohl's, Anthropologie, Macy's, and gift stores around the world.

From the outside, it looked like I had made it. And in many ways, I had.

Yet, there was still a quiet voice inside me that kept saying there was more for me. Even though I couldn't quite put my finger on it, I knew there was more meaning to be found in my artwork.

When Life Cracked Open

As my art business grew, life shifted in big ways. Around this time, I got divorced, sold my house, and moved back to Chester County, PA, to be closer to my family. For a while, I lived alone and worked from home. This felt so safe and simple, like I had created a life that worked for my nervous system (even though I didn't know that language yet).

Then I met someone and started a new relationship—not an easy feat for someone in their fifties.

In January of 2021, I lost my dad. Not long after, my mom had a heart attack. Around the same time, I was forced to leave the beautiful little cottage I had been renting on a thirty-acre horse farm. Within a short span of time, the ground beneath me dissolved—then I got Lyme disease, *again*.

It felt shocking, and yet the symptoms eventually improved this time around. What I was just beginning to understand through all this was that I was still carrying layers of old stress, trauma, and emotional weight, most of which I still struggled to name. A couple years later, I endured the passing of my mom. This was heartbreaking, but also, in its own painful way, it would become another part of my healing, showing me how much I had already survived and how much I still wanted to heal.

Glimmers of Answers

In the middle of life cracking open in so many ways, small glimmers started showing up, little synchronistic events that pointed me toward answers. One night, I came across a video about something called depersonalization and derealization (DPDR) and heard someone describe an experience that felt exactly like mine: that sense of being slightly disconnected from reality, like there was a thin glass wall between me and the world around me. For the first time, I realized I wasn't crazy.

I went on to find out that DPDR is often connected to chronic anxiety and long-term nervous system dysregulation, and then later learned that parts of my brain and nervous system had been stuck in a protective loop for years, trying to keep me safe long after the danger had passed. These realizations changed everything.

Where Everything Came Together

So, I dove in with all I had to learn about nervous system regulation. By practicing some simple techniques, little by little, my body started to respond: My mind felt clearer, my body felt calmer, and I began having moments where I felt more like myself. To my delight and relief, those moments slowly began to last longer. As these things go, nothing happened overnight, but I could feel that something *real* was shifting.

As my nervous system learned to settle, I naturally used my art differently. It stopped being about creating a finished product and transformed into a quiet form of support and self-care.

I painted slower, using repetition and allowing simple, predictable movements to lead the process. I noticed that when I painted this way, my breath would soften, my shoulders would relax, and my mind would become quieter. Painting became so much more than just a way for me to express my creativity; it became a way to tend to my nervous system and a new way to quietly heal in my daily life.

This was the beginning of what eventually became "Paint Your Way to Peace," my online journey into healing the nervous system through watercolor, a toolkit of rituals where painting evolves from just making art and turns into a gentle tool for calming your nervous system, easing you out of survival mode, and creating a felt sense of safety in your body, mind, and heart.

This book brings all those rituals together in one place. It's the result of a long road for me, moving from illness to insight, from surviving daily life to healing in my daily hobby, and from painting in bed to creating a career where I get to now share this gentle practice with you.

What I learned along this winding, difficult path is that healing yourself is not about fixing everything yourself. More often, it's about finding simple rituals and tools that help you feel safe inside yourself. For me, the most powerful tool is painting rituals, and now I get to place those in your hands!

place where you could set things down, take a breath, and gently relax.

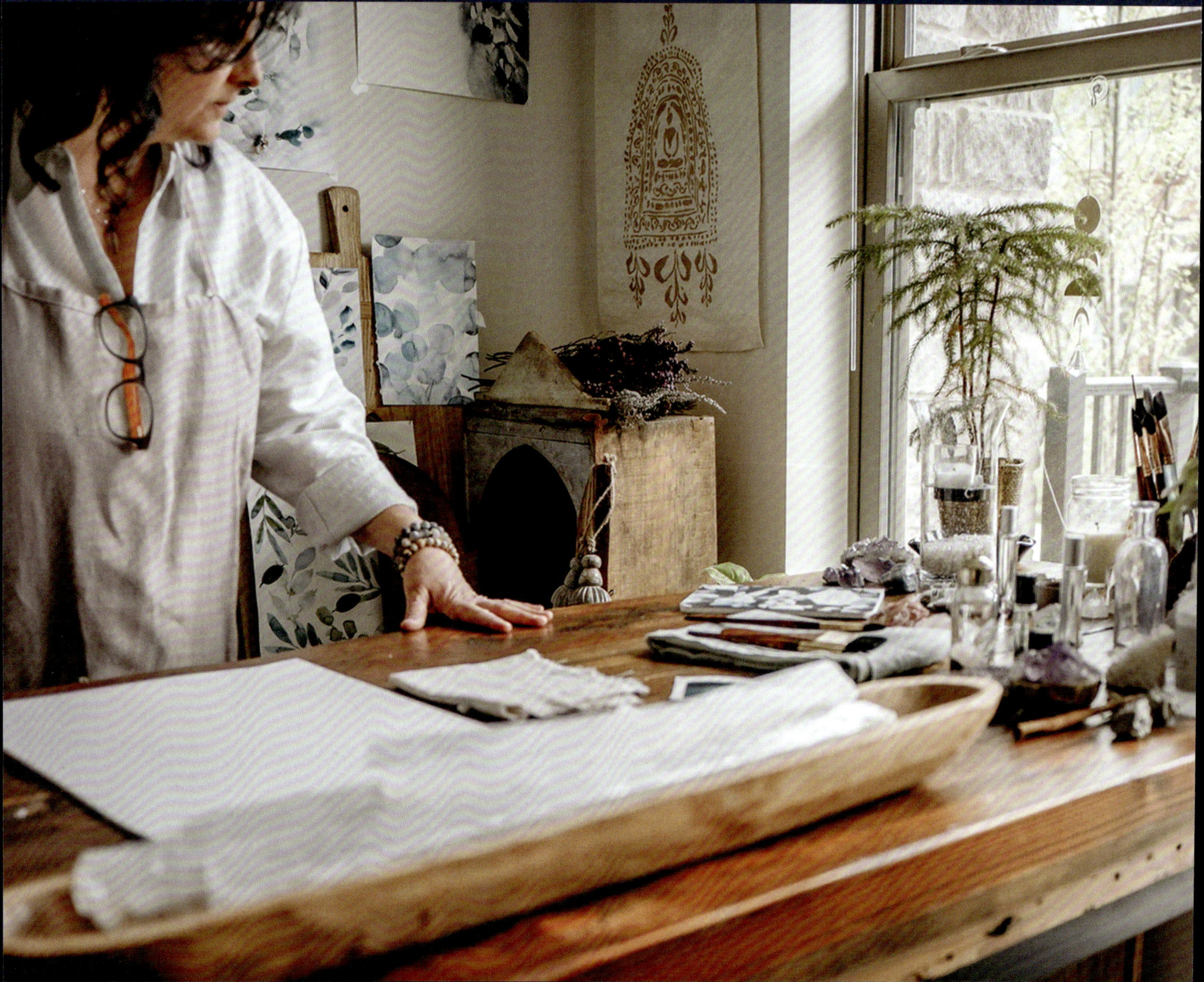

2

This book is not meant to be rushed. It is not a program you have to move through quickly, and it is not something you need to finish in order to receive its benefits.

Think of it as a gentle companion rather than another thing on your to-do list.

You are invited to move through it at your own pace and in your own rhythm, in a way that feels supportive to your nervous system. Begin at the start and move through slowly, or open to the lesson that feels most relevant in the moment. You may find yourself returning to the same lesson again and again, especially during stressful times. There is no wrong way to do this.

Each lesson introduces a simple nervous system regulation tool, followed by a painting exercise, and then guides you into a *painting meditation*. Basically, you can learn the technique, practice until you feel comfortable, and then move into the slower, more peaceful experience of painting as meditation. You will also find gentle moments for integration and journal prompts, offering you space to pause and notice what you experienced.

Some days you may paint for twenty minutes. Some days, five minutes may be enough, or you may simply set up your space and breathe. All of it counts.

You may notice different things as you work with these practices. Some days you may feel calmer. Some days, you may notice emotions rising, tenderness, or restlessness. Some days you may not notice much at all. All of these experiences are normal, and what matters most is that you are showing up for yourself.

Take your time and breathe through it. This book is for your self-care. Trust the process.

A Gentle Safety Note

This book is intended to be a supportive and educational resource and is not a substitute for medical, psychological, or mental health care. I am not diagnosing, treating, or curing any condition, and I encourage you to continue working with qualified healthcare professionals for your individual needs. As you explore the lessons and exercises, you are invited to listen to your body with kindness and to move at a pace that feels safe for you. If at any point something feels overwhelming or activating, it is okay to pause, to slow down, or to seek additional support. You know yourself best.

Understanding Your Nervous System

Your nervous system is the part of you that is always sensing, listening, and responding to your inner and outer world, quietly gathering information and constantly asking a very simple question: Am I safe right now, or am I in danger?

Long before your thinking mind has time to analyze a situation, your nervous system has already taken in signals from your body, your breath, your heart, your memories, your past experiences, and the environment around you, and it begins organizing your internal world based on what it perceives.

When your nervous system senses safety, your body naturally shifts into a state that supports rest, digestion, repair, creativity, and connection. This is a state often referred to as the *parasympathetic nervous system* or *rest and digest*. This is where your breath flows more freely, your muscles soften, your digestion works more smoothly, your immune system functions more effectively, and your mind tends to feel clearer and steadier. In this state, you may notice that you feel more present in your body, more emotionally available, and more able to respond to life with flexibility instead of bracing against it.

When your nervous system senses danger, whether that danger is real in the present moment or connected to past experiences that have not yet been fully processed, your body shifts into a protective state called the *sympathetic nervous system*. This state is where fight, flight, and freeze responses live:

- *Fight* can show up as irritation, anger, frustration, or the urge to push through.
- *Flight* can feel like anxiety, restlessness, overthinking, or the need to stay busy.
- *Freeze* can feel like heaviness, exhaustion, numbness, brain fog, or a sense of being disconnected or stuck.

These responses are not mistakes, and they are not signs that something is wrong with you. They are intelligent survival strategies that developed to help you cope, endure, and get through moments that felt overwhelming or unsafe.

At some point in your life, your nervous system learned that certain patterns helped you survive. Even if those situations are no longer happening, the body can continue running the same protective programs out of habit. It is simply trying to keep you safe in the only way it knows how.

Nervous system regulation is the gentle process of helping your body recognize when it is safe again, so it can gradually move out of chronic survival mode and into a more settled, balanced state.

It is not about forcing yourself to calm down, controlling your thoughts, or fixing who you are, but about offering your body consistent, compassionate signals of safety over time. This matters because healing does not happen only in the mind.

Your nervous system is the bridge between your mind, your body, and your heart. When it is overwhelmed or stuck in survival mode, you may notice that your thoughts feel busy, foggy, or repetitive; your body feels tense, heavy, exhausted, or disconnected; and your emotional world feels guarded, tender, shut down, or easily overwhelmed. As your nervous system begins to regulate, even in small ways, you may start to notice that your thoughts quiet, your breath deepens, your body feels a little safer, and your emotional world feels more accessible and less threatening.

This is why many healing approaches that truly work are body-based and experiential rather than purely intellectual; they meet the nervous system where it lives. Practices such as brain retraining, mindfulness, somatic work, heart-centered practices like HeartMath, breathwork, gentle movement, sound, and rhythm all work in slightly different ways, but they share a common purpose: They help send messages of safety to the nervous system. They all aid the creation of new, more supportive patterns.

Nervous system regulation tools are simply gentle practices that support this process, including things like slow breathing, progressive muscle relaxation, humming or toning, micro-movements, orienting to the room, bilateral movement, heart-focused breathing, and rhythmic, repetitive motion, all of which help remind the body that there is no emergency in this moment.

These tools are not meant to make everything disappear, and they are not about achieving a perfect state of calm. They are about creating small shifts and small openings that, over time, begin to add up in meaningful ways. You may start to notice fewer intense spikes, shorter recovery times after stress, and longer stretches of ease, which is what real, sustainable healing often looks like.

In this book, you will be working with watercolor as one of your nervous system regulation tools, because the water, brush, slow movements, and repetition naturally ease the nervous system, offering predictability in a way the body understands. You do not need to understand all of this perfectly, and you do not need to do it right. You only need to show up, move gently, and allow the process to meet you where you are. Your nervous system already knows how to heal. You are simply learning how to support it.

Watercolor as a Nervous System Tool

For a long time, I didn't think of watercolor painting as something connected to healing, and I certainly did not think of it in terms of the nervous system. I simply noticed that when I painted slowly and repetitively, something inside me began to relax. It wasn't the finished painting that created that shift; it was the experience of moving the brush across the paper, of watching the water spread and color bloom, and of allowing my hands to repeat the same simple shapes over and over again. The process itself became the point. Without fully understanding why, I was giving my nervous system something it had been craving for a long time, which was rhythm, predictability, and calm.

Watercolor is uniquely suited to this kind of work because it does not respond well to force or control. It invites you into a relationship with the water, with patience, and with a certain kind of surrender that asks you to loosen your grip both physically and emotionally. When you press too hard, the paper resists, and when you move too quickly, the water does its own thing anyway. Over time, you begin to realize that gentle movement works better than tension and that allowing creates more beauty than gripping ever could.

As you dip your brush into the water and the color moves slowly across the page, your body begins to settle into the steady rhythm of that movement. The repetition gives your mind something simple to follow, which reduces the need to analyze or problem-solve, and your nervous system begins to receive subtle signals that there is no emergency in this moment.

Because watercolor unfolds naturally in front of you, your attention is gently drawn into the present moment. You notice how the brush feels in your hand, how the water pools at the edge of a stroke, how one color softly blends into another, and in that noticing, your awareness shifts from mental loops into a sensory experience. This movement from thinking to sensing is one of the most powerful ways to support regulation, because the nervous system responds to what is happening in the body more readily than to what is happening in the mind.

There is also something deeply regulating about simplicity. When you are repeating an oval, painting horizontal lines, or creating soft circular shapes again and again, you are reducing decision-making and offering your mind a small, manageable task. In that simplicity, the need to get it right fades into the background, and you relax.

You may notice that as you paint, your shoulders drop without you telling them to, your jaw unclenches, your breathing becomes quieter, and your body feels more supported by the chair beneath you. You may notice that thoughts lose some of their intensity or that emotions feel a little less overwhelming.

When you return to painting again and again with this intention of slowness and repetition, your nervous system begins to associate the act of picking up a brush with safety and care. The simple ritual of gathering your supplies, dipping into water, and watching color spread becomes a familiar pattern that signals to your body that it can relax. Eventually, even the sight of your paint set may begin to evoke a quiet sense of calm because your system has learned through experience that this is a space where it is allowed to rest.

This is why the exercises in this book are intentionally simple and repetitive rather than technically complex. They are designed to support your nervous system first and your artistic skill second. The goal is not to create a perfect painting, but to create a felt sense of safety inside your body while you paint.

In this way, watercolor becomes more than a creative outlet. It becomes a companion in your healing, a steady doorway back into your breath, your body, and your inner world. You do not need experience, talent, or a plan. You need only a willingness to move slowly, to let the water guide you, and to trust that something gentle and meaningful is happening beneath the surface.

That is enough.

Creating Your Sacred Space: Small Rituals Support Your Painting Practice

I began to notice that the way I entered my painting time mattered just as much as what I painted. On the days when I rushed into it or treated it like another task on a long to-do list, it often felt harder to settle into it. On the days when I took a few moments to prepare my space with care, I could feel myself start to relax before I even picked up a brush. I didn't think of this as a ritual at first. I simply found myself naturally wanting to create a comforting space. I wanted to light a candle, put on gentle music, and make a cup of tea in my favorite mug before I began. Without realizing it, I was offering small signals of safety to my nervous system, signals that told my body this was a different kind of moment, one where I didn't need to do anything but slow down and be present.

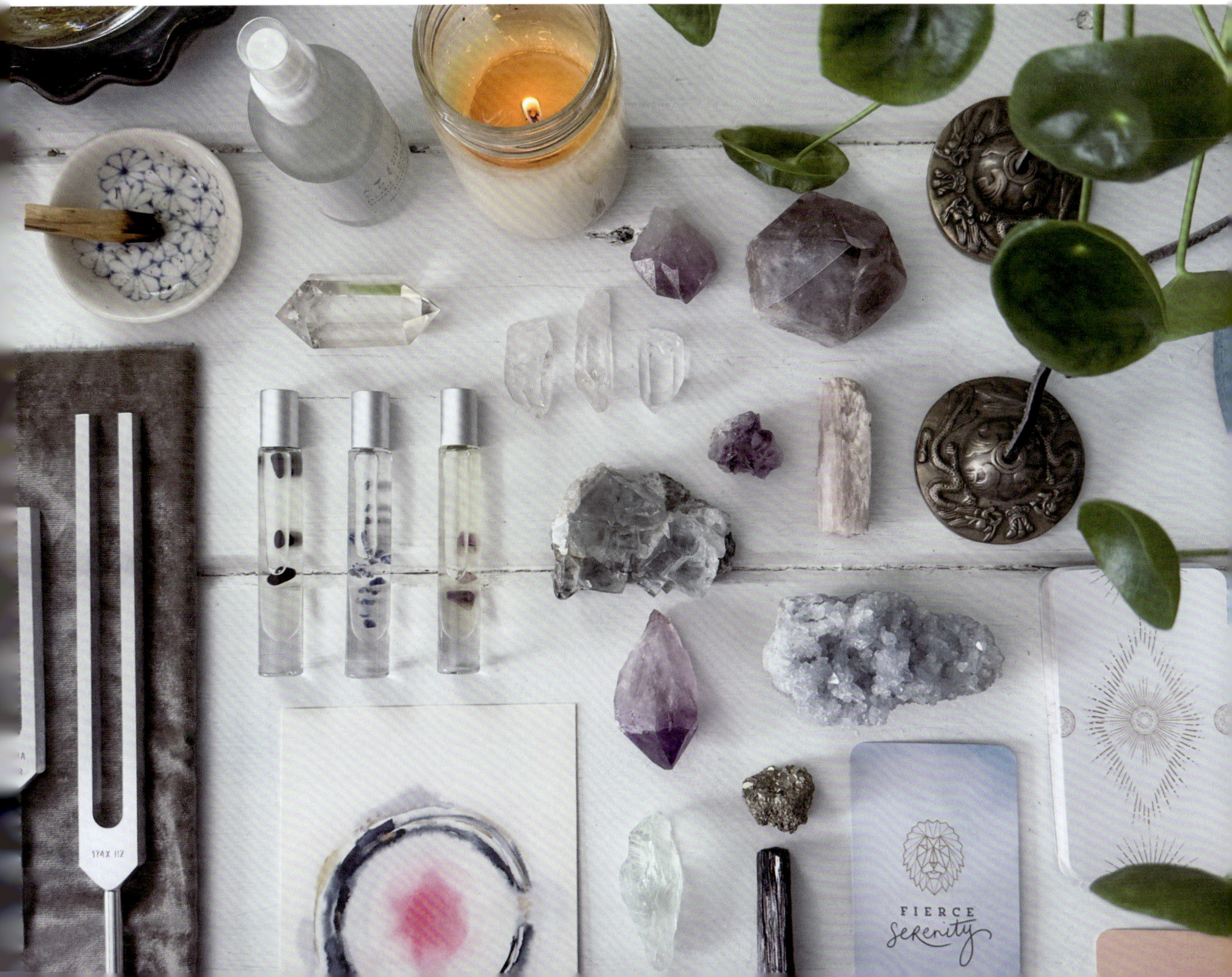

I also began working with objects that carried a subtle sense of meaning for me, such as crystals, essential oils, flower essences, and tuning forks, because they helped me drop more easily into that quiet space. They became gentle reminders that this time was sacred in a very simple way. What I learned through my own experience is that these tools are not separate from the painting meditation. They are part of it. They welcome you into the space and help ground you there.

When you consistently prepare your space in a way that feels calming and intentional, your nervous system begins to recognize the pattern. The simple act of setting out your paints, lighting a candle, or turning on your music can begin to signal that it is safe.

Your sacred space does not need to look like mine, and it doesn't need to be elaborate or perfect. It only needs to feel good to you. It might be a small corner of a table, a spot by a window, or a place you return to again and again because it feels familiar or is easy to work with. What matters most is the feeling of the space, not how it looks.

You are not creating the perfect environment. You are creating a small sanctuary for yourself, and that, in itself, is an act of self-care and a form of healing.

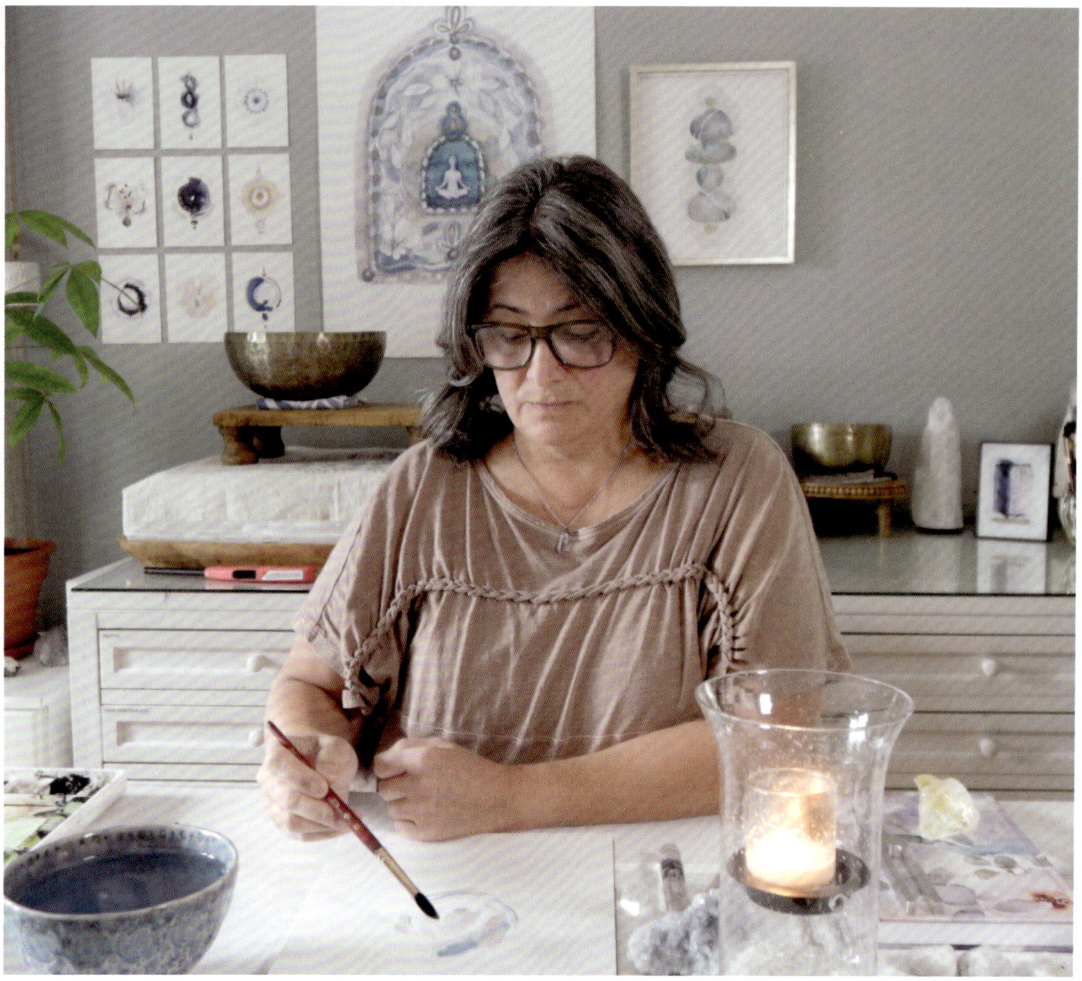

The Painting Meditation

When I first began painting in this slower, more intentional way, I didn't know what I was doing, and I certainly didn't think of it as meditation. I only knew that when I allowed myself to sit quietly with my paints and repeat simple shapes without any pressure to create something impressive, something inside me began to settle in a way that felt both subtle yet profound.

I realized that what was calming me was not the finished painting, but the experience of being fully absorbed in the movement itself. It felt similar to the way people describe meditation, except instead of focusing on my breath alone, I was focusing on the rhythm of my brush and watching the paint and water move across the paper.

A painting meditation is not about creating a picture or capturing a perfect composition. It is an intentional practice where the process becomes the point. Rather than striving toward a result, you are invited to slow down enough to notice how you are holding the brush, how your shoulders feel, how your breath moves as you paint, and what shifts inside you as repetition begins to create its own quiet rhythm.

For me, painting meditation became a doorway into presence during a time when sitting still in silence felt almost impossible. My mind was often busy, and my body carried layers of tension, but when I allowed myself to move slowly with water and color, I could feel my nervous system responding in a way that felt natural rather than forced. The brush gave my mind something simple to follow, and the repetition gave my body something predictable to trust.

As I continued practicing in this way, I began to understand that a painting meditation is less about doing and more about being. It is a space where you are not trying to improve yourself, not trying to produce something worthy, but simply allowing your body and nervous system to soften through intentional movement. The image that appears on the page is secondary to the experience unfolding within you.

When I pair this kind of painting with small rituals, such as lighting a candle or taking a few slow breaths before I begin, the meditation deepens almost effortlessly. The act of sitting down with my paints starts to feel like stepping into a familiar sanctuary where I know my body is allowed to relax.

Gathering Your Materials

You don't need much to begin. Because I know many people are curious, I will share the materials I use, but none of these exact supplies are required.

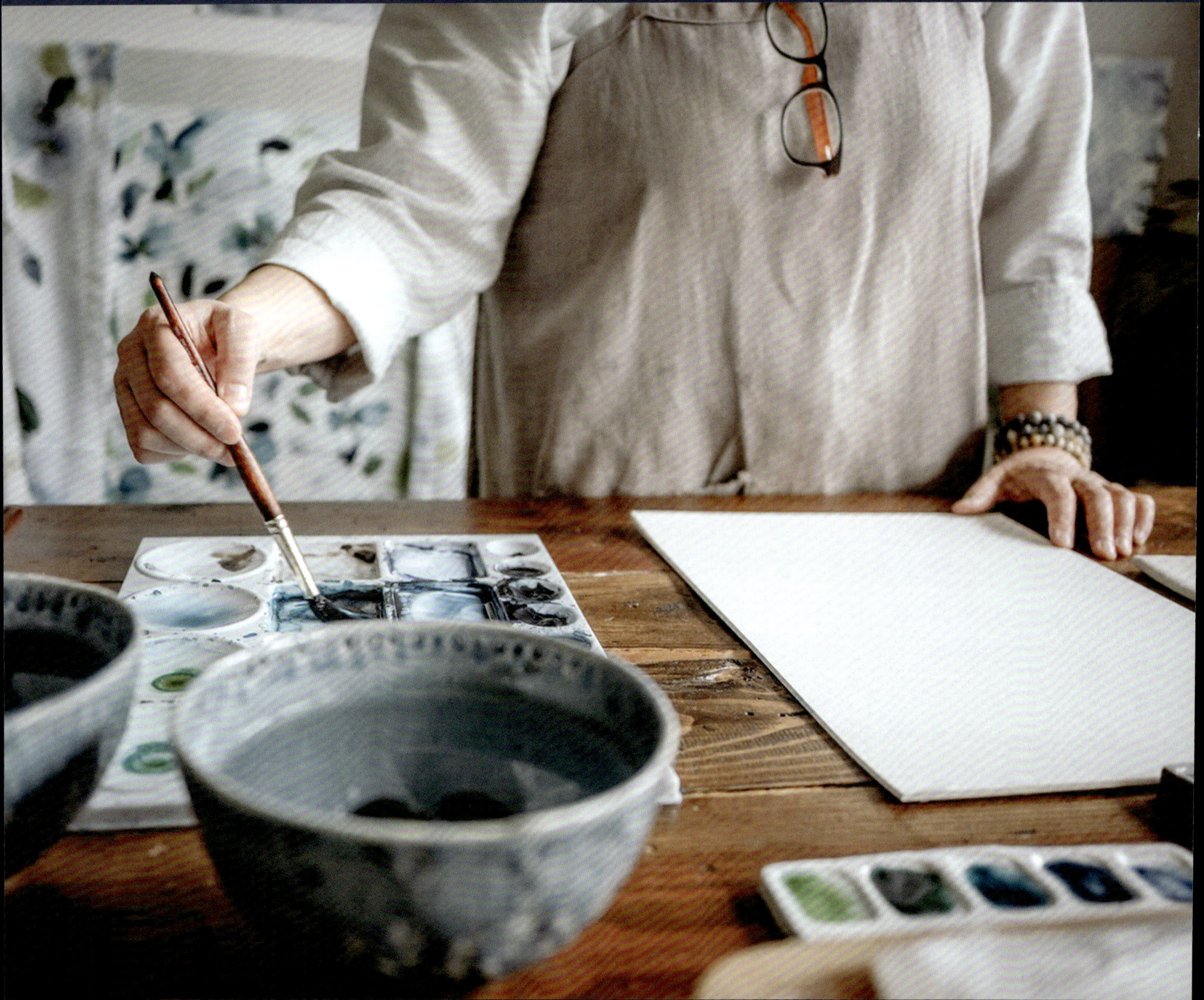

3

I use professional-grade materials because of my art business. You don't have to. Student-grade paints, economical brushes, and basic watercolor paper work beautifully for the book's lessons. Your painting is not about the quality of your supplies. It is about the process and the healing nature of watercolors. Use what you have. If you choose to purchase anything, let it be simple and within your comfort level. You may naturally discover materials you enjoy. There is no rush.

What matters most cannot be bought.

Watercolor Paint

I use a mix of professional and student-grade watercolor paints. Some of my favorite brands are Winsor & Newton (both professional and student grade), Schmincke, and Holbein. I move between these brands freely and usually choose paint based on color rather than brand. If a color speaks to me, I use it.

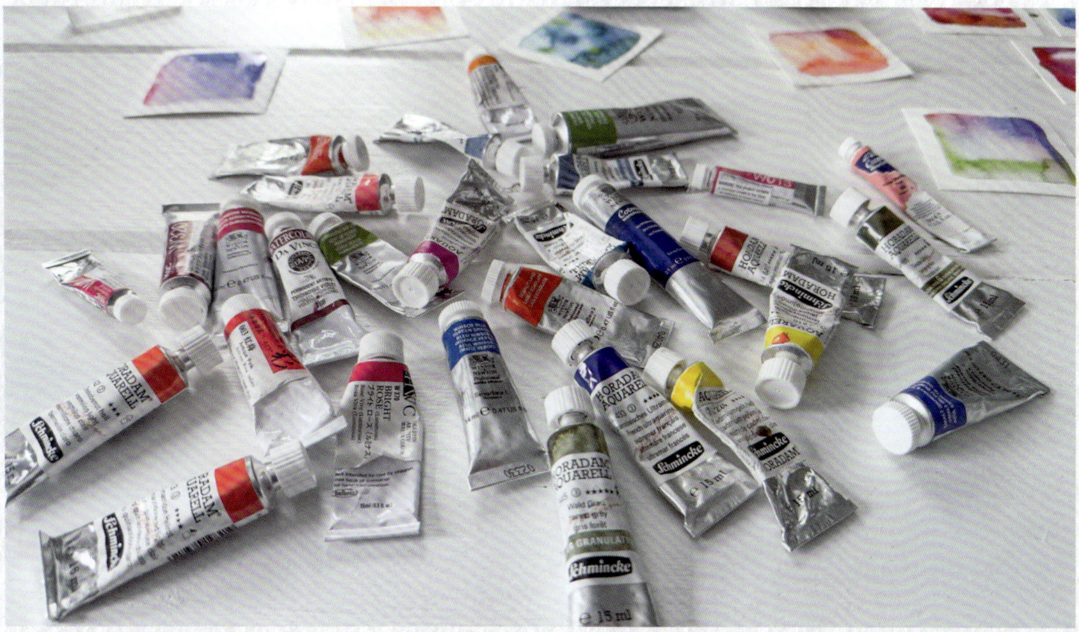

I prefer tube paints, because I like being able to squeeze out paint and mix custom colors on my palette. This is especially helpful in my art licensing work, where I often build specific color palettes for collections. That said, pan paints are wonderful too, and they are often the easiest place to start if you are new to watercolor.

Tube Paints

Tube paints come in small tubes filled with wet watercolor paint. You squeeze a little paint onto a palette, add water, and mix as needed. Tube paints are great if you enjoy mixing colors and experimenting with custom blends. They also last a long time because you need only a small amount at a time.

Pan Paints

Pan paints are small, dried blocks of watercolor that sit inside a palette or case. You activate them by adding water with your brush. They usually come in sets that include a range of colors, which makes them simple and convenient. You open the set, add water, and begin painting.

If you are totally new to watercolor, pan paints are a great place to start. If you do not currently own any paints, start with a small, affordable pan set. That is more than enough to begin, and you can always add individual colors later if you feel called to. What matters most is not how many colors you have or what brand they are. The important part is that the process feels calming, and you don't get overwhelmed. It's easy to feel overwhelmed when buying art supplies.

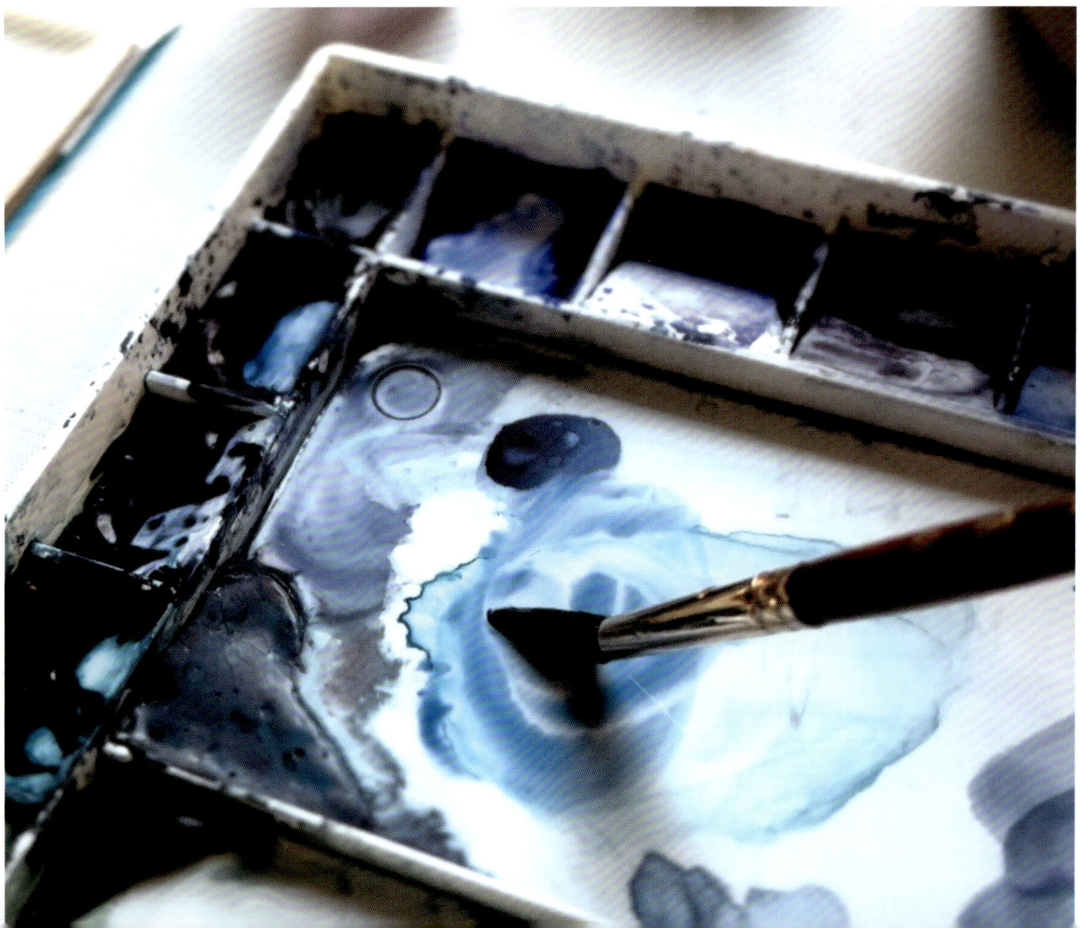

Paint Colors

For reference, here are the colors I use throughout the book:

1. Sap Green (Winsor & Newton)
2. Olive Green (Winsor & Newton)
3. Shadow Green (Holbein)
4. Burnt Umber (Winsor & Newton)
5. Prussian Green (Schmincke)
6. Deep Sea Indigo (Schmincke)
7. Ultramarine Blue (Winsor & Newton, Cotman)
8. Indanthrene Blue (Winsor & Newton)
9. Quinacridone Magenta (Winsor & Newton)
10. Crimson Lake (Holbein)
11. Quinacridone Violet (Schmincke)
12. Winsor Violet (Winsor & Newton)
13. Winsor Yellow (Winsor & Newton)
14. Cadmium Yellow Orange (Holbein)
15. Scarlet Lake (Winsor & Newton)
16. Opera Rose (DaVinci)

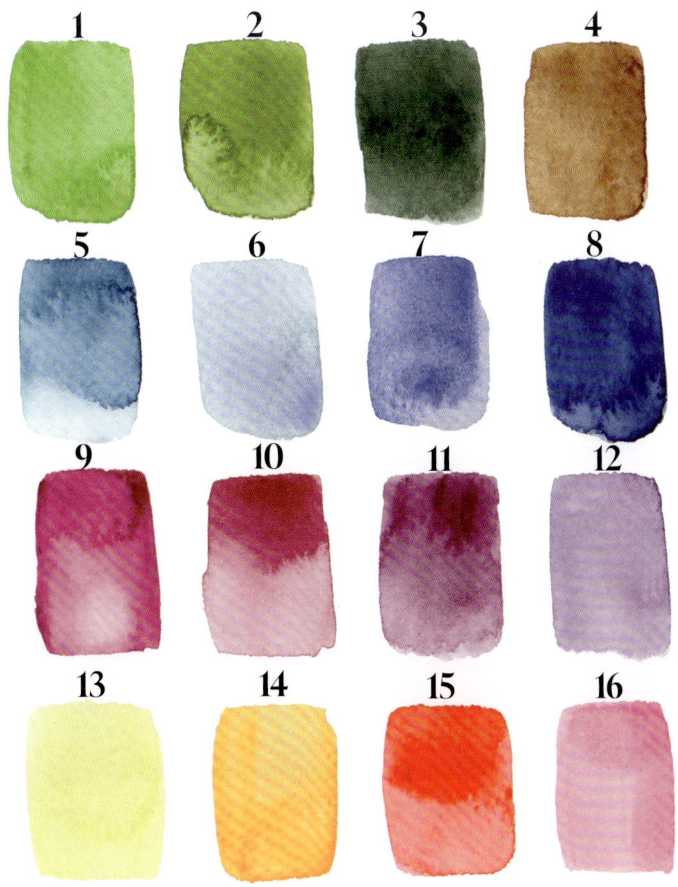

Throughout the book, however, I won't mention the specific paints I used for the lessons. Why? Because you do not need to use the exact same colors as me to receive the benefits of the practice. The lessons are not about creating something perfect or matching a specific palette. They are about slowing down, exploring the movement of paint and water, and allowing yourself to be present with the process. Let your intuition guide you. Use whatever colors you already have. Or, if a particular one of my colors just calls to you, find and try it. Either way, the simple act of painting is what matters most.

Watercolor Brushes

Over the years, I've experimented with a lot of different brushes. The ones I reach for most often are the Princeton Neptune Synthetic Squirrel brushes in round and flat shapes. I love how soft they feel and how they move across the paper. Round brushes are my favorite, and I use size 8 and size 10 rounds the most. What I love about these brushes is the fat belly. They hold a lot of water, which is perfect for loose, watery painting. At the same time, they come to a beautiful point, so you can still do more detailed work. If you can get only one brush for this book, I recommend a round size 10. It will work for all of the lessons, even the ones where I use a flat brush.

When I do use flat brushes, I usually reach for a 1/2-inch or 1-inch flat. That said, you do not need these exact brushes. Any soft, round, or flat watercolor brush will work. Use what you have. More than anything, I want your brush to feel comfortable in your hand and capable of holding plenty of water. The softness and water capacity will support the loose, flowing style you'll explore throughout this book.

Waterbrush

A *waterbrush* is a brush with a hollow handle that holds water inside. Instead of dipping into a cup of water, you gently squeeze the handle, and water flows down into the bristles.

I mainly use waterbrushes for detail work and mark-making. They are easy to control and keep a nice point, which makes them great for small lines, dots, and gentle accents. I usually reach for a regular brush for loose washes and larger areas, and I use a waterbrush when I want to add small details. For you and this book, a waterbrush is completely optional. A regular watercolor brush and a cup of water will work just as well.

Gel Pen

I love using a white gel pen for mark-making once the paint has dried. There is something about working with white on top of watercolor that really resonates with me. It feels light, quiet, and a little bit magical. That said, you are not limited to white. Feel free to use whatever color pen you are drawn to. Let your intuition and imagination guide you. I typically use a size 10 gel pen, but they are also sold in sets with different sizes. Those work great too.

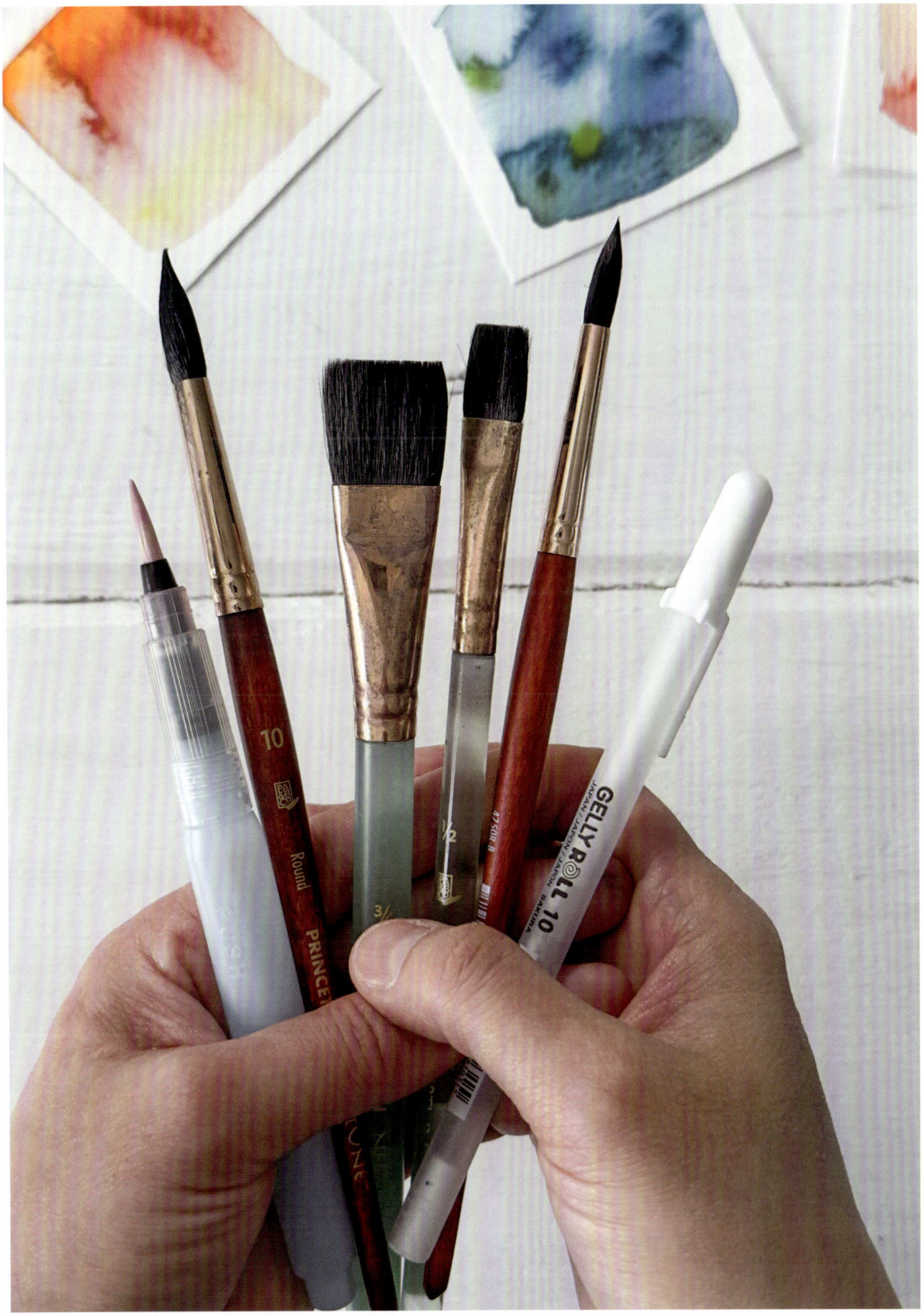
10
Round
GELLY ROLL 10

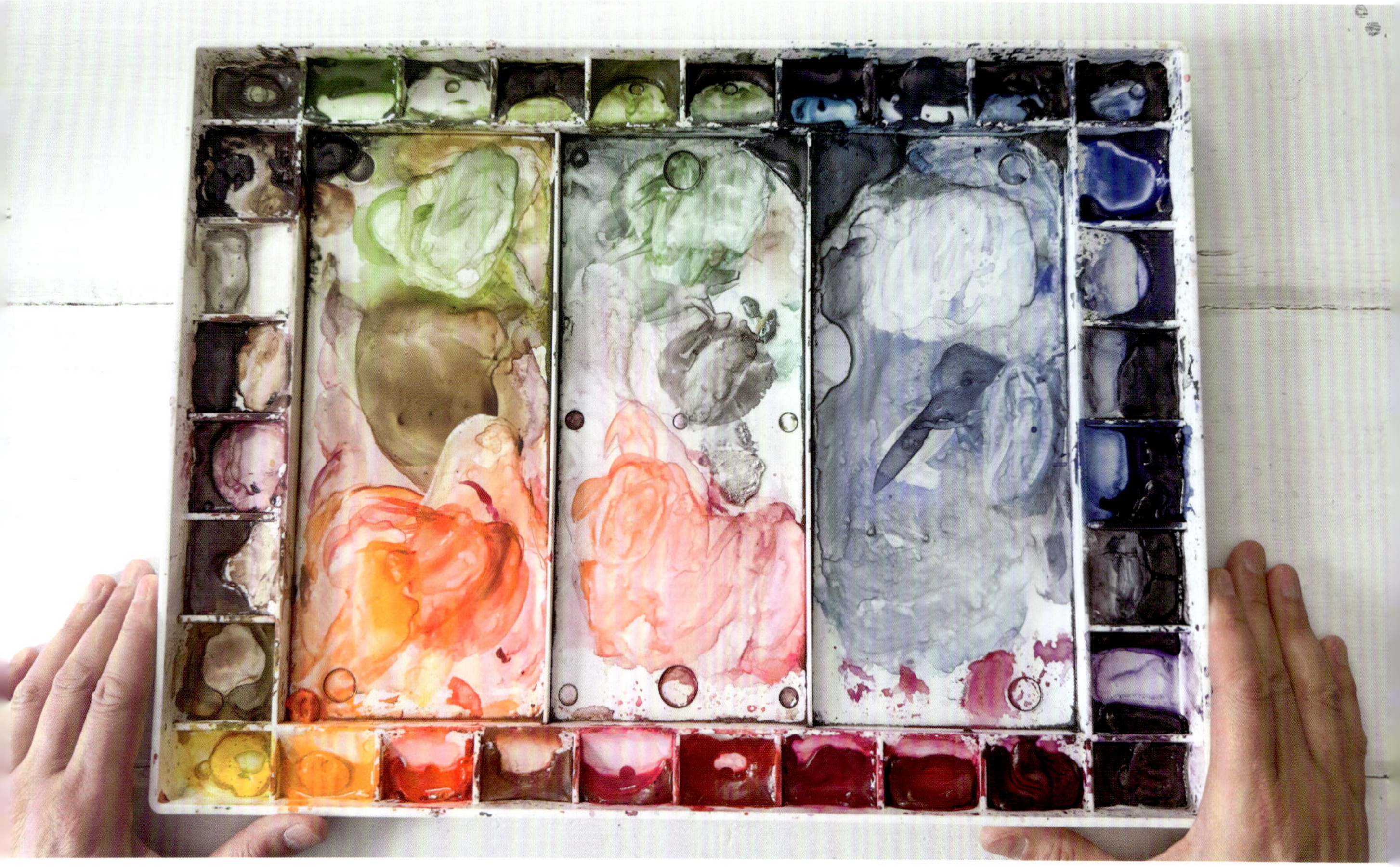

Watercolor Palette

I use the Masterson Aqua Pro Watercolor Palette in my own practice. It has 32 paint wells around the outer edge, divided mixing areas in the center, along with a lid. I love having a wide range of colors available when I'm painting and enough space to mix freely. I also enjoy working with a smaller palette at times. A smaller palette is perfect when I want to work with a limited selection of colors. It keeps my choices simple and makes the process feel more focused and easier. When there are fewer colors in front of me, I spend less time deciding and more time painting.

That said, you do not need either of these exact palettes. If you are using pan paints, you can use the palette that comes with your set. A ceramic plate, a paper dish, or any simple mixing surface works just as well. Use whatever feels easy and supportive for you. Sometimes having fewer options creates more freedom.

Watercolor Paper

Watercolor paper really does matter, because it affects how water sits on the surface, how paint is absorbed, and how everything dries as you work. All of that shapes how the painting experience feels. I have experimented with a lot of different watercolor papers over the years. For a long time, I was looking for two things: one paper I could use for my professional work and a more economical paper that gave similar results for my healing and practice work. I found it and highly recommend the Canson XL Watercolor Pads. The price is great, and the paper feels surprisingly luxe for an economical option. It has a subtle texture that gives the paint something to hold onto without getting in the way of the finished results. The thing I love most about this paper is that I can paint right in the pad. I don't need to tape it down. It has minimal curling, which is impressive with the amount of water I use. For this book, I used the 9-x-12-inch pad, but I also work in larger sizes depending on the project.

As you gather your materials, remember that nothing needs to be perfect. I want this to feel simple, accessible, and supportive, wherever you are starting from. More than anything, I want your supplies to feel easy rather than another thing to figure out. This practice is about slowing down and giving yourself space to explore.

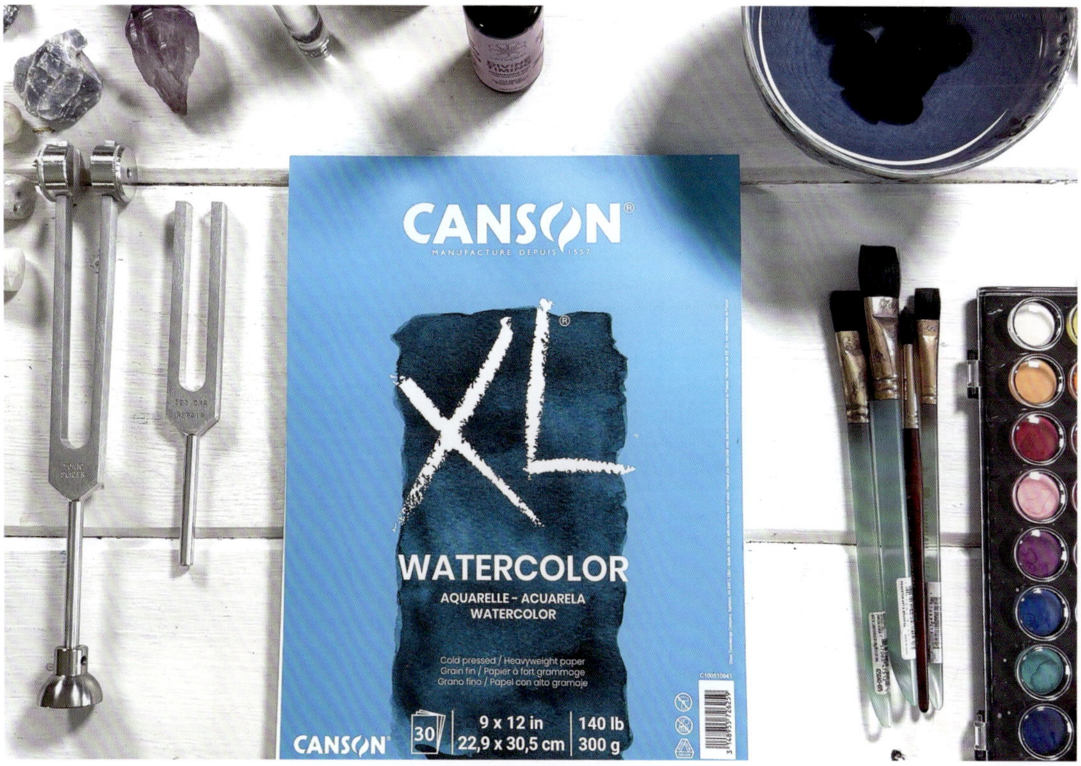

A Few Simple Techniques

No experience needed. No perfection required. The simple techniques you will learn in this chapter will open the door to the quiet magic of watercolor painting. They are here to support you as you begin exploring watercolor in a simple, relaxed way.

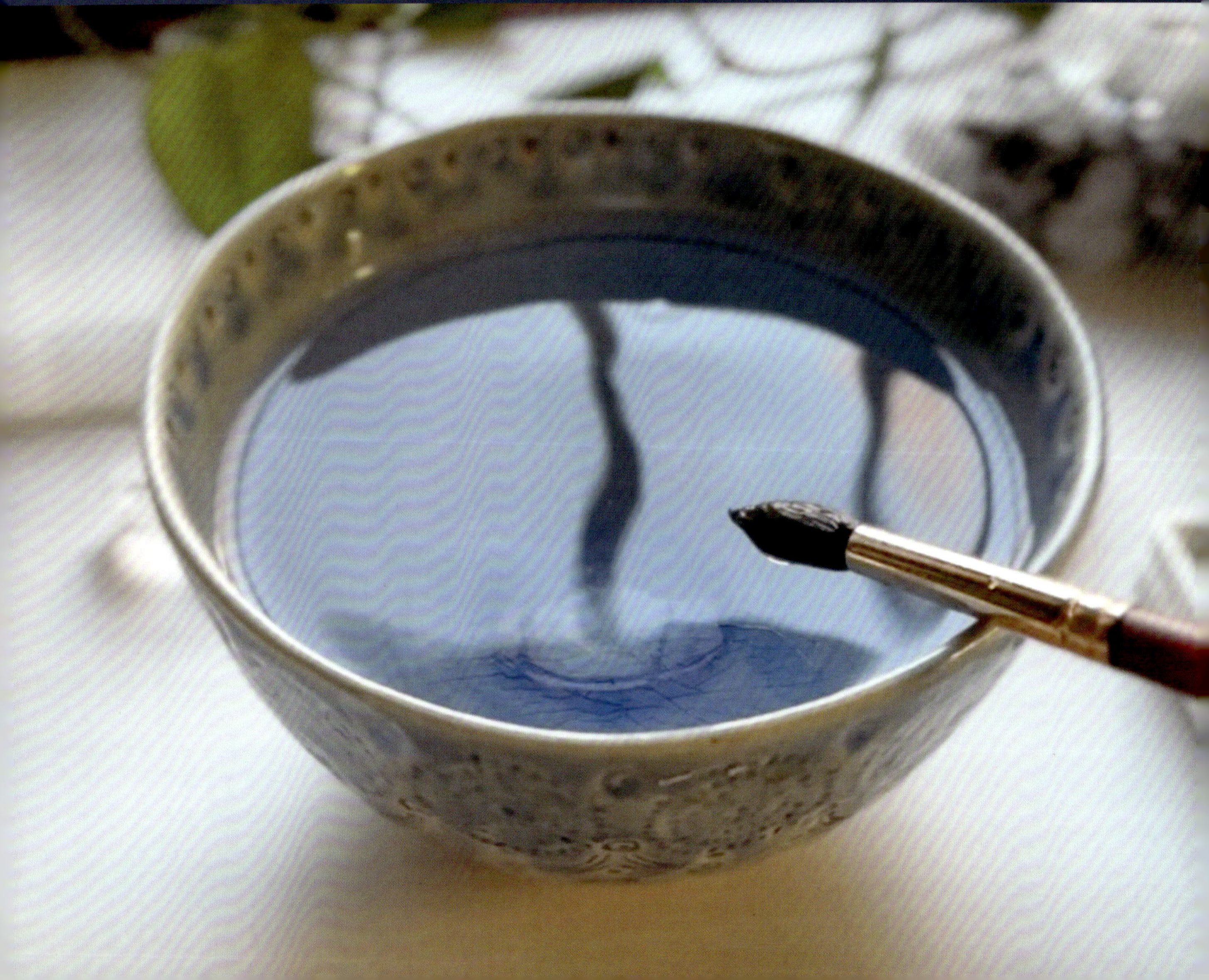

4

They are here to help you feel more comfortable with water, paint, and movement so you can relax into the painting process.

The techniques are simple ways of exploring how watercolor behaves and how your body feels as you paint. Think of them as small invitations—invitations to slow down, soften your grip, and become curious about watercolor painting. Watercolor is a responsive medium. It reacts to water, time, and touch. When you begin to understand these simple relationships, painting becomes less about control and more about collaboration.

I often say: *Let the materials do the work for you.* That is the thing I love most about watercolor. You can lay down color in a wet area of your paper, and the watercolor will move and respond on its own. When I try to control the outcome, interrupt the way the color is spreading, or hurry the drying phase, it usually takes the life out of what the watercolor is trying to express.

This chapter focuses on a few foundational ways of working:

- Use plenty of water.
- Place color and let it move.
- Allow colors to meet and blend.
- Soften and blur edges.

Nothing here is meant to be mastered. You may move through these practice routines once or return to them many times. Let this chapter be a place where you build trust. Trust in the water. Trust in the paint. Most importantly, trust in yourself. When you're ready, begin by using lots of water.

You don't need to practice perfectly.

You don't need to get anything "right."

All you need is the willingness to show up and play.

Don't Be Afraid of the Water: Learn to Trust the Flow

For me, water is the key to painting in this loose style. It creates the most beautiful effects when it is allowed to wander and move. Resist trying to control it, and don't "fix it" with your brush. Let the paints dry naturally and in their own way. When I paint, the thing I love most about watercolor is the water itself. Water carries the pigment; it creates movement and makes space for unexpected beauty. I always say: *Don't be afraid of your water.* The more water you use, the more watercolor begins to do what it does best: spread, soften, blend, and surprise you. This loose, flowing style depends on water. There is no room for control or perfectionism here. This simple practice lesson is about getting familiar with what water feels like, how it moves, and how it changes your relationship with the brush.

What You'll Explore

You'll explore the difference between painting with mostly water and painting with mostly paint and begin to feel why water is the key to working in a soft, loose way.

Water knows how to move. You only have to let it.

thoughts

How to Practice

STEP ONE: LET'S DIVE IN

Before dipping your brush into the water, hold it in your hand and take a moment to feel its weight. Next, dip the brush, and let it fill with water. Now notice the weight of the brush again. It feels heavier, more solid. Being aware of the brush in your hand, how it feels, what your grip is like, and the weight of it helps you slow down and feel into your body. This kind of sensing brings your attention out of your head and into your direct experience, which is naturally regulating for the nervous system.

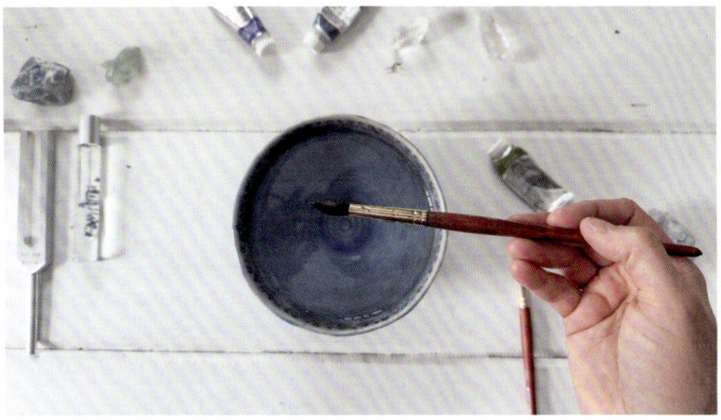

As you begin to feel the brush and notice subtle shifts, you start building a quiet relationship with your materials. When I am in the flow, I can often tell what is happening with my brush without looking. I instinctively know if I need more water, or if I am holding too tightly and need to soften my grip and take a breath. This gentle sensing supports nervous system regulation and your relationship with the materials. Over time, this awareness grows on its own.

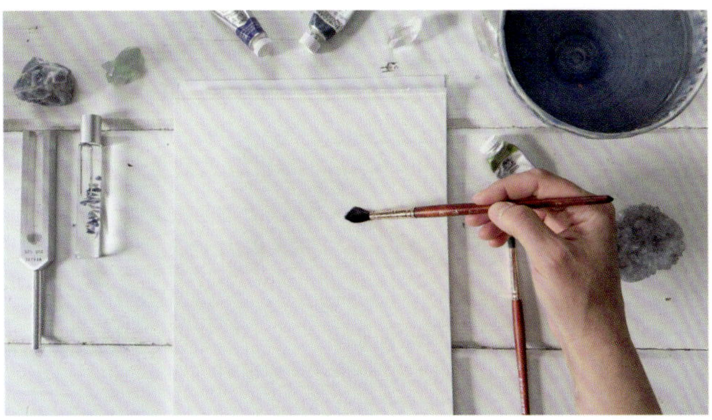

STEP TWO: FEEL THE WATER

Fill your brush up with water and move it along the paper in a wave motion. Feel what the brush feels like on the paper when it's filled with water. It glides. It feels smooth. It feels light. Let yourself really sense this.

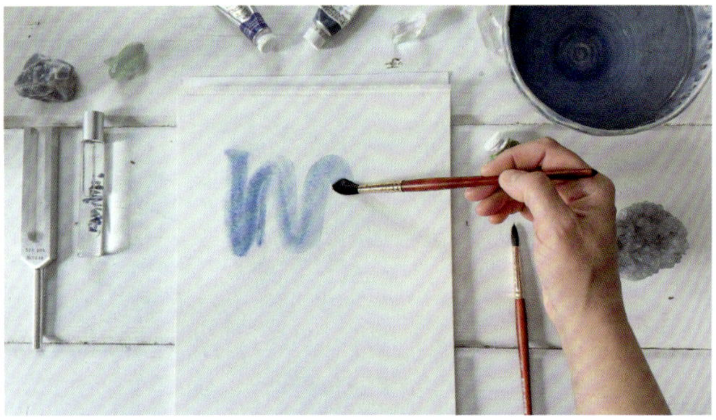

STEP THREE: MAKE A WASH

Add a tiny bit of color to your brush and repeat the same movement. Notice how it feels. With more water and less paint, the brush still glides. It still feels smooth. It still feels light. This is the feeling you are looking for: ease and flow.

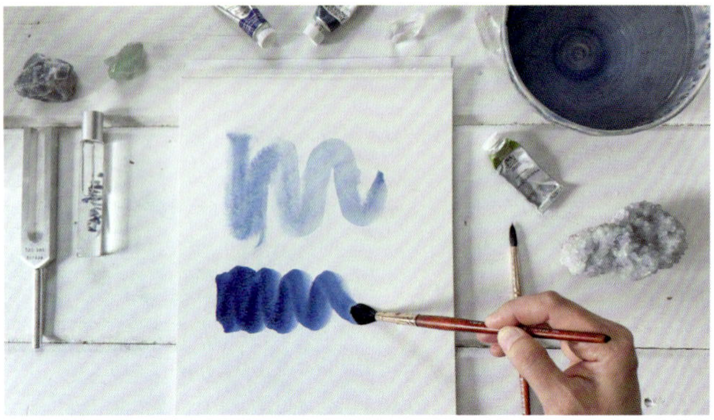

STEP FOUR: SATURATE WITH PAINT

Now, pull most of the water off your brush so there is only a small amount left—just enough to help pick up the paint. Repeat the same wave motion. Notice how your brush feels this time. The paint may feel a little sticky, a little drier, and almost like it is gripping the paper. There is nothing wrong with this.

At times you will want more paint on your brush and other times more water. I simply want you to be able to feel the difference. I also want you to see that you do not need to be afraid of using a lot of water. Water carries paint beautifully. It helps color spread, it helps the colors to blend, and it helps edges to soften and blur. Have fun getting to know your materials and begin building a relationship with them. Let the water guide you. Trust the process.

Color Swatches: A Gentle Introduction to Dripping

For me, *dripping* is really about placing paint and seeing what happens. You place color into a wet area and watch it move. You let it blend with what is already there. There is no rushing, or forcing, or fixing—just being. It is a soft conversation between water and paint. Color swatches are a simple way to explore this relationship and create little abstract paintings. It's fun to explore how to place color, add water, and observe how watercolor responds. Each square becomes a tiny world of movement and possibility. This practice lesson helps you get comfortable moving back and forth between laying down soft swashes of color and gently dripping in additional color or clear water.

What You'll Explore

You'll explore how color behaves when placed onto wet paper and how moving between swashing and dripping allows the painting to slowly evolve on its own.

Place the color. Watch it move.

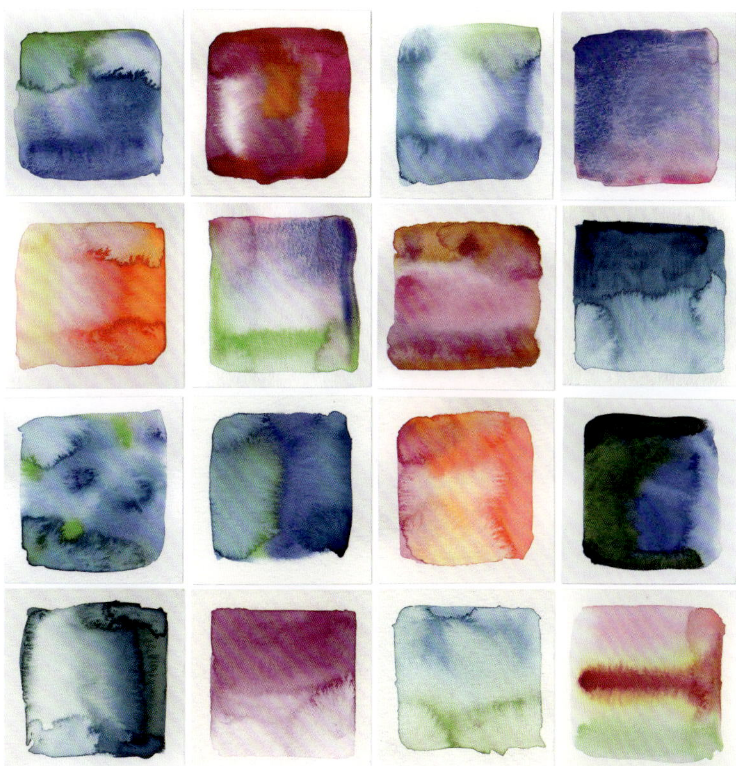

How to Practice

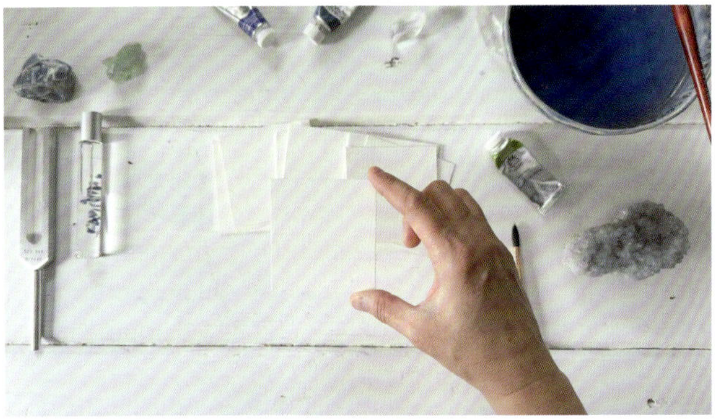

STEP ONE: CUT YOUR SWATCHES

Cut or tear your watercolor paper into 3-inch squares. You can prepare several at once and place them in front of you, or work with one square at a time.

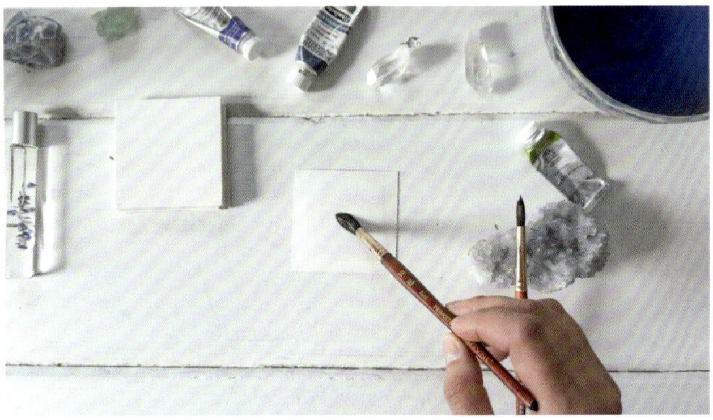

STEP TWO: BEGIN WITH WATER

On one square, paint a small square in the center using clear water. Use plenty of water so the surface looks shiny and wet. This wet area will carry the color.

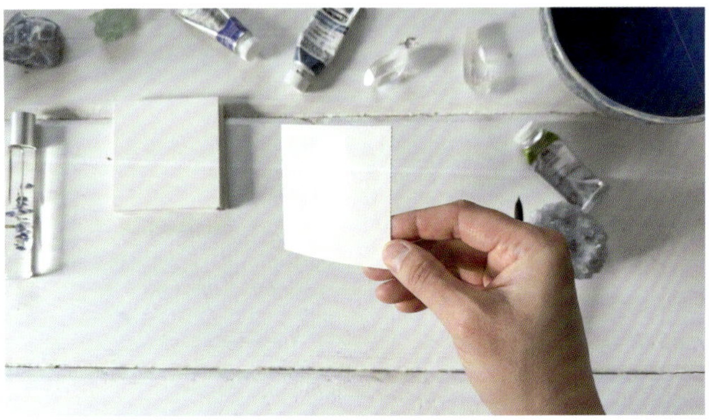

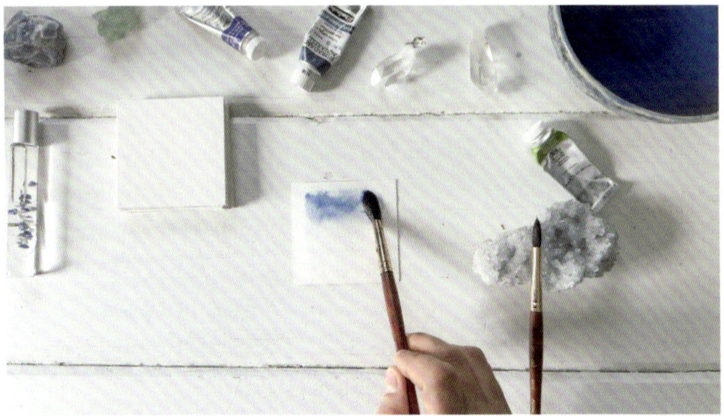

STEP THREE: LAY DOWN COLOR

Choose a color and place a soft swash into the wet area. Watch as the paint begins to spread.

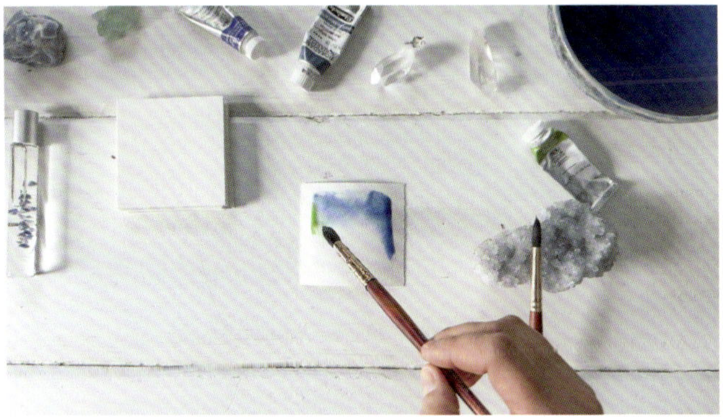

STEP FOUR: DRIP AND RESPOND

Load your brush with watery paint in another color. Gently touch the tip of the brush to the wet area so a drop releases.

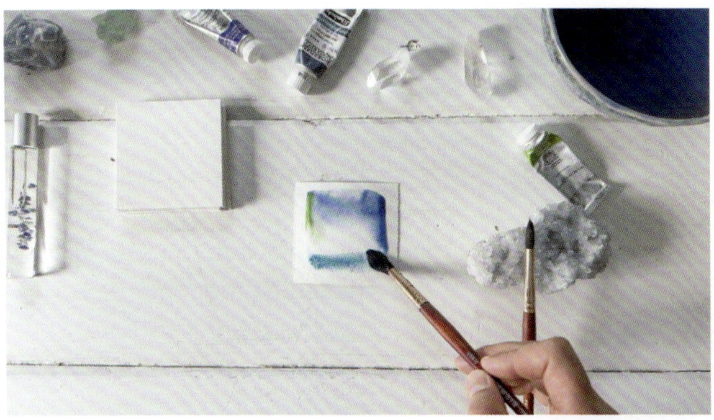

STEP FIVE: COMPLETE THE SWATCH

Add another swash of color, and see what happens. Move back and forth between swashing and dripping, letting each action respond to what is already on the paper.

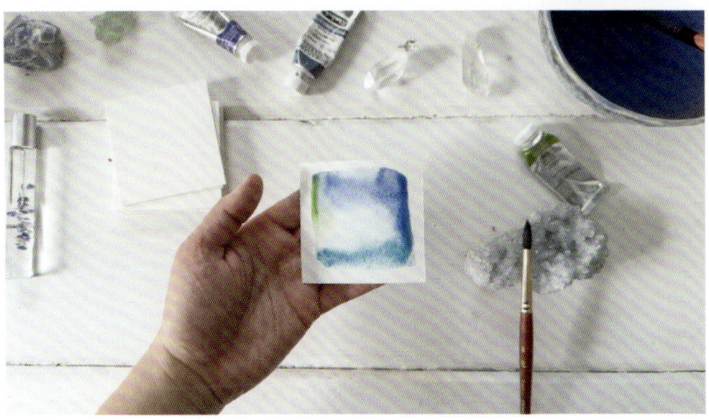

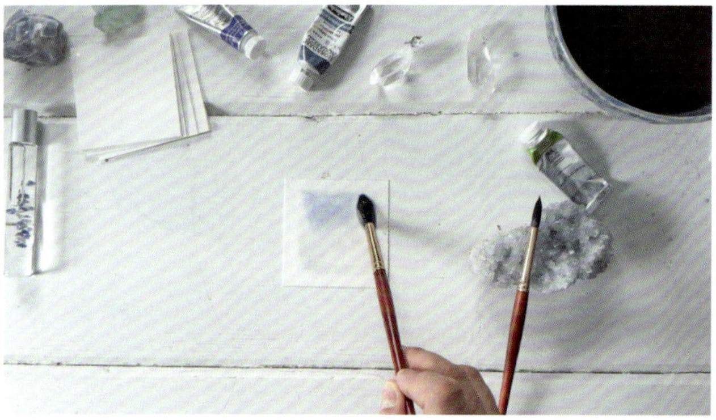

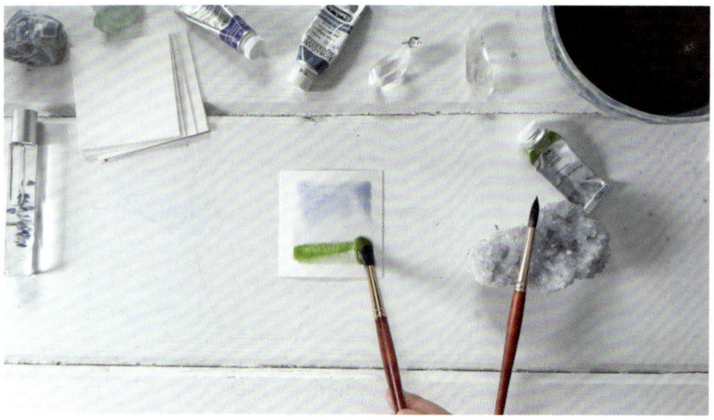

STEP SIX: KEEP GOING

Try another one. This can be whatever you want it to be. Play with water, dripping, and color placement. Slowly explore water and color until the square feels complete to you. Place a light wash of blue on the top of the square. Add a swash of green to the bottom of the square like grass in a landscape.

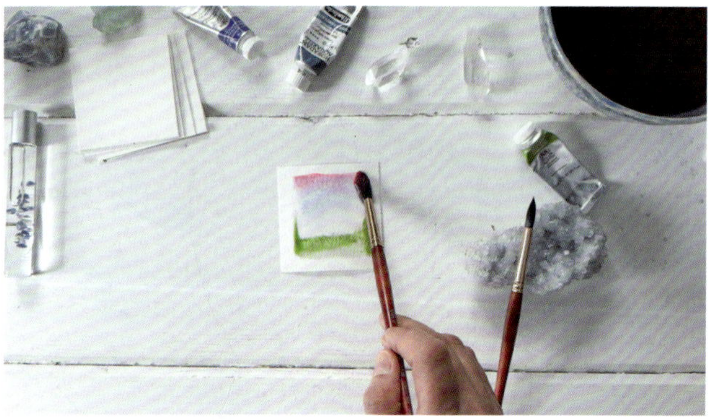

STEP SEVEN: LET YOUR INTUITION GUIDE YOU

Add a swash of bright pink to the top and see how it blends with the blue to create a hint of purple. Note: This is why you want to use a lot of water—that little hint of magic won't happen if your paint is too dry.

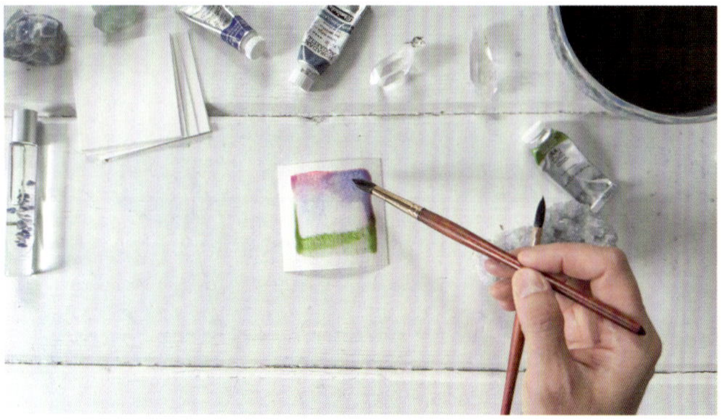

STEP EIGHT: DRIP COLOR, AND LET IT GO

Drip in some blue with plenty of water. I love what happened with mine. See how the water dripped down the side of the swatch. That is a good thing! Once your little swatch is done, you can pick it up and see where the paint travels. Now, set it aside, and let it dry naturally while you move onto your next square.

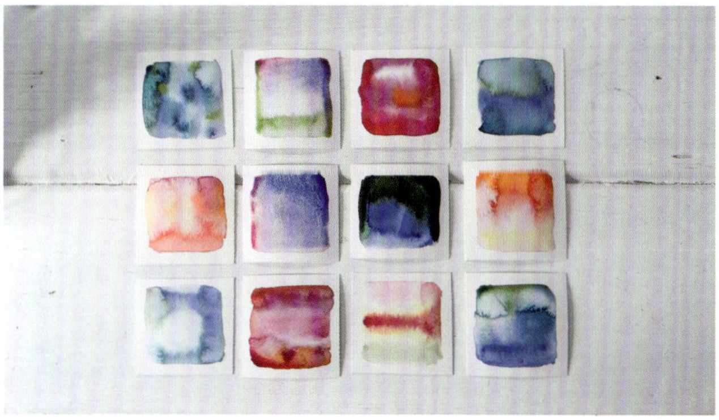

STEP NINE: MAKE A BUNCH OF THEM

Repeat the same simple process with each swatch. I have so many of these swatches and love pulling them out and playing with them. The swatches will become a visual record of your time with the practice lesson.

thoughts

Blurring the Edges: Practice with Softening

Blurring the edges is a simple way of using clean water to soften where the color ends and the paper begins. This practice lesson uses circles, color, and plenty of water to explore how edges dissolve, how colors blend, and how watercolor responds when you step back and let the materials do the work for you. It is not about precision. It's about letting go.

What You'll Explore

You'll explore painting simple circles, then using clean water to gently blur the edges, watching how color spreads, blends, and softens on its own.

As the edges soften, so do you.

How to Practice

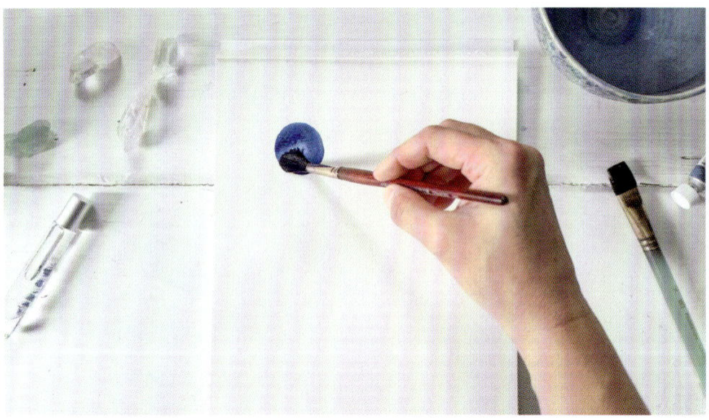

STEP ONE: START WITH A CIRCLE

Choose a color and paint a loose circle on your paper. Use plenty of water so the paint stays wet and movable.

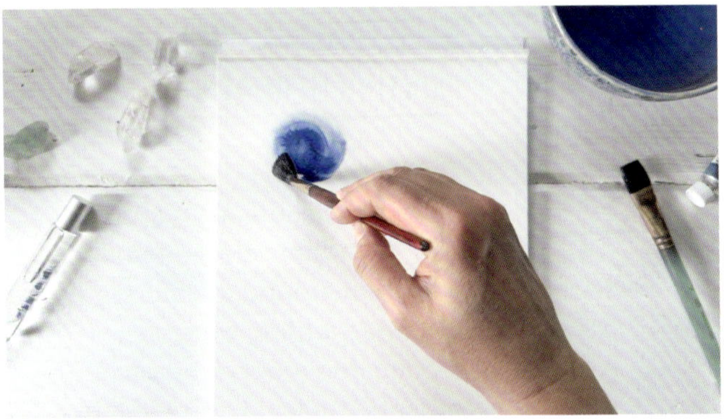

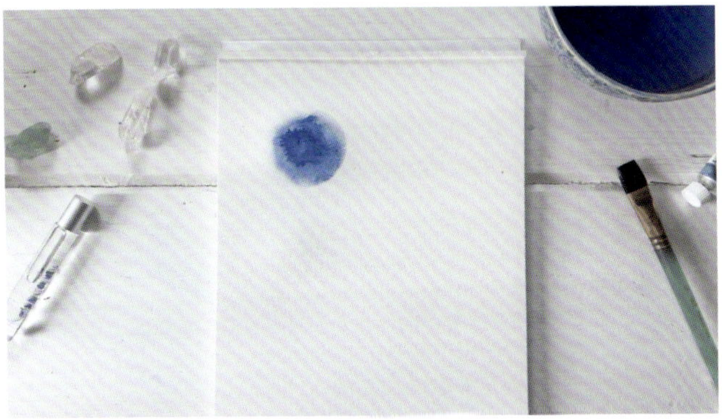

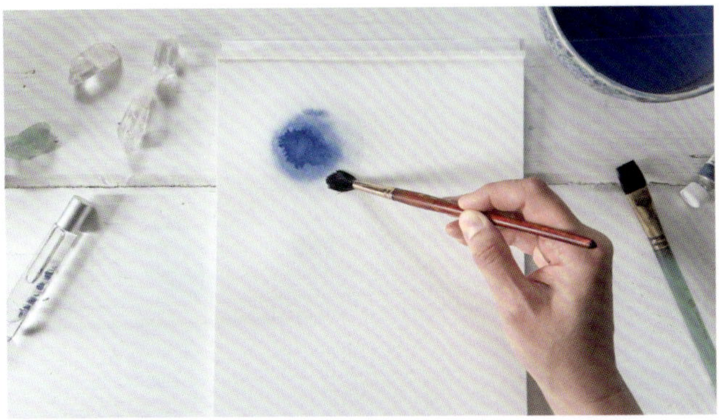

STEP TWO: KISS THE EDGE

Clean your brush. Gently touch the clean, damp brush to the edge of the painted circle. Think of this as "kissing" the edge with water. Move around the circle, and watch what happens. The color begins to soften and spread outward. The edge starts to blur. Continue going around the edge with clean water until you feel like it's complete.

STEP THREE: ENJOY LITTLE PAINTING MEDITATIONS

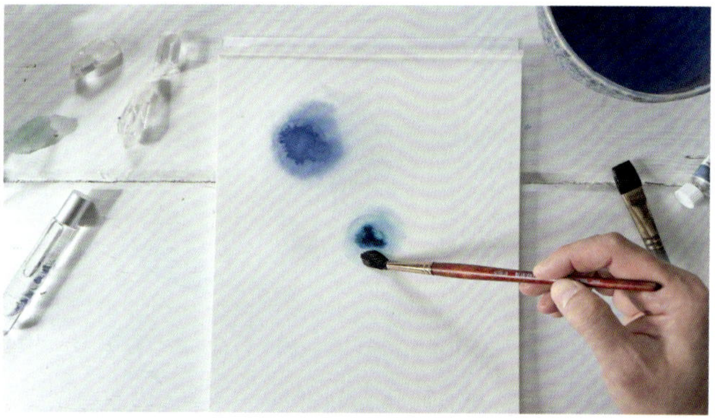

Try another one: Pick a color and paint a circle. Clean your brush and blur the edge. Select another color and paint around the blurred edge. Continue adding water as you go around and around the circle. This process can feel very meditative. Don't try to control the outcome; let the colors dry.

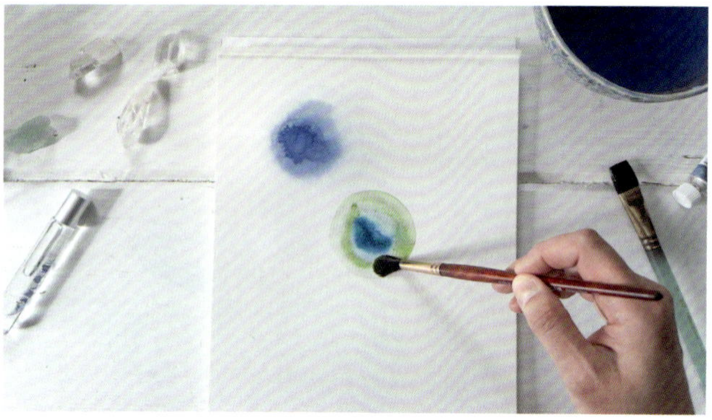

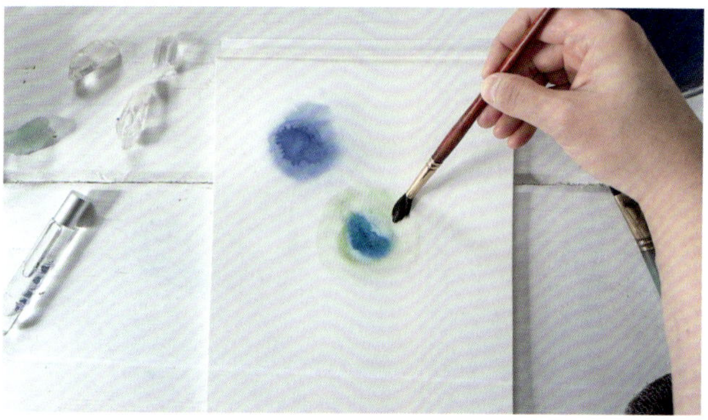

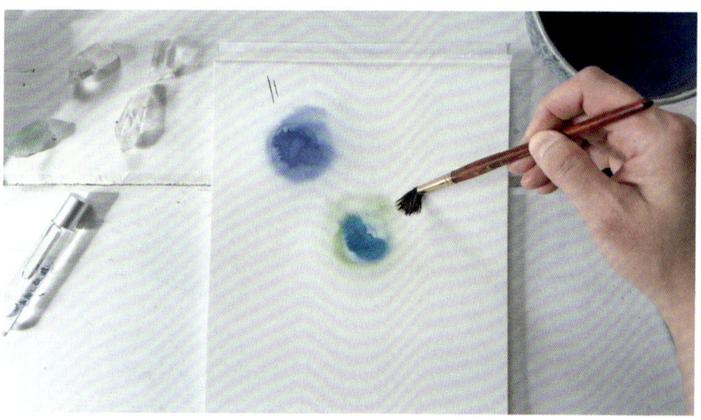

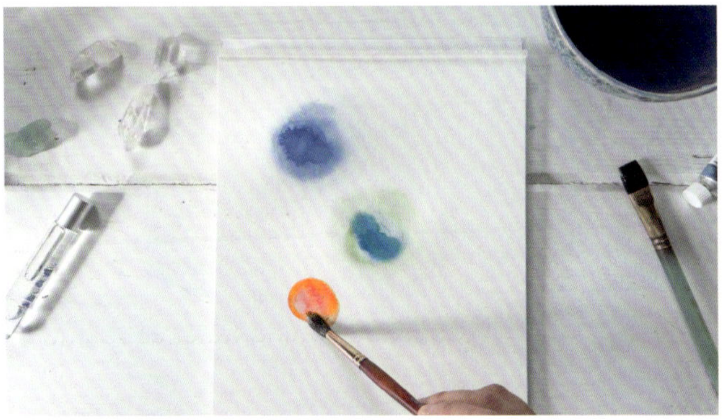

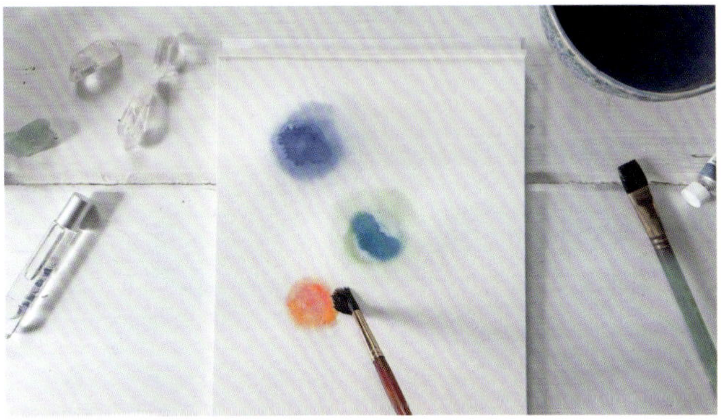

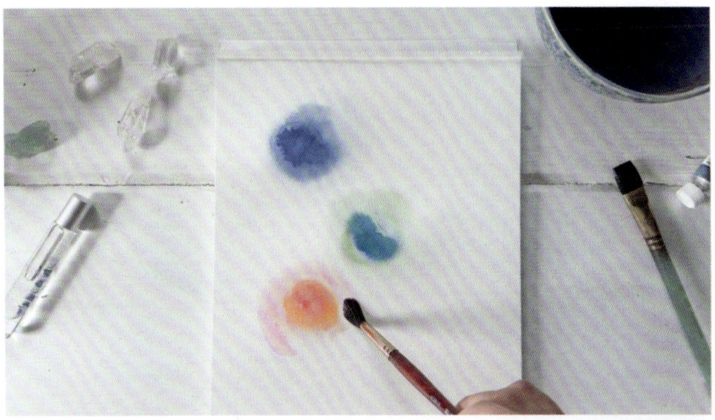

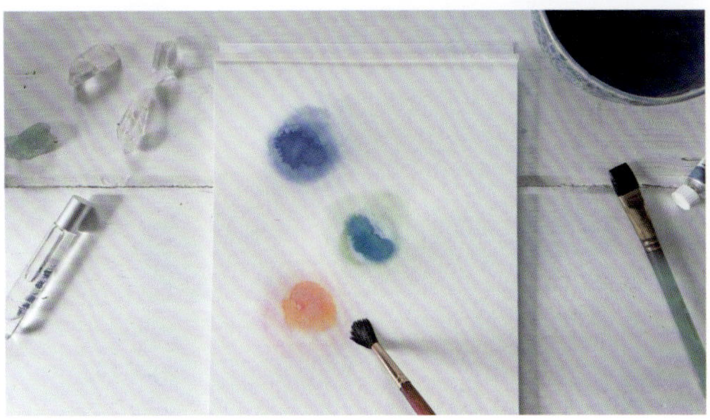

STEP FOUR: SWITCH UP THE COLOR

Let's play with more colors. Pick a warm color to start this one (I chose pink). Paint a circle, and then go around the circle with another warm color (orange for me). Clean your brush and blur the edge with clean water. Next, add some of your first color to the blurred edge. Use plenty of water to carry the color, and move your brush around and around the center until you feel ready to stop.

STEP FIVE: WATCH FOR THE MAGIC

Continue playing, and fill up your paper. On my next circle, I used orange in the center and a saturated red around it, then I blurred the edge with lots of water and continued to go around the circle until it felt complete. Finally, I had some fun with bright pink and then blurred the edge. You can see how blurring the edges softens the circle and how the water creates magical effects.

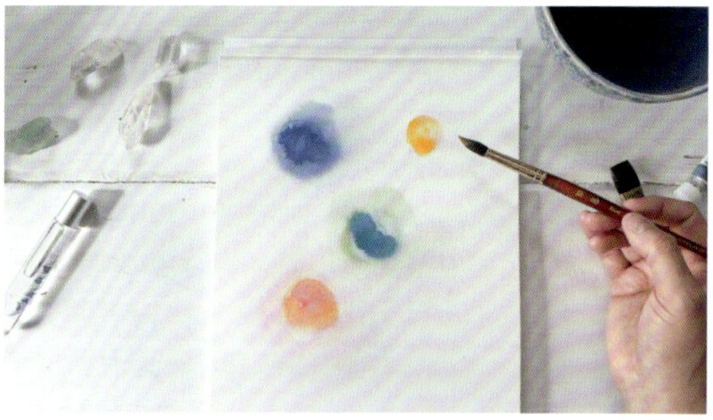
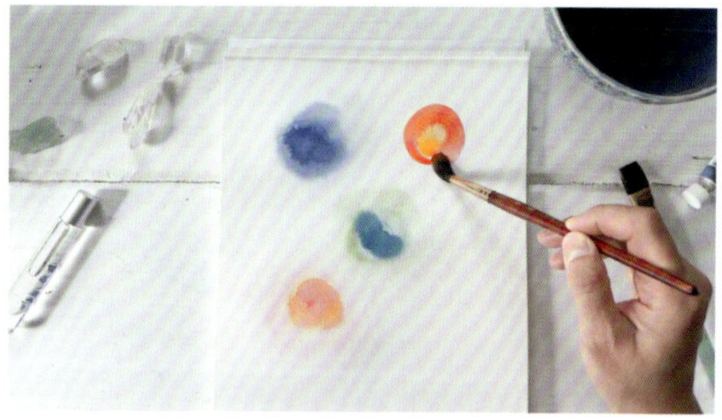
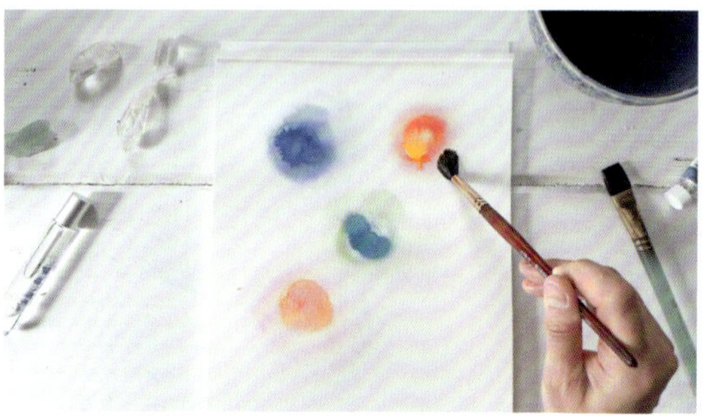
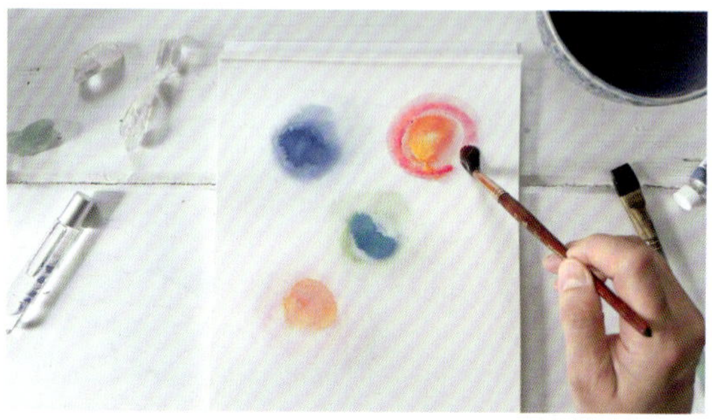
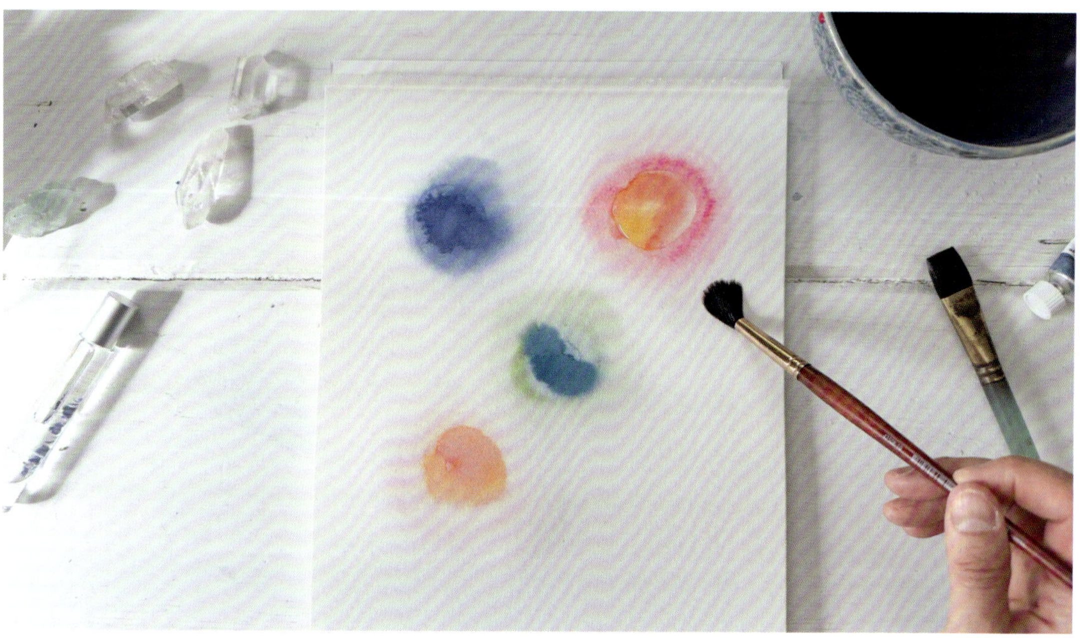

STEP SIX: PRACTICE ALCHEMY

Start with a blue circle. While it is still wet, surround it with a nice saturated green. Now blur the edge. Rinse your brush, grab some more water, and blur again. Watch how the water creates soft, unexpected effects along the edge of the circle. This is a beautiful example of the magical qualities of water and the quiet alchemy that happens when water and paint meet. If you tried to control this circle, you would never get this exact effect. This is what becomes possible when you let the materials do the work for you.

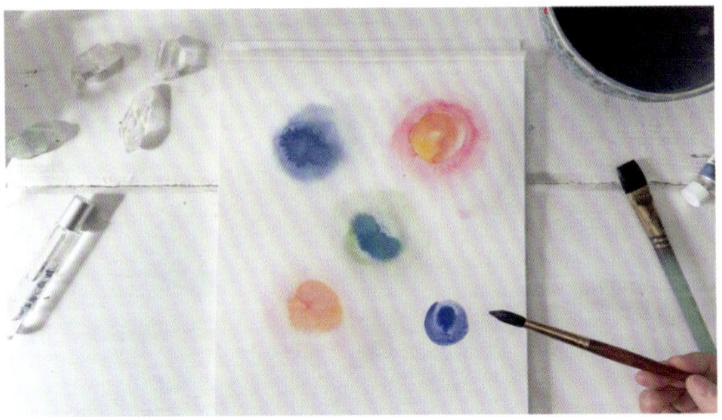

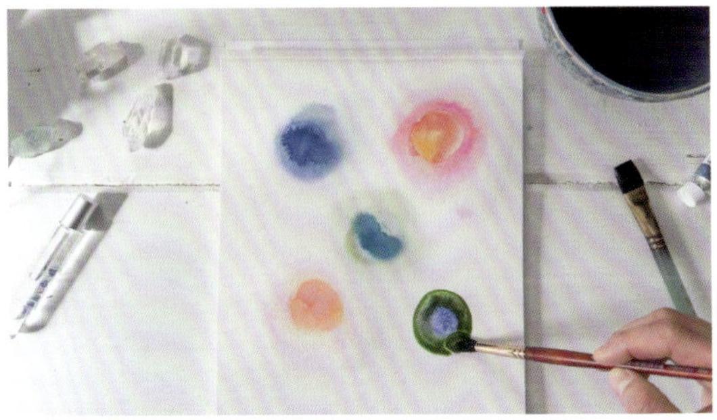

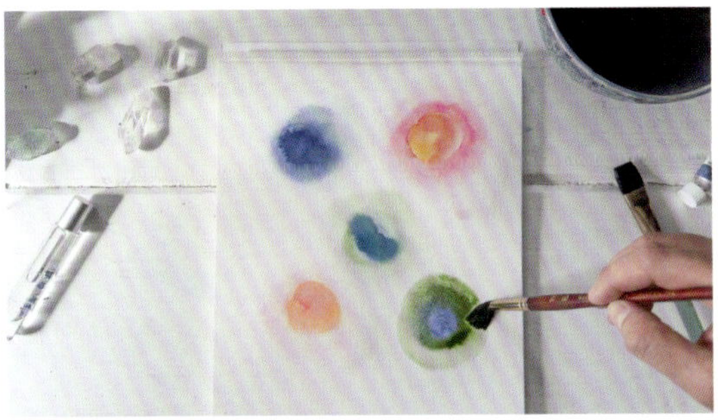

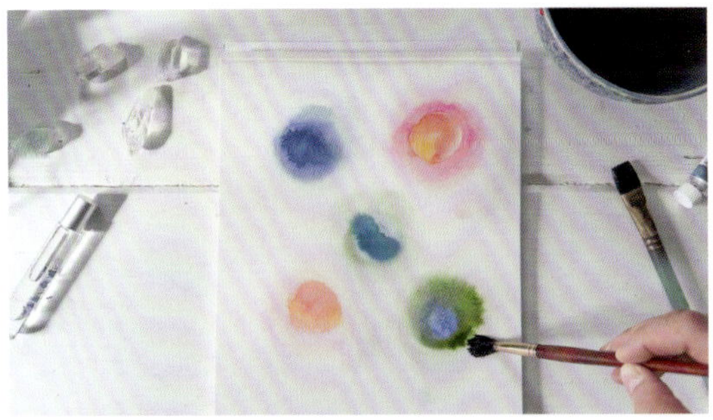

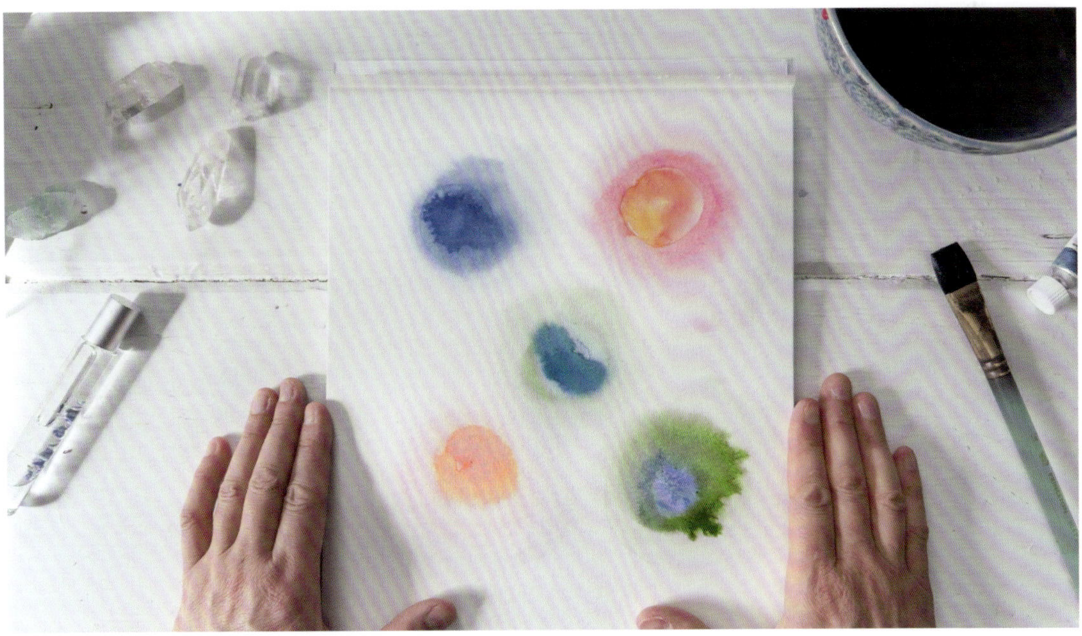

Slow Down, Soften, and Flow

These practice lessons are simple, but they are powerful. They teach you how to slow down, how to soften your grip, and how to let the materials do the work. Return to them anytime you need to remember how to flow. When you're ready, move on to the painting lessons.

thoughts

PART TWO

The Painting Practice

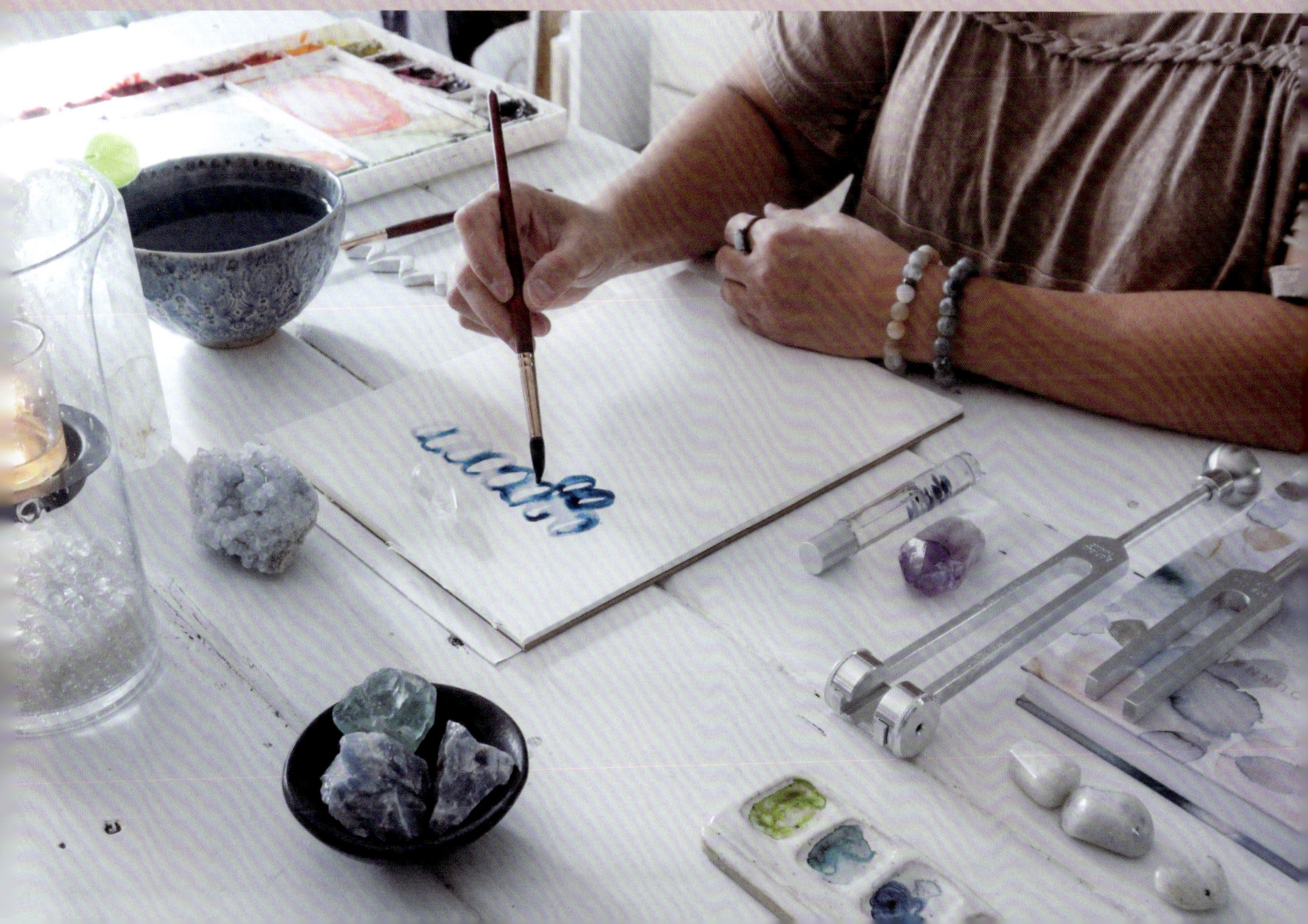

Part Two is divided into three sections in which you'll learn how to combine watercolor painting with breath work and body awareness to help quiet your mind, connect with your body, and open your heart with gentleness. For all the lessons, begin with small steps, practicing the "How to Try It" exercises for 30 to 60 seconds as a start. Let's take a closer look at what you'll learn in each section.

Calm Your Mind

In this section of the painting practice, we begin by gently calming the mind. When the nervous system has been under long periods of stress, the mind often stays busy, scanning, planning, replaying, and trying to keep us safe, even when nothing is wrong in the present moment. The lessons in Chapters 5 through 9 are invitations to offer your mind a softer place to rest and to create a little more space inside the noise.

Through slow, mindful painting exercises, simple breathing practices, and gentle pattern-based movement, you'll explore what it feels like to stay present with your brush and with yourself. Repetition, rhythm, and predictable marks give your mind one small, steady place to land, which naturally helps ease mental chatter without force or effort.

These practices are not about stopping your thoughts or making your mind perfectly still. They are about softening the intensity of thinking and allowing moments of calm awareness to arise in their own time. Over time, this supports nervous system regulation, eases anxious patterns, and builds a foundation of inner stillness that you can return to whenever you need it. Think of this section as creating gentle doorways back to quiet, one brushstroke at a time.

Connect to Your Body

In Chapters 10 through 14 of the painting practice, the focus begins to shift from thinking to sensing. Many of us spend a great deal of time living from the neck up, while slowly losing touch with what our bodies are feeling. These lessons invite you to come back into a gentle relationship with your body in a slow, safe, and supportive way. Using watercolor as a grounding and regulating tool, you'll explore intuitive painting exercises, breathwork, and simple body-based practices that help you notice sensation, soften tension, and build a felt sense of safety from the inside. As your brush moves across the page, you may begin to notice your shoulders relaxing, your breath deepening, and your body settling in small but meaningful ways. This part of your journey is not about fixing your body or forcing release. It is about listening. It is about learning how to be with your body with a little more curiosity, kindness, and patience, and allowing art to become a gentle bridge back into presence. Here, painting becomes a way to anchor into your body's wisdom, ease stress and anxiety, and cultivate a sense of steadiness you can carry with you beyond the page.

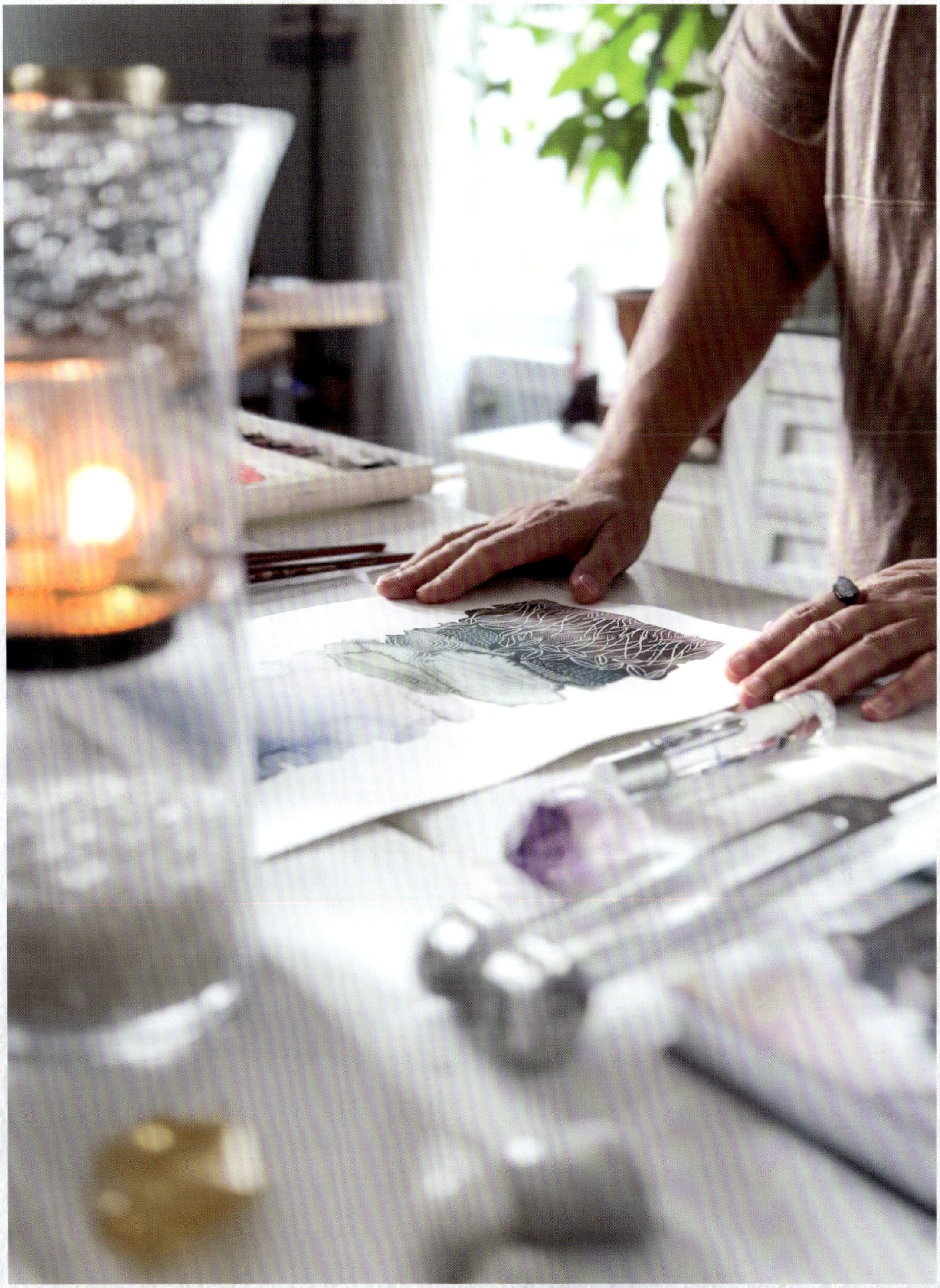

Open Your Heart

In Chapters 15 through 19, the final part of the painting practice, the invitation is to gently turn toward your emotional world with softness and care. The heart and nervous system are deeply connected, and when the heart feels guarded or overwhelmed, the body often stays on alert. When the heart begins to feel safe enough to open, the nervous system can soften as well.

Through heart-centered breathing, compassionate awareness, and guided watercolor exercises inspired by HeartMath and intuitive painting, you'll explore ways to meet your emotions without needing to analyze or fix them. Color, shape, and movement become a simple language for what you may not have words for, allowing feeling to move in a contained and supported way.

This section is not about forcing positive emotions or trying to feel a certain way. It is about creating space for whatever is present, whether that is tenderness, grief, gratitude, longing, joy, or something in between. As you layer color onto the page, you are also gently opening space within yourself for self-compassion, connection, and deeper healing.

Here, painting becomes an act of devotion to your own heart.

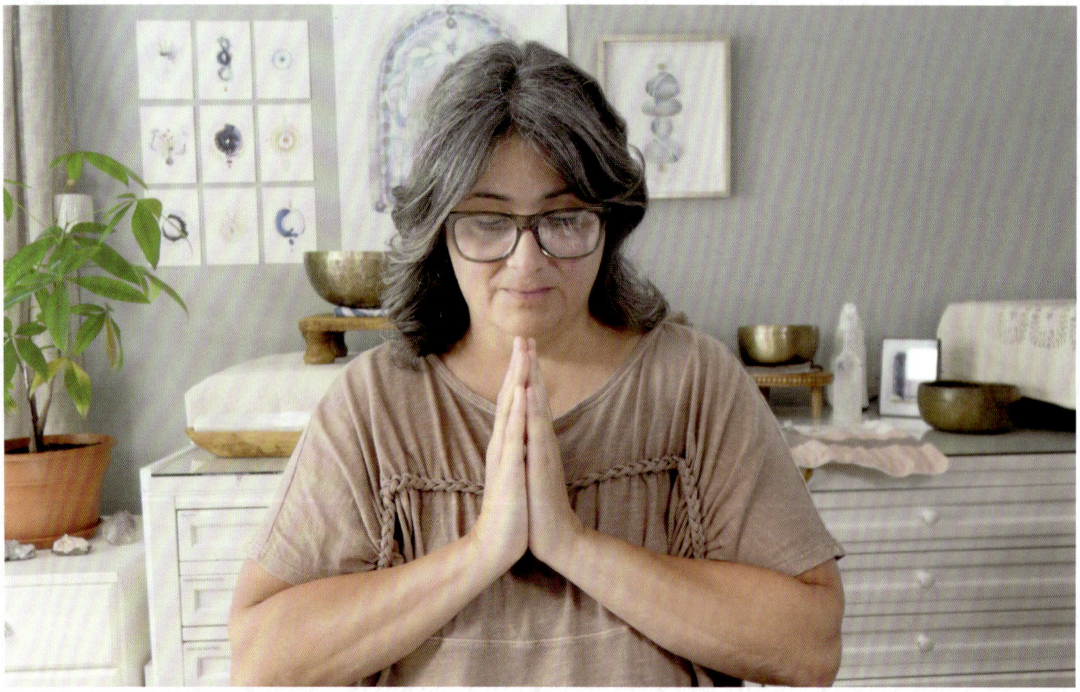

NERVOUS SYSTEM REGULATION TOOL

5

4–6 Breath

With the 4–6 Breath technique, you inhale softly for four counts through your nose and exhale slowly through your mouth for six, like blowing gently on a candle flame. The slightly longer exhale signals safety to your nervous system and helps your body unwind.

BENEFITS

- **Calms the body.** The extended exhale activates the parasympathetic response, easing stress and tension.
- **Steadies your rhythm.** Each breath becomes the metronome for your brush, syncing breath and movement.
- **Releases control.** A longer out-breath helps loosen perfectionism and invites flow.
- **Supports presence.** The breath keeps you anchored in this moment: one inhale, one exhale, one mark.

HOW TO TRY IT

- Sit comfortably and soften your shoulders.
- Inhale gently through your nose for four counts.
- Exhale slowly through your mouth for six counts, soft and steady.
- Repeat for four to six breath cycles.
- Let the brush follow the pace of your breathing as you paint.

WHEN IT'S USEFUL

Use the 4–6 Breath technique before or during painting, when you feel rushed, tense, or overthinking. Use it anytime you want to slow down, find ease, and let your marks move with your breath.

Restful Rhythms

SOOTHE THE MIND WITH REPETITIVE SHAPES

Let steady shapes become your resting place. As your brush repeats, your breath lengthens, and your mind softens.

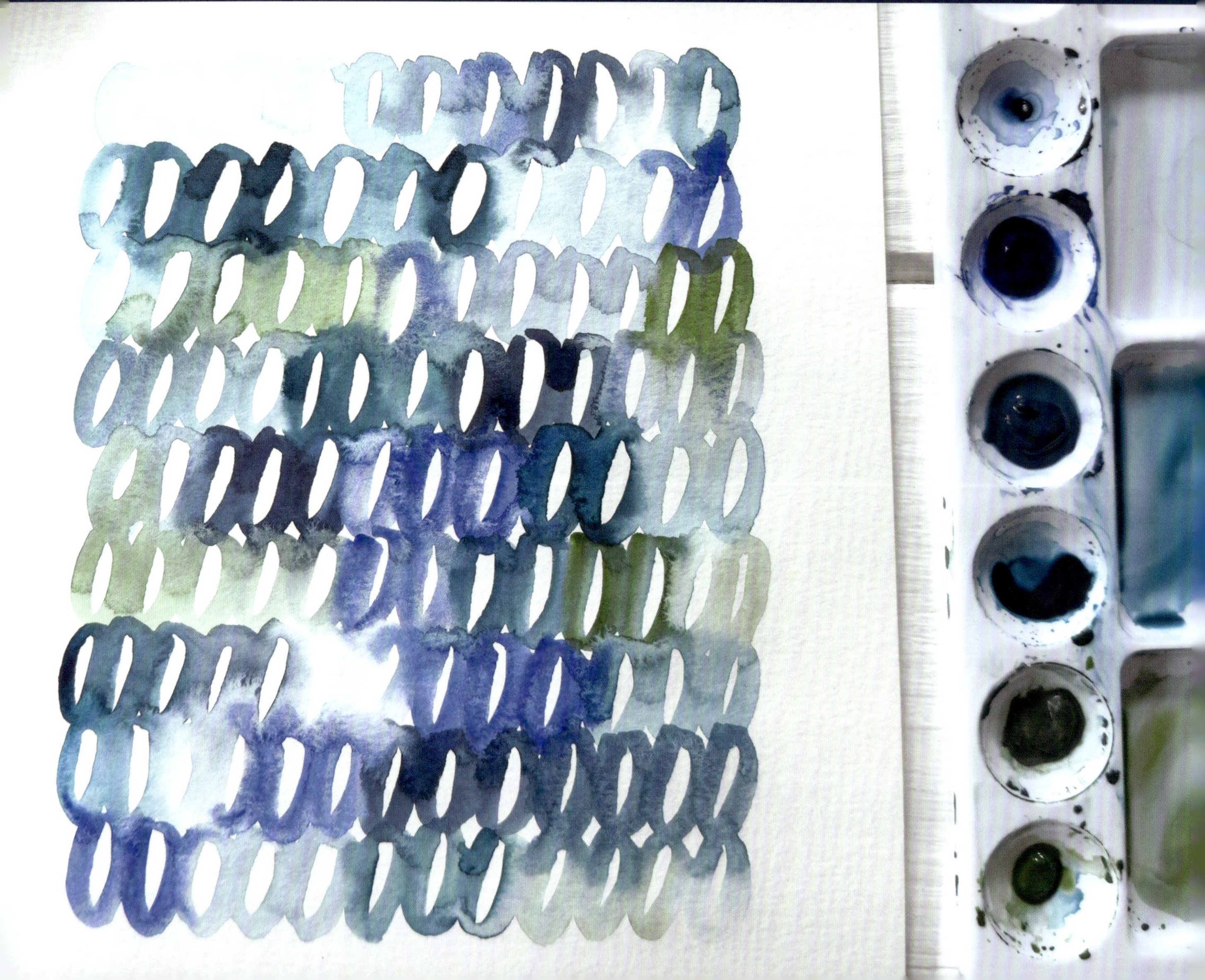

WHAT YOU'LL LEARN

- A calming, repetitive shape practice that invites flow with minimal decisions
- A simple way to drip-in color and let water do the work
- How to paint wet-on-wet
- How playing with value adds interest and variety

In this session, you will build a calming rhythm with simple, repeated oval shapes so you can settle in without overthinking. I'll show you how to drip in color and let the water do the work for you. You will explore how to paint wet-on-wet to explore how the paint reacts to water with gentle blooms, and how to play with value to add interest and variety to your painting.

WHAT YOU MIGHT FEEL

- A natural lengthening of your exhale
- Shoulders and jaw releasing as you get lost in the process
- Appreciation for the imperfections you will see as each mark dries in unique and beautiful ways

HOW THIS SESSION FLOWS

- Let's begin with a short technique tutorial. I'll walk you through the exercise and share simple ways to add variety with little shifts in spacing, value, and wet-on-wet techniques. When you feel comfortable, move on to the painting meditation. Pair the techniques with gentle 4–6 breaths, a soft mantra, peaceful music, and a kinder pace that loosens your grip, relaxes your body, and quiets your mind.

Soft, rhythmic circles; a softening breath.
We'll let the water lead and see where it wants to carry us. Nothing needs to be perfect here.

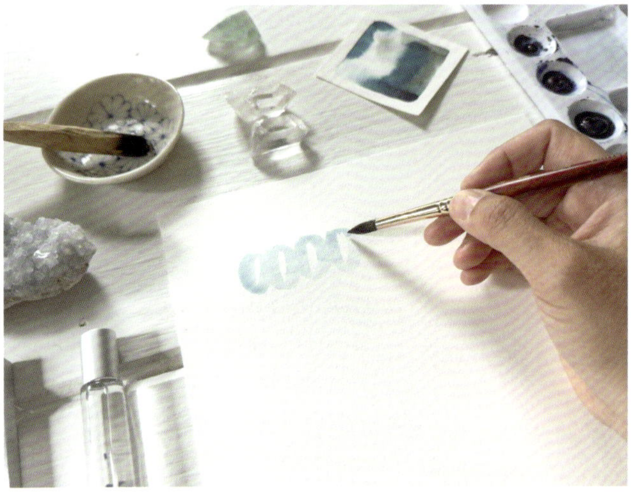

STEP ONE: PAINT THE FIRST OVALS

Mix a light, tea-strength color of your favorite blue. Let your brush hold a good amount of water. You need enough water so that it sits on top of the paper. Begin wherever it feels comfortable on the page. Paint three or four test ovals about 1 inch tall with a gentle, consistent tilt. Aim for them all to be a similar size, but remember, they don't have to be perfect. Beauty is found in the imperfections of your paintings.

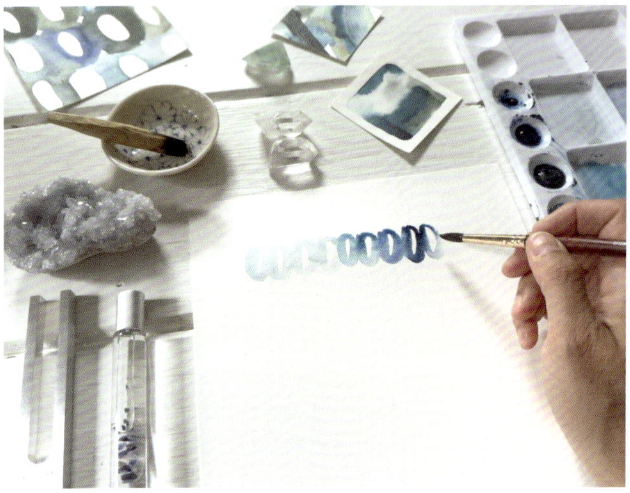

STEP TWO: MAKE A ROW

Continue painting a row of ovals at an unhurried pace. Let the ovals touch and overlap slightly. Start with the light wash. As you progress, change up your color, and watch how the colors interact with each other.

Slowness is safety.
When you slow the mark,
your body hears "it's okay."

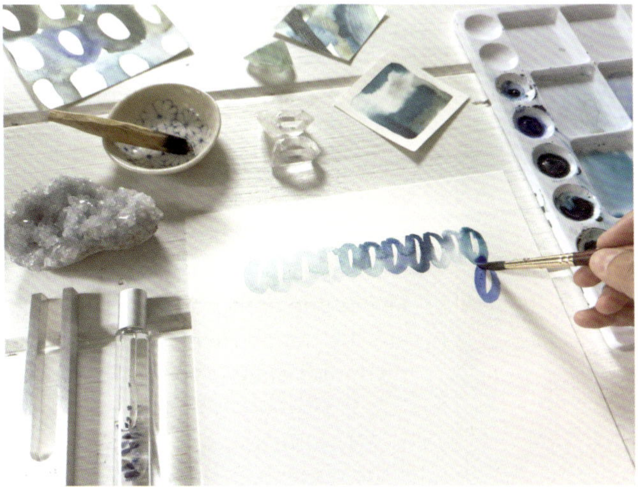

STEP THREE: BUILD THE FIELD

Once you complete your first row, start another row directly below the last oval on the right side and work your way to the left in the opposite direction of the line above. This step engages your brain in an unexpected way, promoting gentle bilateral stimulation that steadies your focus and brings you into the present moment.

Stack additional rows below, allowing each row to touch the one above. The ovals won't align perfectly. Some will be right under the above oval, and some will look like stacking bricks. There is no wrong way of doing this. I find that the less perfect my painting, the more interest it offers.

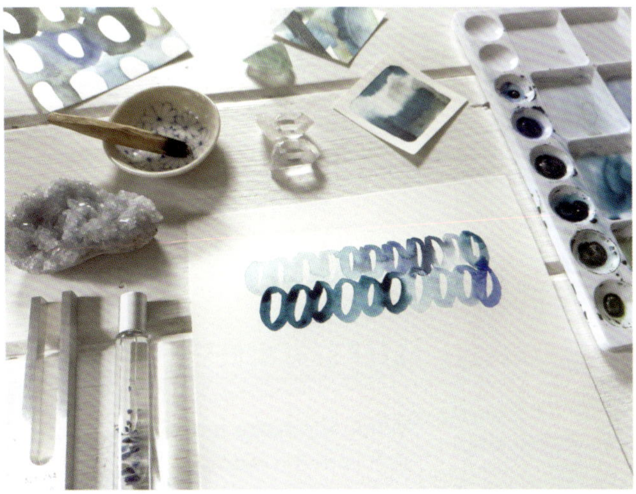

STEP FOUR: PLAY WITH VALUE

There are no rules while you are painting in this way–just opportunities to play. Try playing with value. Paint a few ovals in a light wash, add in a darker wash of the same color, and then add an even darker wash of that color. Experience the flow of color, one into another. How does that feel?

Gentle Reminder

Slow down your tempo.

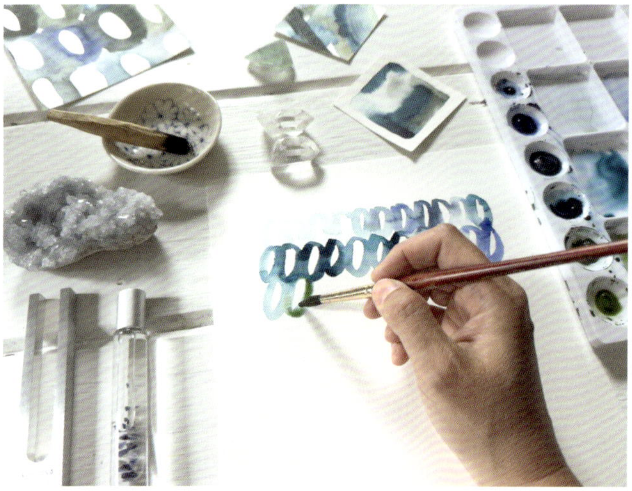

STEP FIVE: DRIP IN COLOR

As you paint, play with dripping color into already wet ovals and watch what happens. Drip in a darker blue or a different color at one edge of the oval and let it feather across the shape. Remember to drip color into spots that are still wet. Then, return to your rhythmic painting.

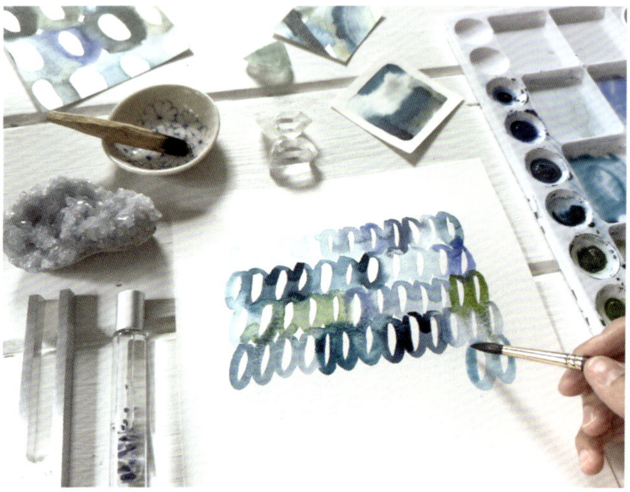

STEP SIX: CONTINUE PLAYING

Fill up your page with rows of ovals. Each row can be an experiment of color, value, and pace. Get to know your materials. Feel the weight of your brush when it is full of water. Feel the texture of the paper as you paint. Drip in different colors and see how they interact with each other. Get lost in the process of play and exploration.

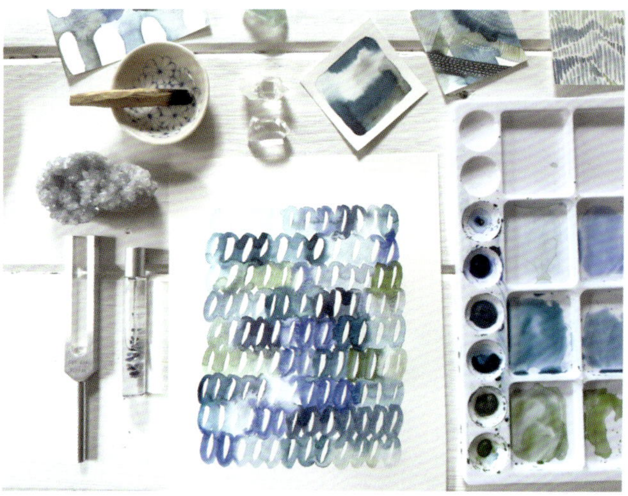

STEP SEVEN: REST AND REVISIT

When the page feels complete, rest with it a moment. Watch where color met color, how water carried the paint, how edges dried each in their own way. Visit the places you worried over and see the beauty that arrived there. When you're ready, let the journal pages hold what you felt.

Painting Meditation: Restful Rhythms

Put on soft-frequency music. Gather what soothes you: a candle, a favorite stone, a drop of oil. Take a deep breath in for 4, then blow gently out through your mouth for 6, like you're softening a candle flame. Pick up your brush, add water and color, and begin wherever your hand wants to land.

Paint in a slow, rhythmic procession. Keep your pace unhurried and your rhythm steady. Let the breath set the tempo. Play as you go, use more water, less water, a shift in color, a touch of deeper value, then return to the rhythm. If you feel overwhelmed or you see something you want to fix, pause, breathe, and loosen your grip. Surrender a little more of the outcome and let the water lead. Release perfectionism; choose peace and calm.

If words help, repeat a mantra: "I am calm and at peace." If mantras don't resonate, simply count with each oval—1, 2, 3, 4, 5, 6—and let the counting carry you. Follow curiosity, not control. When your energy fades or the page feels complete, stop. Take one deep cleansing breath in and release.

Integration

Sit with what you made. Notice how the colors touched, how the water carried them, how edges dried in their own beautiful way. Let what you once called a mistake show you its quiet charm. When you're ready, reflect on the journal pages.

Journal Prompts

- Where do you feel calmer in your body right now?
- What did the water do on the page that surprised or pleased you?
- What did you let go of while you painted?
- How did the painting meditation feel different than just painting with technique in mind?

thoughts

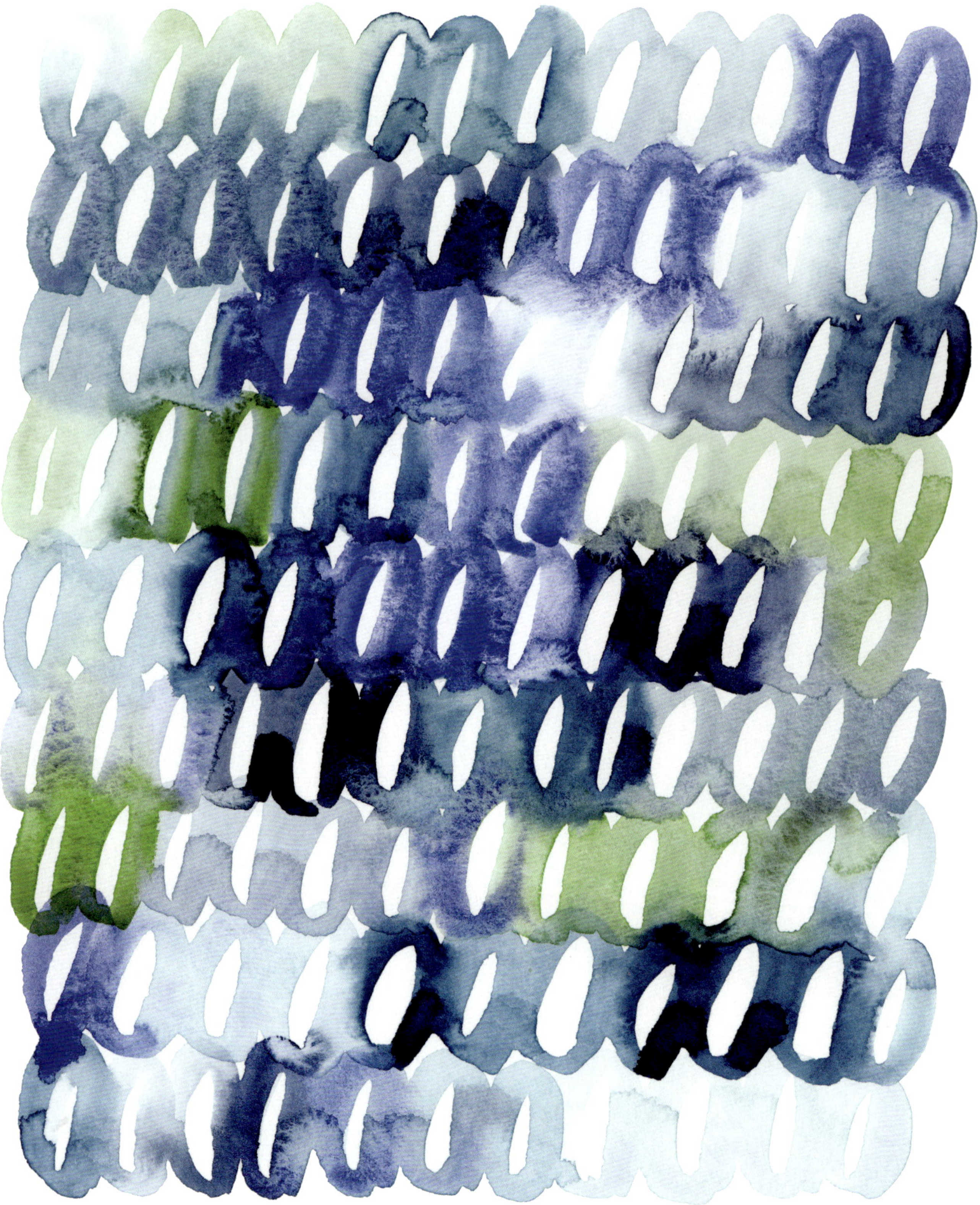

6

NERVOUS SYSTEM REGULATION TOOL

Counting

With the Counting technique, you give your mind the simple job of counting steadily. The predictability of counting helps your whole system settle.

BENEFITS

- **Quiets mental noise.** A gentle count anchors attention, interrupting worry loops and overthinking.
- **Steadies your pace.** Numbers act like a metronome, syncing breath and hand so you move slower and kinder.
- **Signals safety.** A steady rhythm (especially on the exhale) tells your body it's okay to downshift. Watch as the shoulders drop, and the jaw softens.
- **Supports presence.** Counting keeps you present, instead of spiraling into "what ifs." The monkey mind quiets as the counting takes priority.

HOW TO TRY IT

- Sit comfortably and soften your shoulders.
- Inhale gently through your nose.
- On the exhale, count in your head: 1, 2, 3, 4, 5, 6.
- Repeat for four to six breath cycles.

Prefer fewer numbers? Try 1, 2, 3, 4, or count every other breath.

If numbers feel tense, switch to a soft phrase like "I'm safe to slow down."

WHEN IT'S USEFUL

Use the Counting technique when stress spikes, you have a busy mind, perfectionism creeps in, or anytime you want a calm, repeatable rhythm to bring you back to the present.

Counting Calm

QUIET THE MIND WITH COUNTING MARKS

Let steady counts become your resting place. One tick, one number, one breath, your pace slows, your mind gets quiet, and your body softens.

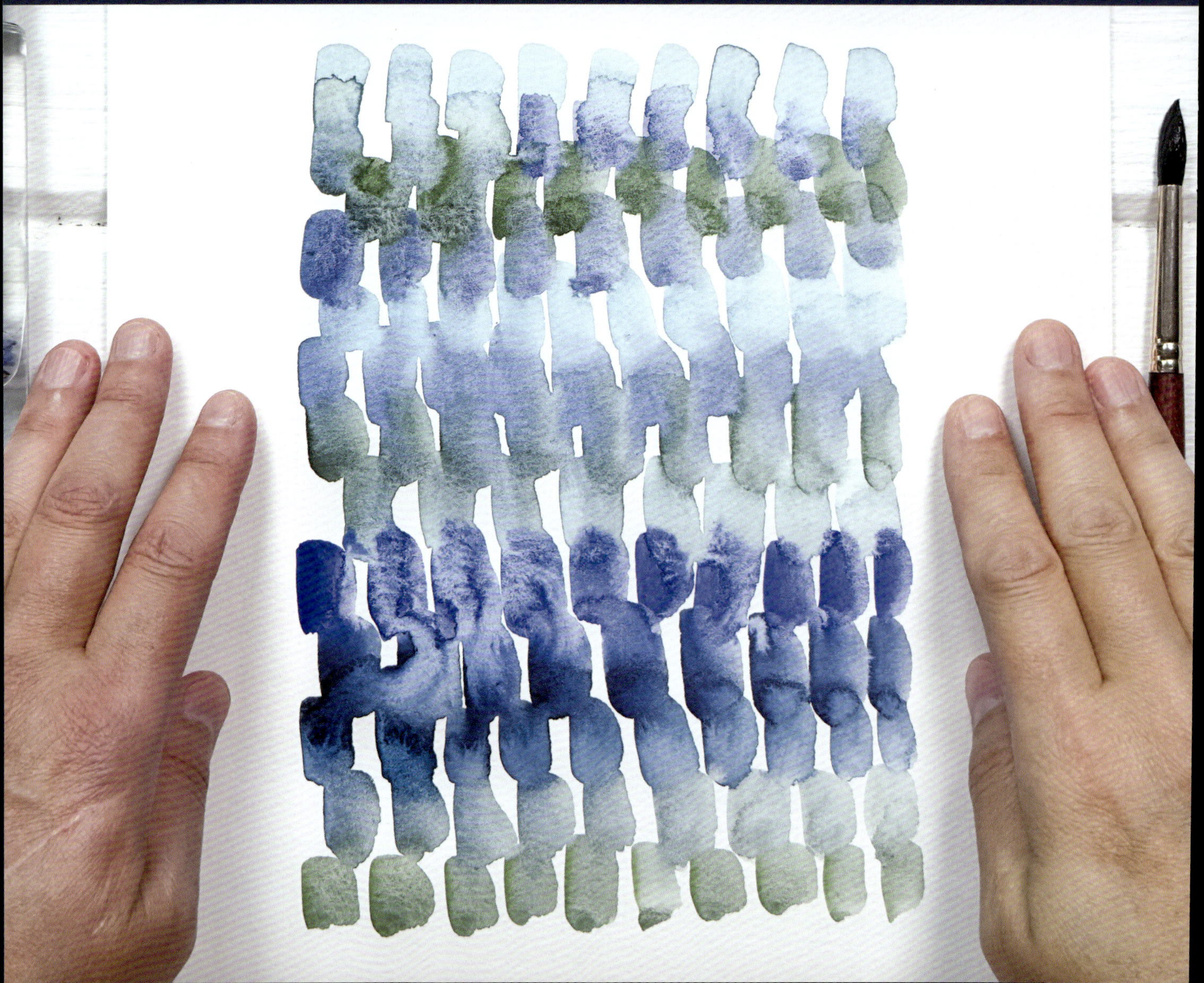

WHAT YOU'LL LEARN

- A slow, repetitive mark-making practice using counted tick marks
- How to build single-color rows so your rhythm stays uninterrupted
- To let go of perfectionism
- How to use value so each row feels different while the whole piece stays unified

In this session, you will paint small tick marks while you count. Each tick mark will be a count that leads to the next mark. Place each mark and move on; the water will do its quiet magic. You will keep each row a single color, which will allow you to stay with the rhythm without stopping to switch paints. The simple left-to-right pattern gives your brain something easy to follow, which helps your nervous system downshift. As you keep the pace slow and let your exhale guide the mark, the thinking mind quiets, your shoulders drop, and you come back to the present moment.

WHAT YOU MIGHT FEEL

- A quieter mind as counting takes the lead, and your brain settles
- A steadier pace that softens your muscles and relaxes your body
- Relief in the simplicity of doing one small thing at a time without worry or fear

HOW THIS SESSION FLOWS

Let's begin with a short technique tutorial. I'll show you the exercise and share tips on how to let go of control and trust the process. When you feel comfortable with the exercise, move into the painting meditation: Pair the technique with quiet counting, peaceful music, and a kinder pace that loosens your grip, relaxes your body, and calms your mind.

One tick, one number.
Keep it steady and let the
counting carry you.

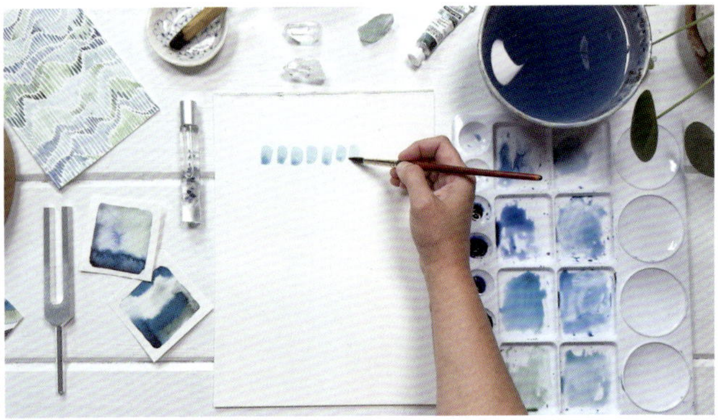

STEP ONE: LAY DOWN YOUR TICK MARKS

Mix a light tea-strength color. Begin by painting tick marks using the side of your brush. The size is up to you. My examples are approximately ¾ of an inch and vary slightly. It's important to let the marks flow from your brush without worry. Let the brush determine the size; don't overthink, just paint. Keep your brush wet; this will allow the color to flow and make beautiful marks when it dries. Keep the marks evenly spaced, with small, breathable gaps in between each mark. Paint with the same color for the entire row.

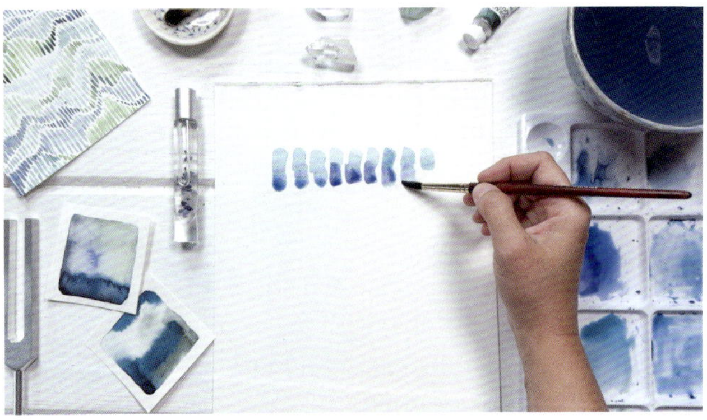

STEP TWO: MARK AND COUNT

Change up the color to make each row feel different. You can adjust the value and make it lighter or darker, or you can keep it at the same value for a more peaceful vibe. There are no wrong decisions here. As you begin the second row, loosen your grip on the brush and breathe softly. As you paint each tick mark, softly count as the brush touches the paper: 1, 2, 3, 4, 5. Feel each mark as you lay down the color, keep your pace slow, your voice quiet, and remember to breathe.

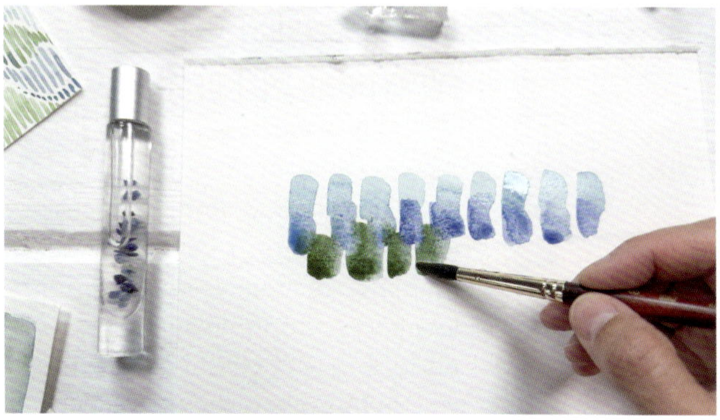

STEP THREE: KEEP GOING

Continue stacking rows. Keep each row touching the row above. Let slight differences in length or tilt add quiet interest. Don't worry about making anything perfect. You can change the color of the row and see how the color from the row *above* mixes with the new row. The more water you use, the easier it is for the mixing magic to happen. Don't be afraid of the water.

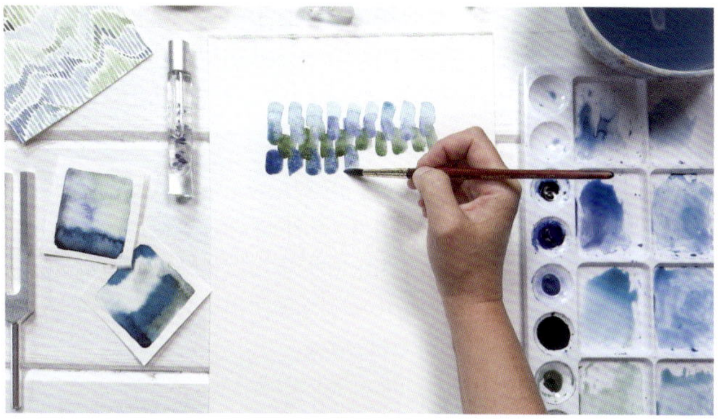

STEP FOUR: PLAY WITH VALUE

As you paint each row, play with the value. Some rows can be light washes, while others are medium tone or dark. Experiment with each row, let your intuition guide you, and don't overthink any of your decisions. It will be beautiful no matter what you do. Don't forget to breathe and let each count calm your mind and body. Continue playing.

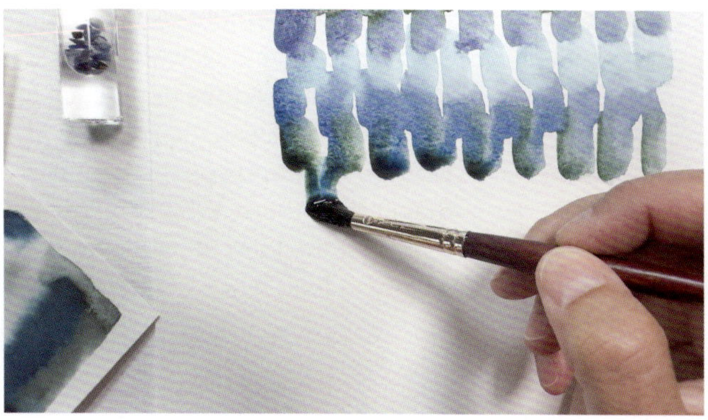

STEP FIVE: SURRENDER TO THE PROCESS

Let the paint and the water do the work for you. Don't try to control the outcome; watch as the magical properties of watercolor transform simple tick marks into a beautiful abstract painting.

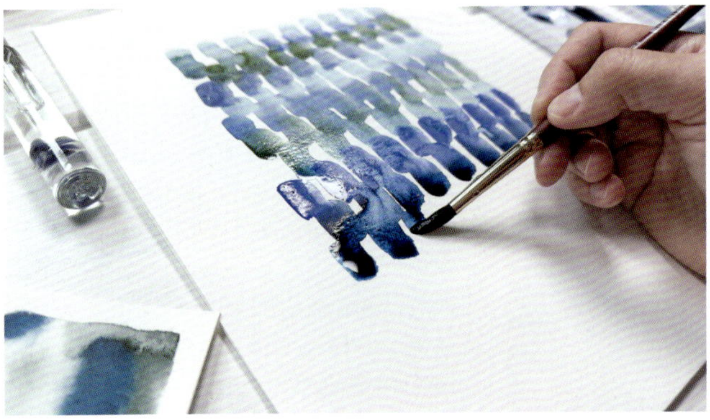

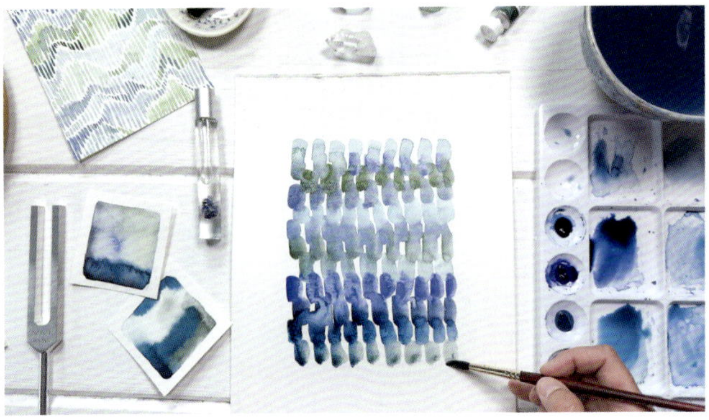

STEP SIX: TRUST THAT EVERYTHING WILL BE OKAY

As you settle into the rhythm of painting and counting, perfection will loosen its grip. Let the wild moments of creative flow happen. Don't try to control every bloom or edge. See where letting go carries you. In this piece, the paint mixes in unexpected ways; it overlaps, there are soft floods of water, and a little chaos that can feel like it's too much. Breathe and loosen your grip. Don't fix or fuss, just place the next mark and keep moving. Trust the drying; what feels messy now often settles into something quietly beautiful.

You can see how that area dried with that swirl of unexpected glamour. The less you try to fix things, the more beautiful your painting will become.

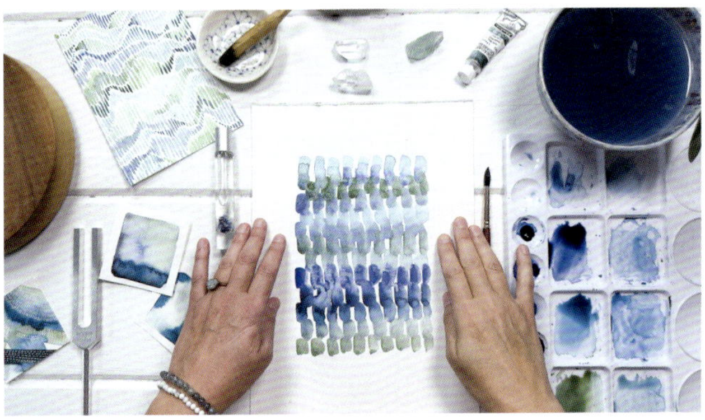

STEP SEVEN: PAUSE AND REFLECT

When the page feels complete, rest with it a moment. Watch where color met color, how water carried the paint, how edges dried each in their own way. Visit the places you worried over and see the beauty that arrived there. When you're ready, let the journal pages hold what you felt.

Painting Meditation: Counting Calm

Put on soft-frequency music or whatever makes you feel happy. Gather what soothes you: a candle, a favorite stone, a drop of oil. Take a deep breath in for 4, then blow gently out for 6, like softening a candle flame. Pick up your brush, add water and color, and begin wherever your hand wants to land.

Paint in a slow, rhythmic procession. Count each tick as you place it: 1, 2, 3, 4, 5, 6... Keep one color per row so you don't break the flow. Let the breath set the pace. Play as you go, slightly more water, a softer or deeper value, a touch of extra space, and then return to the rhythm. If you feel overwhelmed or want to fix something, pause. Breathe. Loosen your grip. Surrender to the process. Let go of perfectionism. If mantras resonate, whisper: "I'm calm and at peace." If not, let the counting carry you. Follow curiosity, not control. When your energy fades or the page feels complete, stop. Take one deep, cleansing breath in, and release.

Integration

Sit with what you made. Notice how the rows flowed, the small differences in each mark, and how value shifts created gentle movement. Let any "mistakes" show you their quiet charm. When you're ready, jot a few lines in your journal.

Journal Prompts

- Did counting change how your body felt? Where do you feel calmer now?
- What did counting do to your mind while you painted? Did it quiet the chatter, steady your focus, or something else?
- Which value (light, mid, deep) felt best to use today, and why?
- What did you let go of while you painted?

thoughts

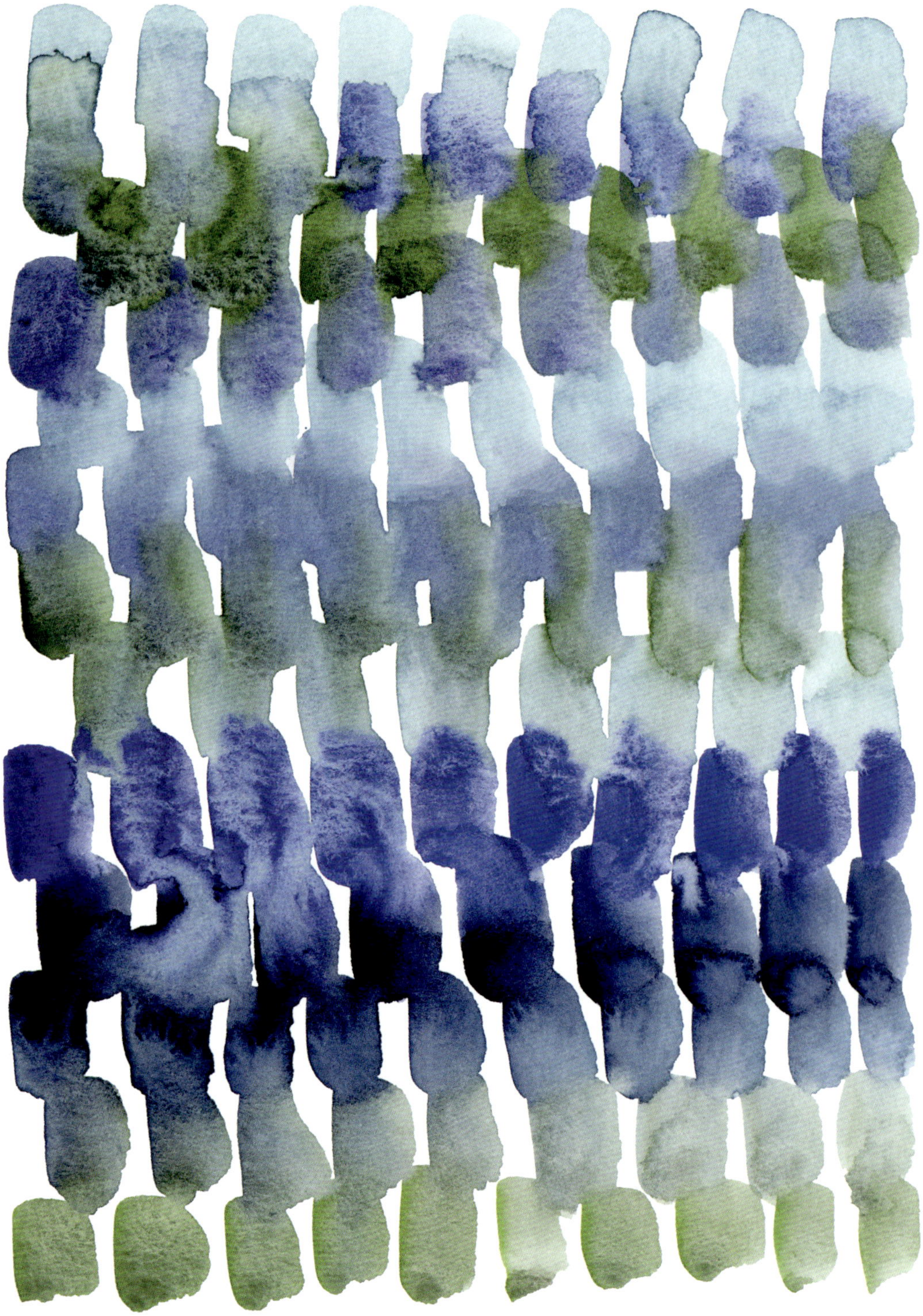

7

NERVOUS SYSTEM REGULATION TOOL

Air Practice

With the Air Practice technique, you give your mind a simple, gentle focus by moving both hands in mirrored motions in the air in front of you. This easy left-right awareness, plus slower breathing, helps your whole system settle.

BENEFITS

- **Quiets mental noise.** Mirrored movement gives your mind a simple track to follow, so worry loops soften.
- **Signals safety.** Slow, even motion with a longer exhale tells your body it's okay to downshift. Shoulders drop, and the jaw softens.
- **Supports presence.** Watching both hands together keeps you here, with this breath and this moment.

HOW TO TRY IT

- Sit comfortably and soften your shoulders.
- Rest both hands on your lap, then hover them out in front of you.
- Inhale gently through your nose.
- On the exhale, move both hands at the same time in small, mirrored motions (like butterfly wings): Start with small circles. Each hand mirrors the other.
- Keep movements slow and even. Let your eyes follow both hands together.
- Try counting with each rotation.
- Try making squares. Pause at each corner and follow the movement with your eyes.
- Remember to take in a few deep breaths during the process.
- Continue alternating circles and squares until the time is up or your energy fades.

WHEN IT'S USEFUL

Use the Air Practice technique before you paint to ground in your body, during a stressful moment, when perfectionism starts to grip, or anytime you want a calm, repeatable reset that brings you back to the present.

Symmetry in Flow

PAINT WITH TWO HANDS

Let mirrored movement become your resting place. Two brushes, one gentle rhythm. Your focus settles, and your mind gets quiet.

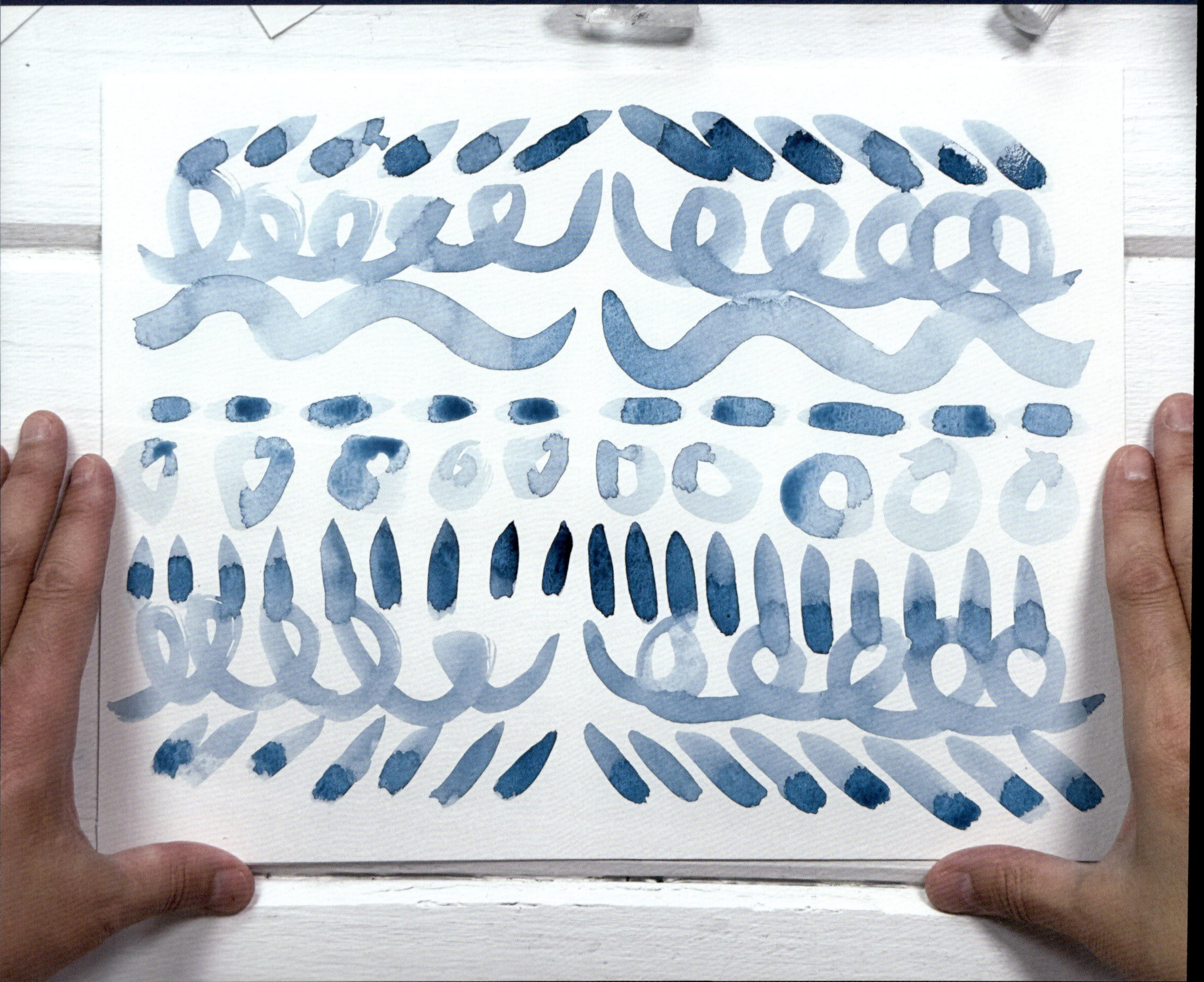

WHAT YOU'LL LEARN

- How to paint with both hands to invite balance and presence into your practice
- A simple way to begin at the center, then let mirrored lines unfold while surrendering to the process
- How to welcome unpredictability from your non-dominant hand
- How to let go of perfectionism and let the paper hold whatever energy it receives

In this session, you will paint with two hands at the same time. Start near the center; it doesn't have to be measured or perfect. Choose one color from your palette, whatever color is calling to you. Let your brush touch the paper and pull soft, mirrored marks across the page, from the center outward. Let one pass suggest the next. Use your intuition and allow the marks to flow. Dashes, lines, dots, or whatever comes out. There are no wrong decisions. Sharing attention between both hands keeps you present, loosens control, and opens room for intuition. When you keep the pace slow and steady, your mind quiets and your body can relax.

Using both hands gives your brain gentle left and right input simultaneously, which can steady attention and help your nervous system downshift. Many people notice easier breathing, softer shoulders, and less pressure to be perfect when both hands are involved.

WHAT YOU MIGHT FEEL

- A calmer, more focused mind as both hands share attention
- Shoulders dropping, jaw softening, and a kinder pace
- Relief as your non-dominant hand leads you past perfection and into play

HOW THIS SESSION FLOWS

We'll begin with a short technique tutorial. I'll show you how to set up two brushes, start at the center, and pull mirrored marks. When you feel comfortable with the technique, move into the painting meditation. Pair the motion with soft music, easy breaths, and a let-go mindset that relaxes your body and quiets your mind.

Two hands, one rhythm.
Let the symmetry carry you
and let perfection go.

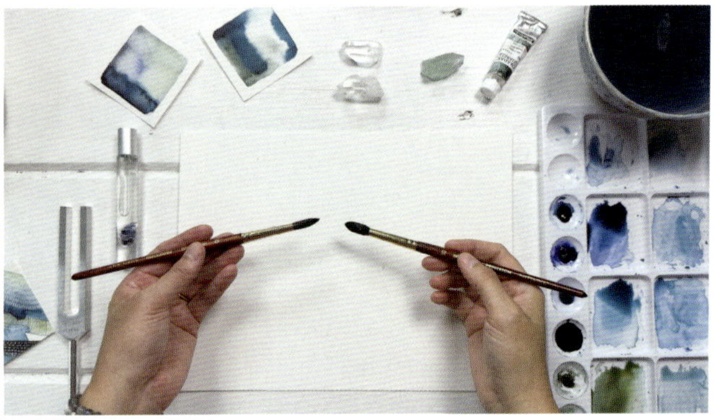

STEP ONE: SET UP TWO BRUSHES

Pick any two brushes. They do not have to match.

Load both brushes with the same color paint at a light, tea-strength mix. Once you feel comfortable with the lesson, you can mix up the colors and play with the values. Keep it simple to start.

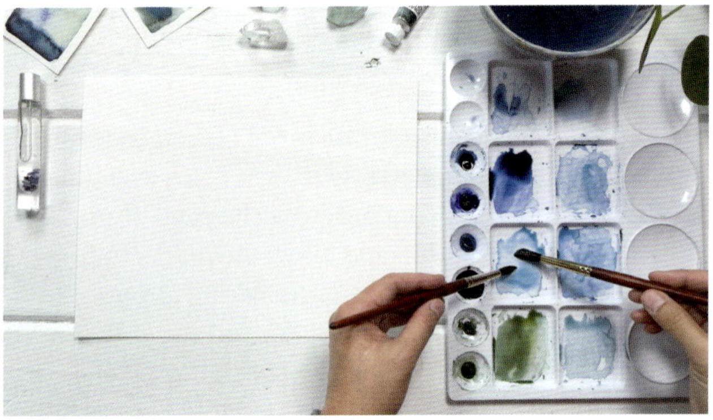

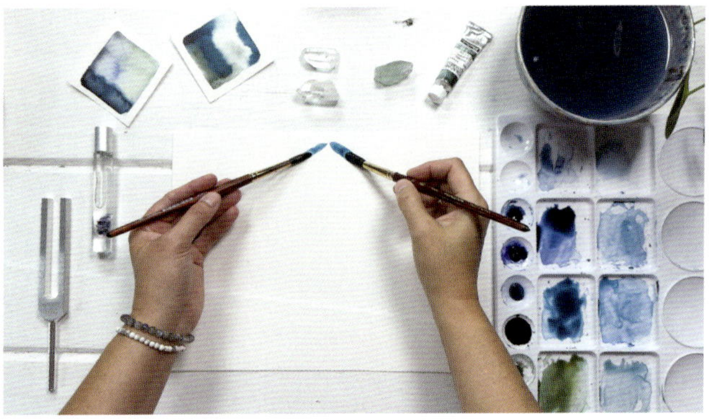

STEP TWO: FIND YOUR CENTER

Place both tips near the middle of the page. Get comfortable. Soften your grip. Let your shoulders drop. Take a deep breath into the count of four and release with a little force to the count of six. Feel the tightness in your body start to release.

Gentle Reminder

Let the water help the color flow

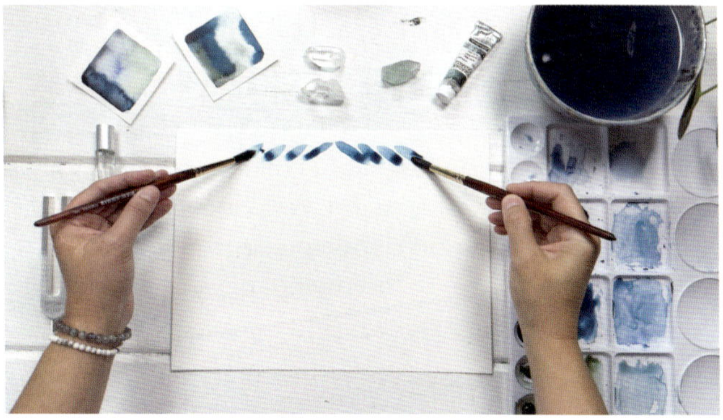

STEP THREE: PULL THE FIRST MIRRORED LINES

Move both hands at the same time. Glide outward from the center, making slanted lines to start. Keep your pace kind and steady. It will feel strange at first, but keep going. The thing I love about this exercise is that you are so focused on making the marks that your thinking mind shuts down and your focus sharpens.

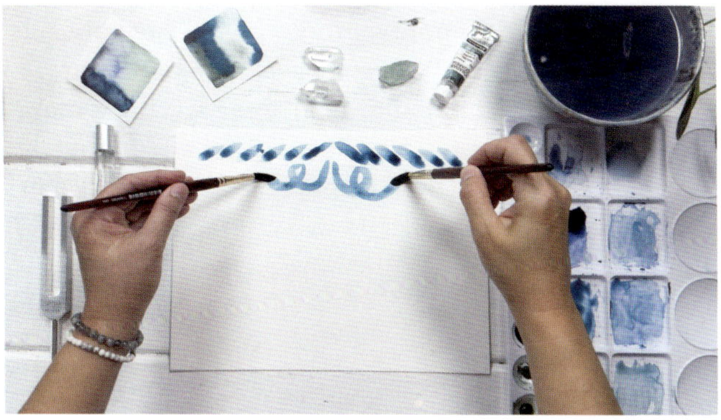

STEP FOUR: REPEAT THE MOTION

Return to the center and start a new line. I chose swirly lines, but you can let your intuition take you wherever you would like to go. Remember to have fun. It will feel weird, so embrace that and smile while you are making your way through.

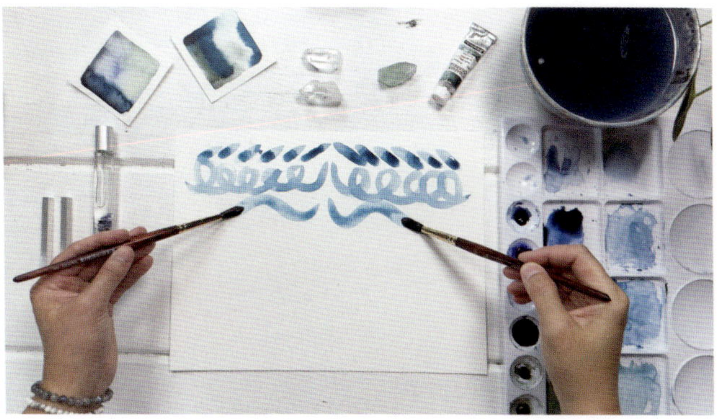

STEP FIVE: MATCH PRESSURE AND LENGTH

Notice if one hand presses harder. Soften it to match the calmer hand. Keep lines "similar enough" without chasing perfect. Yes, I know this sounds easier than it is. It's okay if it looks messy. Embrace the messiness and enjoy the process.

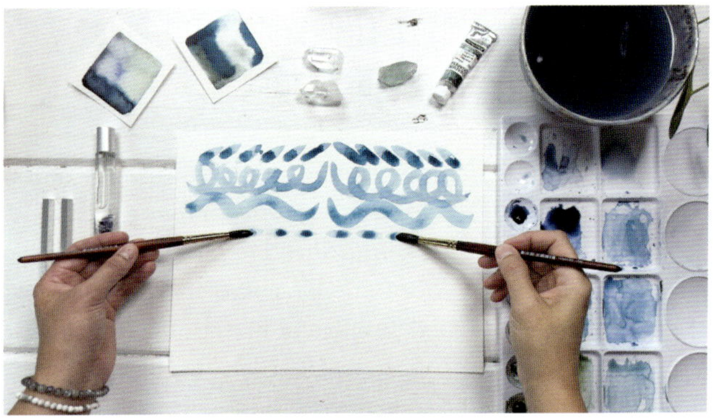

STEP SIX: LET SMALL DIFFERENCES HAPPEN

Allow slight changes in tilt, length, or spacing. Welcome what your non-dominant hand brings. Play with the rhythm of your marks.

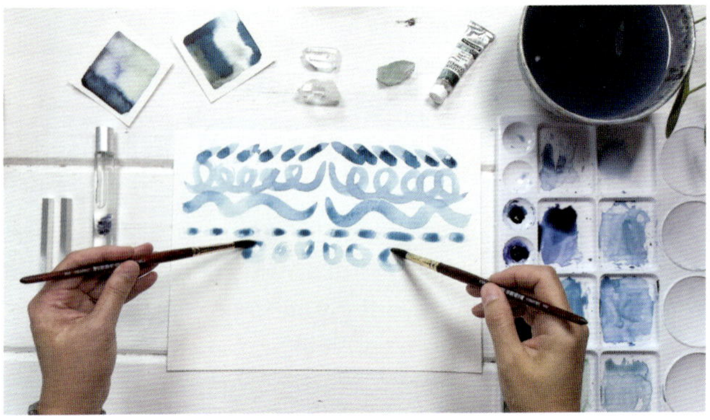

STEP SEVEN: BUILD THE FLOW

Continue from the center, adding more mirrored pulls. Leave pockets of white space so the page can breathe. If an area feels busy, make the next lines lighter and longer. This is where you get to play. What marks do you want to paint next?

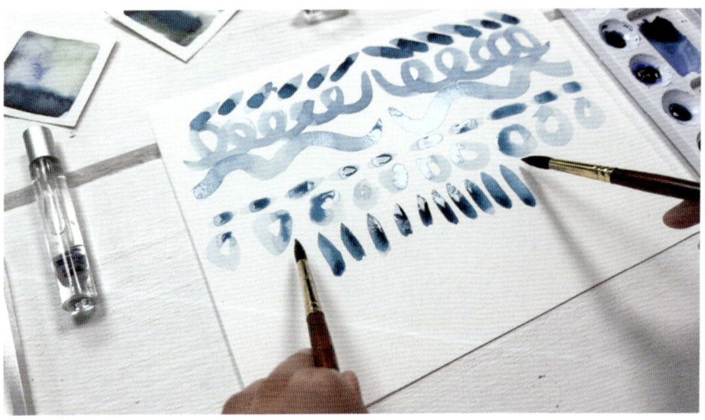

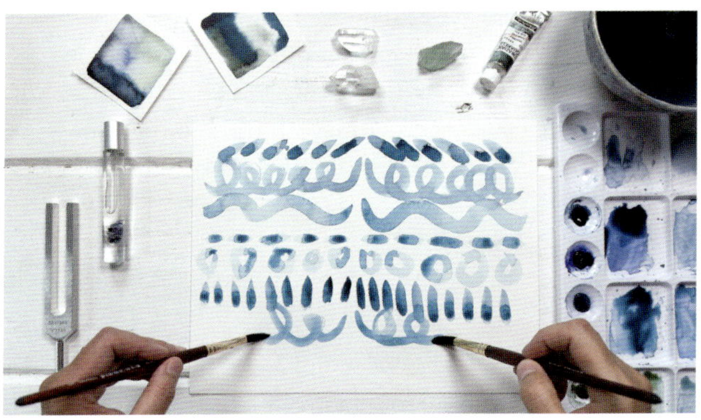

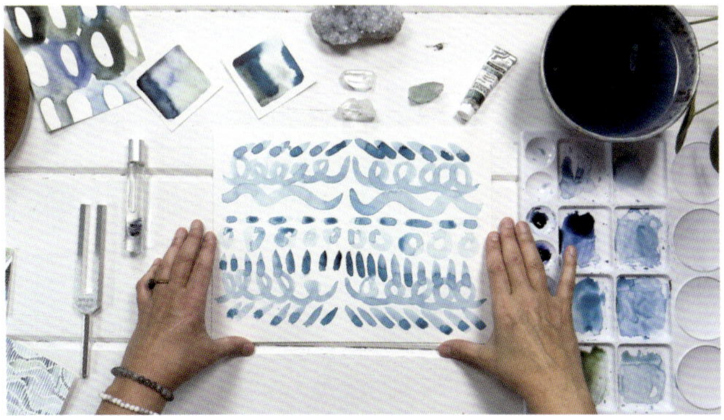

STEP EIGHT: PAUSE AND LOOK

When your energy starts to fade, pause and look at your paper. Notice where the two sides met and where they wandered. Think about the journey you just took through the painting. How do you feel?

Permission Slip

Stop when your energy fades.

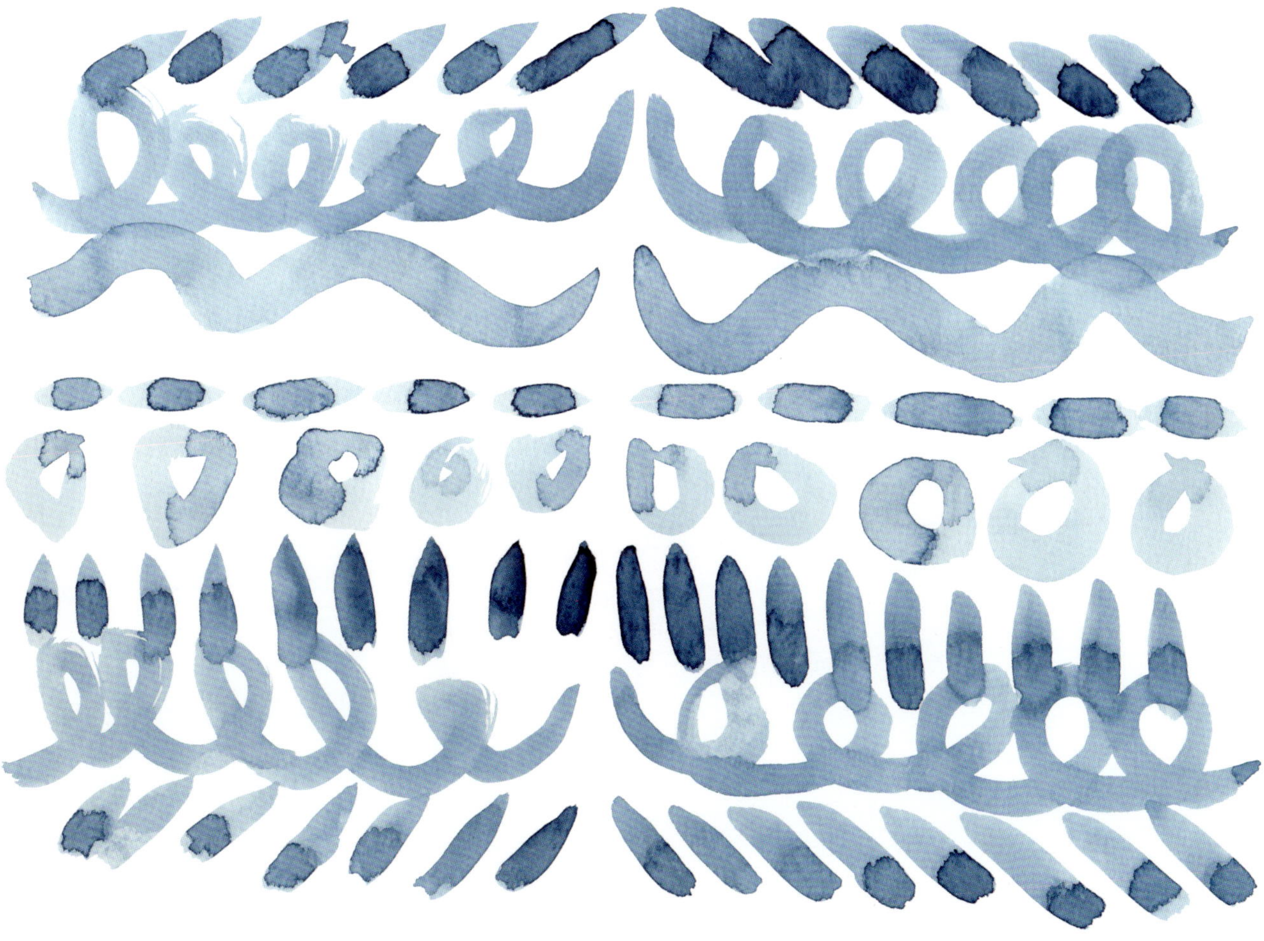

Painting Meditation: Symmetry in Flow

Put on soft-frequency music or whatever makes you feel happy. Gather what soothes you: a candle, a favorite stone, a drop of oil. Sit comfortably. Inhale for four, exhale for six for a few easy cycles. Pick up a brush in each hand. Start near the center. Let both hands move together in a gentle, mirrored rhythm. Keep your pace slow and your body soft. Follow the feeling, not the outcome. If one hand tenses, soften your grip and match the calmer hand. Let water help the paint to flow. Welcome small differences. Stay with the rhythm until your energy fades or the page feels complete.

Integration

Rest with your painting. Notice where the two sides met, where they wandered, and how the water dried on each path. See how small mismatches created life. Take one easy exhale. Name one word for how you feel and jot it in your journal.

Journal Prompts

- How did using two hands change your focus?
- Where did you notice softness in your body after a few minutes?
- What surprised you about the differences between your hands?
- What did you let go of while painting?

Energy Note

White space is rest. Leave pockets of quiet so the page can breathe.

8

NERVOUS SYSTEM REGULATION TOOL

Soft Sigh Out

With the Soft Sigh Out technique, you let the exhale leave as a quiet sigh through the mouth. Make it gentle, easy, and slightly longer than your inhale.

BENEFITS

- **Quiets mental noise.** A soft, steady out breath gives your mind a simple rhythm, so worry loops ease.
- **Releases tension.** The sigh softens the jaw and shoulders.
- **Signals safety.** A longer exhale tells your body it's okay to downshift.
- **Supports presence.** The breath becomes your anchor so you can stay here with this moment.

HOW TO TRY IT

- Sit comfortably and soften your shoulders.
- Inhale lightly through your nose for four.
- Exhale as a quiet sigh through your mouth for six. Think about "softening" a candle, not blowing it out.
- Repeat for four to six breath cycles.

Optional: Place a hand on your heart or belly and feel the rise and fall.

WHEN IT'S USEFUL

Use the Soft Sigh Out technique before you paint to arrive in your body, during a stress spike, when perfectionism starts to grip, or anytime you want a calm, repeatable reset that brings you back to the present.

Links in a Chain

BUILDING CONNECTION THROUGH WATER, COLOR, AND BREATH

Let linked circles become your resting place. One circle at a time, calm and steady. Where they overlap, color meets color, and the water does its quiet magic.

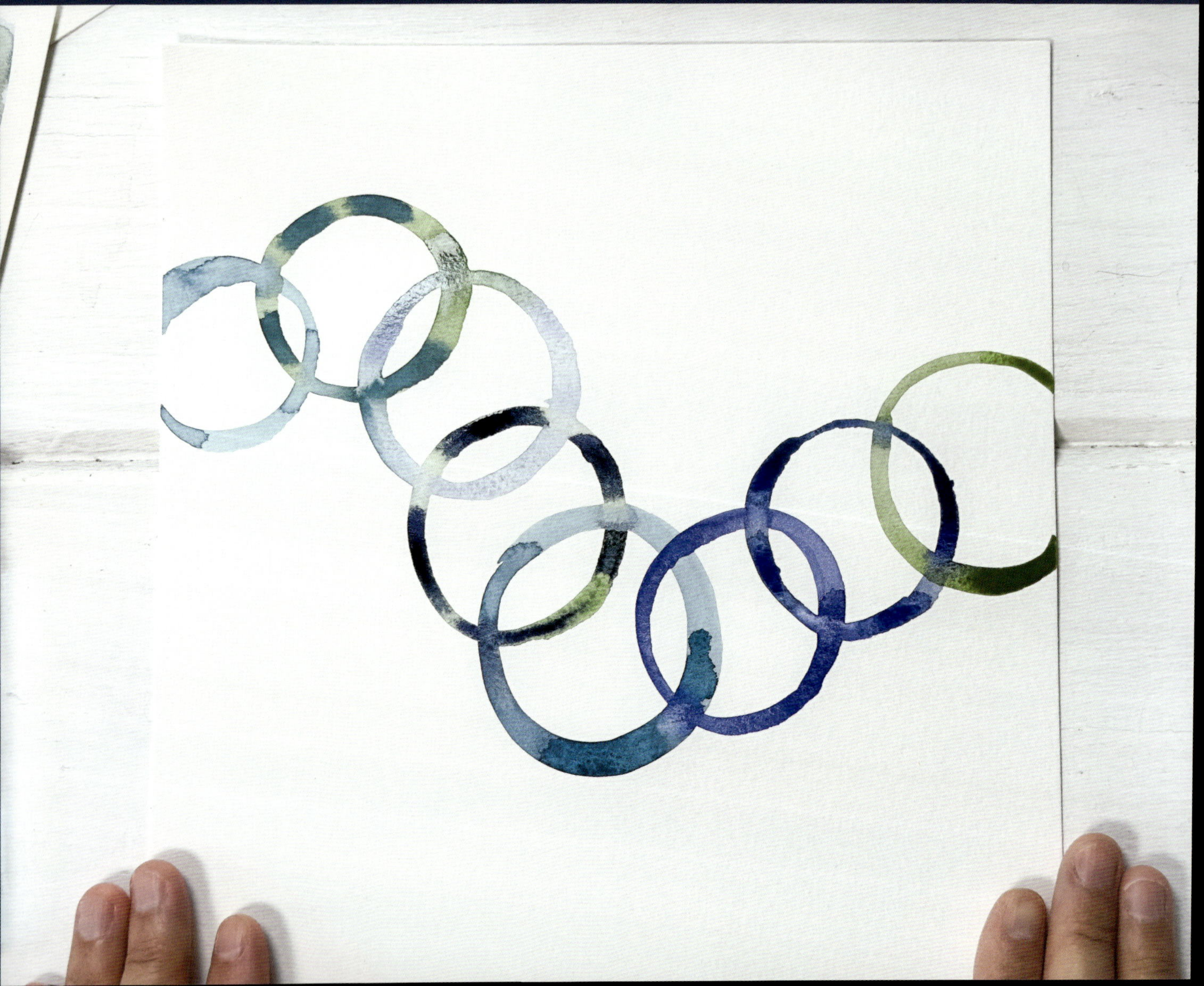

WHAT YOU'LL LEARN

- A slow, repetitive practice of painting simple circle links
- How to place and overlap circles so that the intersections create beautiful mingling
- How to let go of perfectionism and keep moving while the water does the work
- How to use value so each link feels distinct while the whole piece stays unified

In this session, you will paint simple circles that overlap like links in a chain. You place one circle, then the next, letting them meet so color and water can interact on their own. Keep your pace unhurried, notice the soft blends in the overlaps, and let the painting grow link by link. As you move steadily and let your breath guide the pace, the thinking mind gets quieter, your shoulders drop, and you land in the present.

WHAT YOU MIGHT FEEL

- A softer mind as you focus on one circle at a time
- A steady rhythm that relaxes your jaw and shoulders
- Delight in the surprising ways color mingles at the overlaps

HOW THIS SESSION FLOWS

Let's begin with a short technique tutorial. I'll show you the exercise and a few easy ways to add variety in size, spacing, and value. When it feels comfortable in your hands, move into the painting meditation. Pair the technique with a gentle Soft Sigh Out, peaceful music, and a kinder pace that loosens your grip, relaxes your body, and calms your mind.

One circle, then another.
Let the links meet and let the water
show you something beautiful.

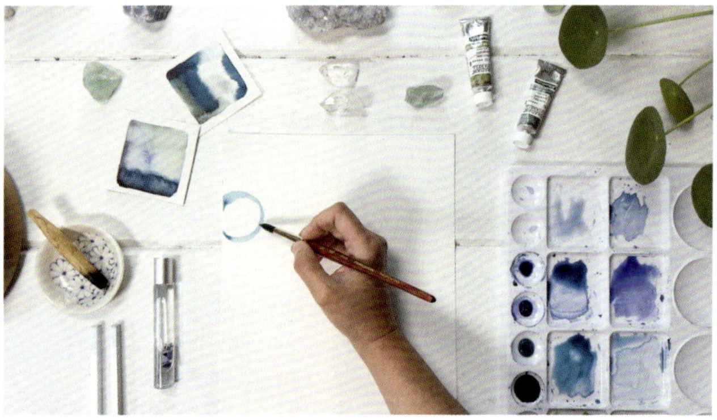

STEP ONE: PAINT THE FIRST CIRCLE

Mix a light, tea-strength color you love. Choose a small circle size that feels easy to repeat. Paint your first circle. Let it be round-ish and relaxed. Do not chase perfection. Keep your grip soft and your pace slow.

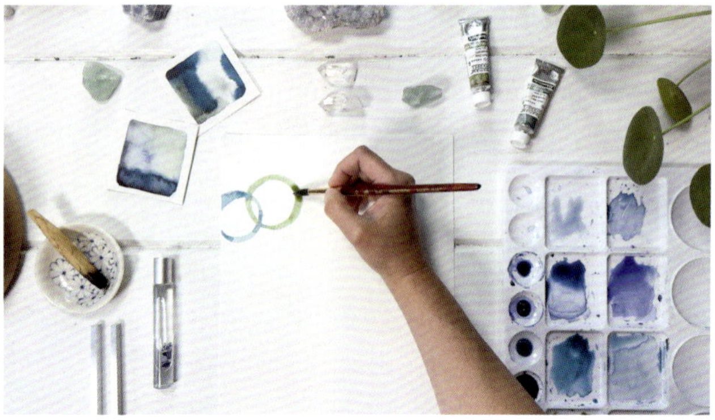

STEP TWO: PLACE THE SECOND CIRCLE AND WATCH THE INTERSECTION

Try a different or darker color. While the first circle is still wet, paint a second circle that gently overlaps the first, allowing the lines to intersect. Watch the intersection as it forms. Notice how the water pulls them together and the colors mix. Let the paint do its thing. Don't fuss with it. Let it go. It will dry in beautiful ways.

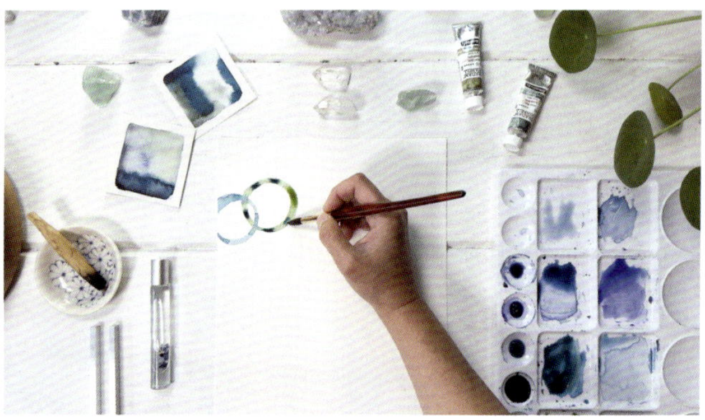

STEP THREE: PLAY WITH DRIPPING COLOR

Take time to experiment with your circles. While my circle is still wet, I drip in some Prussian Green and move to the next circle.

Permission Slip

Messy over perfection.

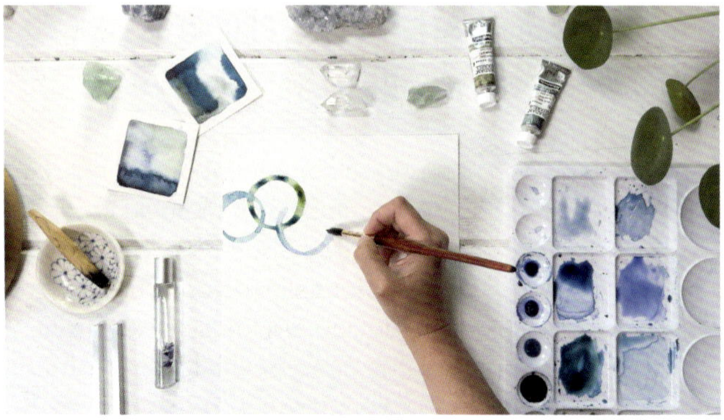

STEP FOUR: BUILD THE CHAIN

Add a third circle that overlaps the second. Continue one circle at a time, each one meeting the circle before it. Follow a loose curve across the paper. Keep moving without worrying. The chain grows link by link. Let your breath flow smoothly and evenly like the circles. Let your shoulders drop and release your tight grip on the brush.

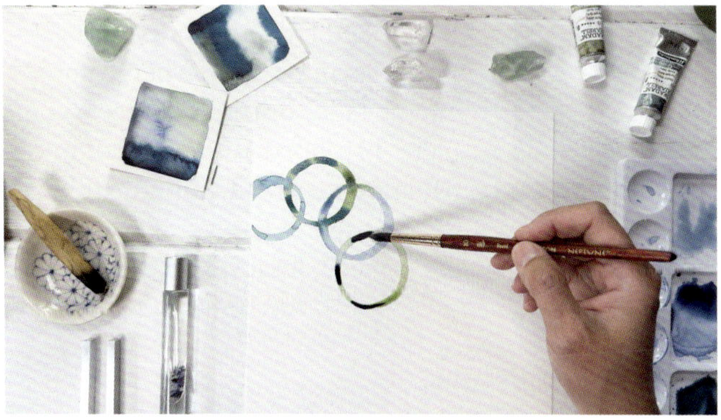

STEP FIVE: PLAY WITH WET-ON-WET

While the circle is still wet, play with dripping more color. Watch as the color spreads and dries, leaving interesting marks.

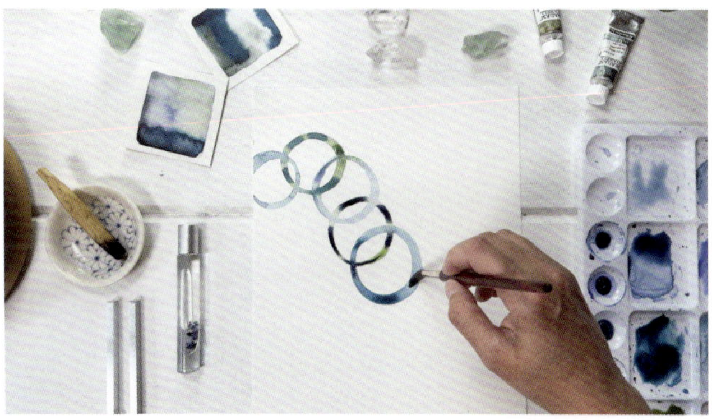

STEP SIX: EXPLORE VALUE AND VARIETY

Introduce a mid-value for a few links, then a deeper value sparingly. Let small differences in size and spacing happen. Keep most links light and mid-toned so the overlaps stay airy.

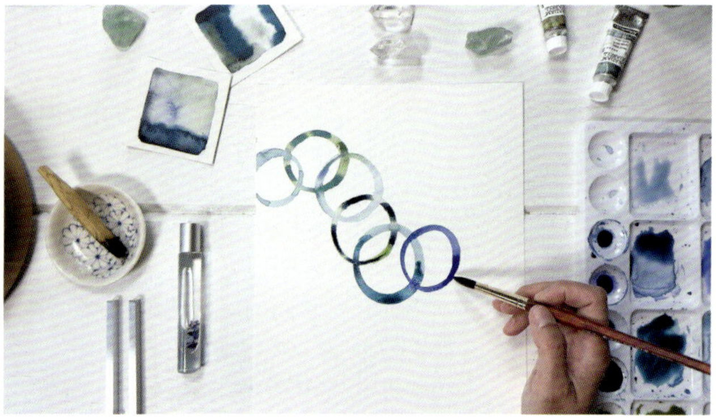

STEP SEVEN: PROGRESS LINK BY LINK

Continue connecting your links. Let your intuition pick the next color. I used Ultramarine Blue, but see what color calls to you. Check in on how you are feeling. Are your breaths deep or shallow? Are your shoulders tense or relaxed?

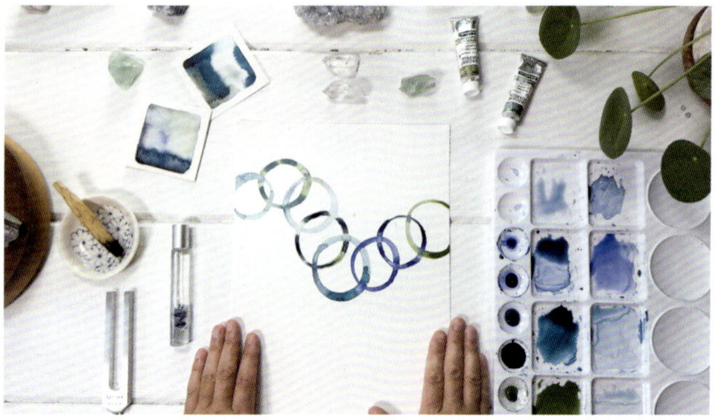

STEP EIGHT: PAUSE AND VIEW

Pause, and look at your painting. Keep playing or stop when your energy fades or the chain feels complete. I stopped at the edge of my paper, but you can continue filling up the page. Whatever you are feeling or need, let it fill up the paper.

Gentle Reminder

Loosen your grip.

Painting Meditation: Links in a Chain

Put on soft-frequency music. Sit comfortably. Try the Soft Sigh Out technique for a few easy breaths. Pick up your brush and begin wherever your hand wants to land. Paint one circle, then the next, letting them overlap like links. Keep your pace slow and steady. Let your breath set the tempo. Watch what happens at the intersections. If you feel the urge to fix, pause. Breathe. Place the next circle and keep moving. Trust the water. Choose soft over perfect. When the chain feels complete, rest with it. Notice where color met color, how the edges dried, and how the overlaps created their own little worlds.

Integration

Sit with your painting. Follow the chain with your eyes, pausing at the overlaps. Notice how the water carried the color and how each meeting dried in its own way. Thank the places you once called mistakes. Take one longer exhale and write a single word for how you feel.

Journal Prompts

- What surprised you at the overlaps today?
- Where did you feel yourself let go a little more?
- Which value felt best to you, and why?

Energy Note

Intersections are invitations to surrender.

thoughts

....

....

....

....

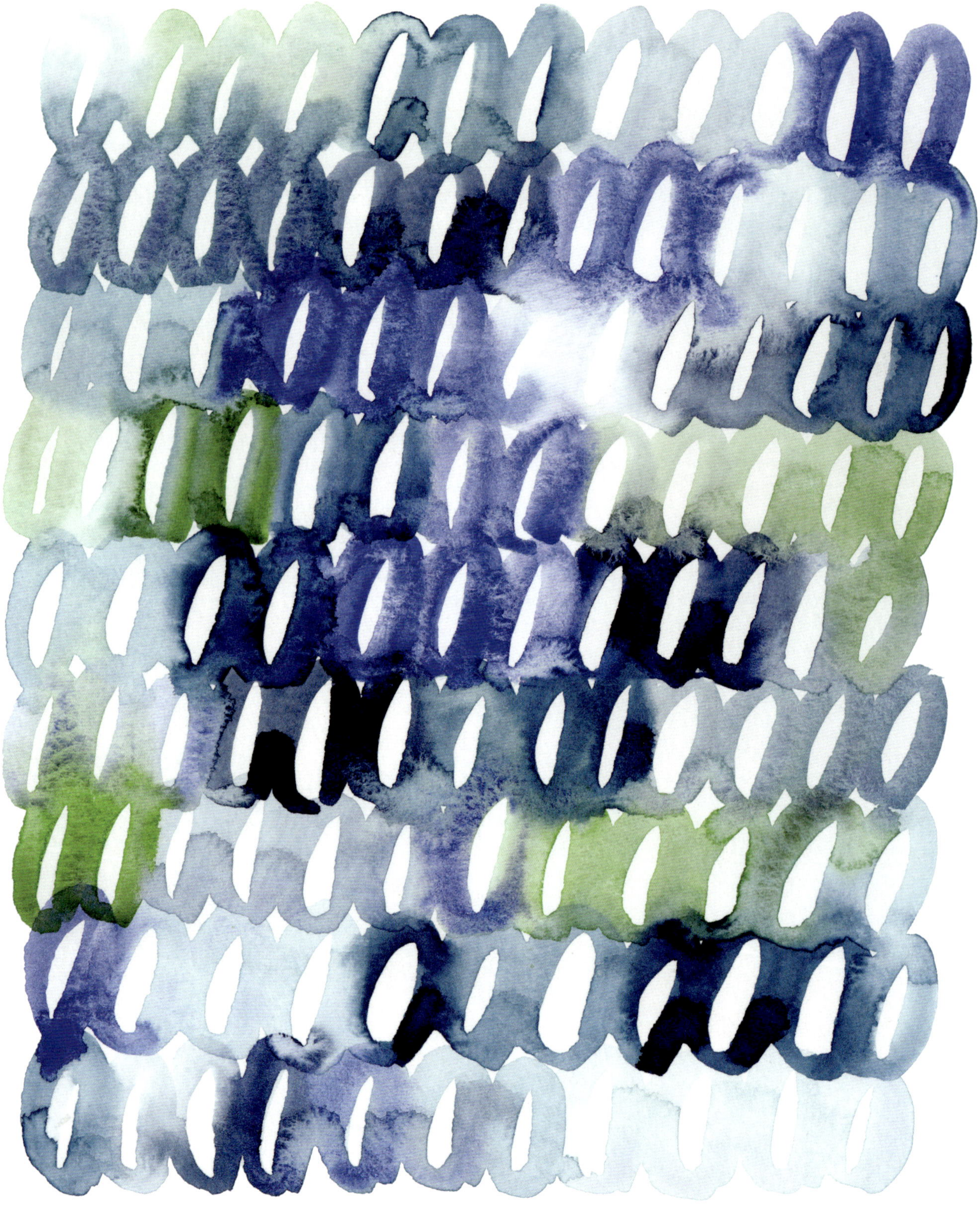

9

NERVOUS SYSTEM REGULATION TOOL

Orienting with Curiosity

With the Orienting with Curiosity technique, you bring your awareness into the present moment by gently noticing what surrounds you. This soft attention tells your body it's safe and opens the senses for painting.

BENEFITS

- **Signals safety.** When your eyes scan the room calmly, your brain registers "I'm not in danger," and the nervous system begins to settle.
- **Expands awareness.** Shifting your gaze from narrow focus to a wider view reduces tension and overcontrol.
- **Invites curiosity.** Noticing color, texture, and light naturally draws you into the creative flow.
- **Supports presence.** The body anchors in the here and now, preparing you to paint from a calm, grounded place.

HOW TO TRY IT

- Sit comfortably and soften your shoulders.
- Let your eyes slowly move around the room.
- Name three things you can see. Name a color, a texture, or a bit of light.
- Let your gaze rest briefly on each one.
- Take a slow, natural breath, and return your focus to the page.
- Begin your first line of painting while holding that quiet curiosity.

WHEN IT'S USEFUL

Use the Orienting with Curiosity technique before painting to shift out of busy thoughts, during moments of tension or self-criticism, or anytime you want to reconnect with safety and the simple beauty around you.

Lines of Ease

PLAY WITHIN THE LINES AND LET THE WATER LEAD THE WAY

Let calm, horizontal bands become your resting place. You paint one line at a time. Stay soft, slow, and open to discovery. As the line settles, you return to it and play within its edges, watching how color and water connect in their own natural rhythm.

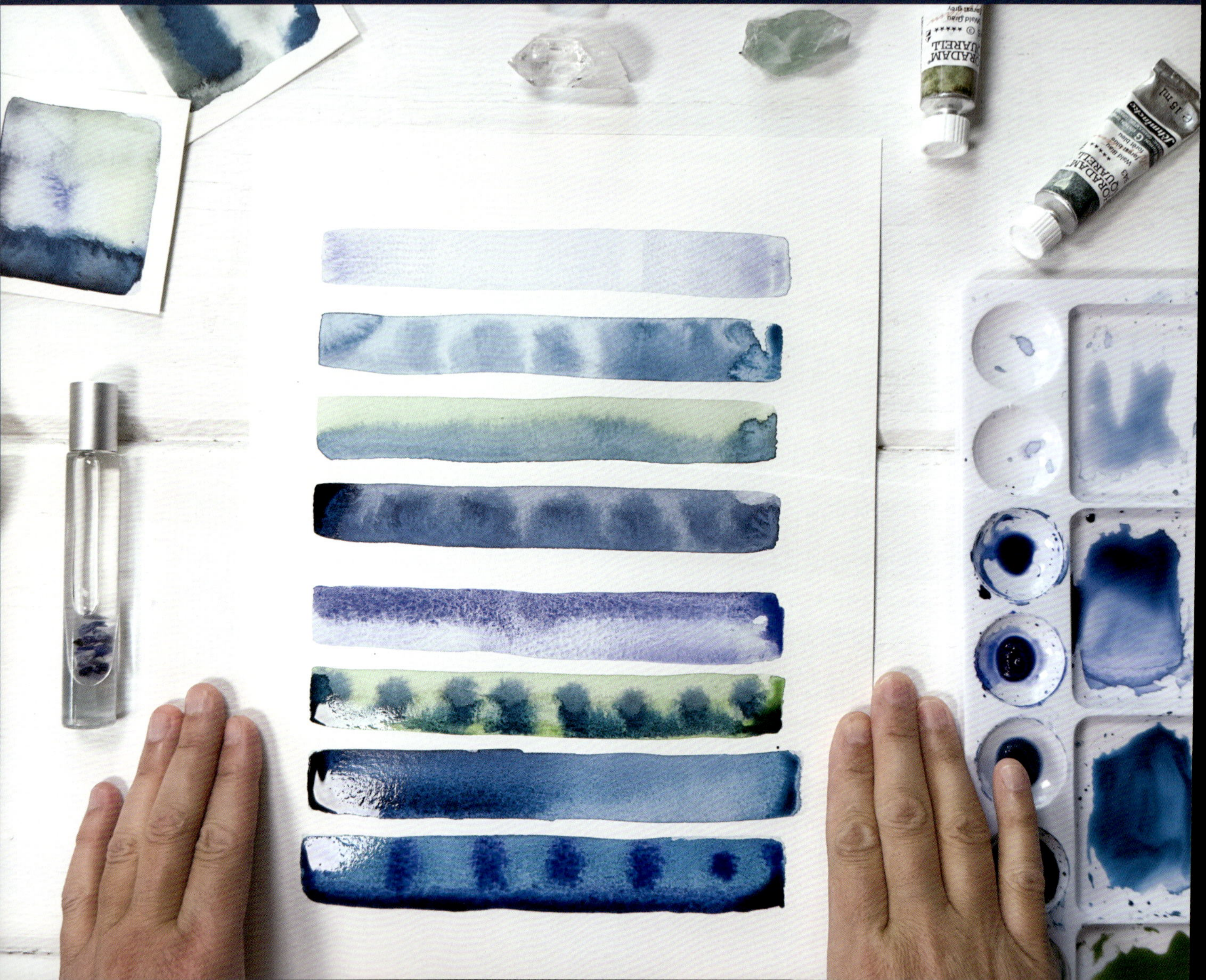

WHAT YOU'LL LEARN

- How to paint horizontal lines that are a little shorter than the page width
- How to play within the lines by dripping, blending, and making marks while the paint is still wet
- How to let go of perfectionism and let the water carry the color
- How to use value and variety so each line feels alive, while the whole piece remains unified

In this session, you'll paint gentle horizontal lines and explore what happens inside them. The first line is simple and still. The next invites a darker blue to drift in. The third might carry a wash of green with a touch of Prussian Blue along one edge. You continue line by line, trying something new each time. Keep the lines wet and loose so the water can move freely, and remember: Don't fear the water. As you work, check in with yourself. Notice your breath. Release your shoulders. Loosen your grip on the brush. Each line is a single moment to connect with your body, your water, and your creative flow.

WHAT YOU MIGHT FEEL

- A sense of calm focus as your rhythm steadies
- Curiosity as color, water, and paper meet in unexpected ways
- Ease as perfectionism softens, and flow takes its place

HOW THIS SESSION FLOWS

Let's begin with a short technique tutorial. I'll walk you through the painting and show you simple ways to play within the lines. When it feels natural, move into the painting meditation. Pair the technique with the nervous system regulation tool, Orienting with Curiosity. Turn on some soft background music, and paint with an unhurried rhythm that helps you stay present, loosen your grip, and let the water take the lead.

One line, one breath.
Keep it wet, stay open, and
let the water surprise you.

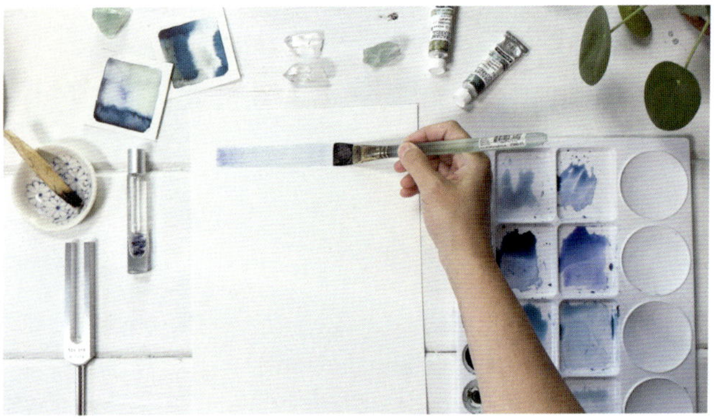

STEP ONE: LAY THE FIRST LINE

Mix a tea-strength wash of your favorite color. I'm using Ultramarine Blue. Paint a 1-inch-tall horizontal line across the page with a flat brush or the side of your round brush. Use plenty of water. Keep it smooth, steady, and simple. Don't worry if the line isn't perfect. It'll add interest to your painting.

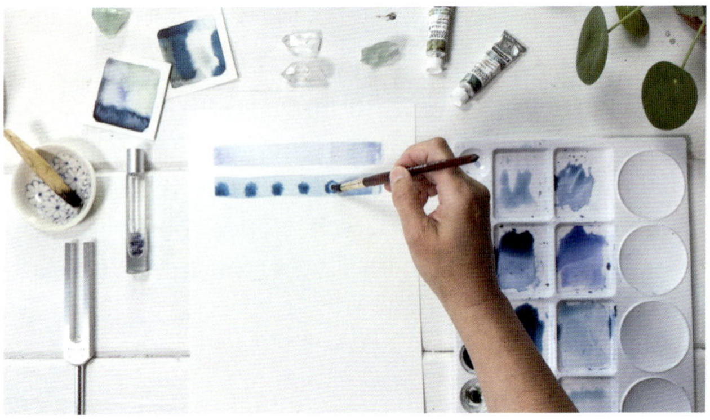

STEP TWO: PLAY INSIDE THE LINE

While the paint is still wet, drip a darker blue line of dots into it. Watch it feather across the band. Let the water carry the pigment; don't chase or control it. If it feels too light, drop in a little more color and let it bloom.

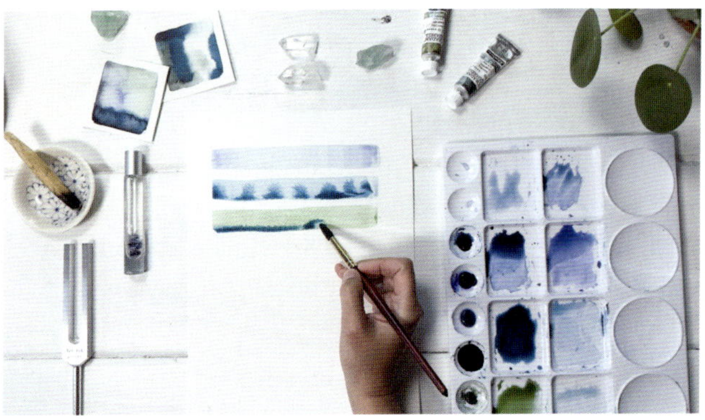

STEP THREE: ADD VARIATION

For the next line, change your color. I used Sap Green with a stroke of Prussian Blue on the edge. Stay curious. Each line can be its own small experiment. Add whatever marks you like.

Permission Slip

Pause between lines, and watch the magic unfold.

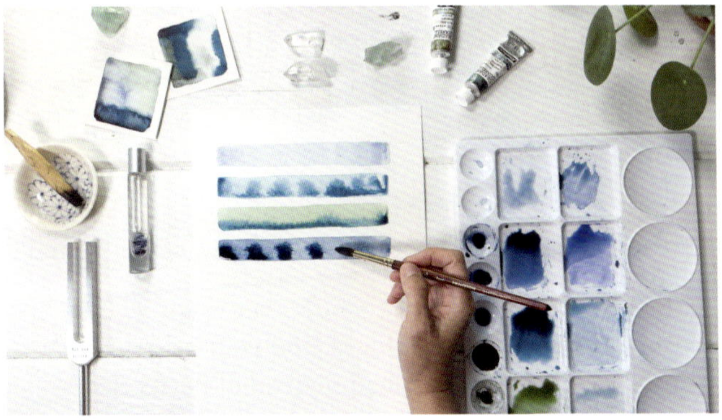

STEP FOUR: CONTINUE THE RHYTHM

Stack line after line. Keep your pace slow and steady. Between lines, pause to check your breath, release your shoulders, and soften your grip.

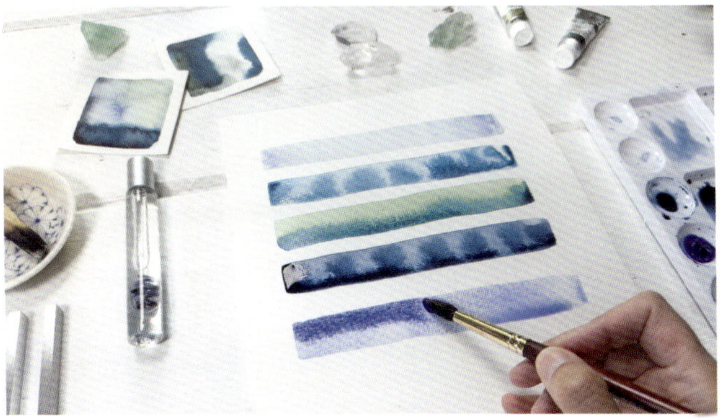

> **Energy Note**
>
> *Play is presence. Each experiment brings you closer to calm.*

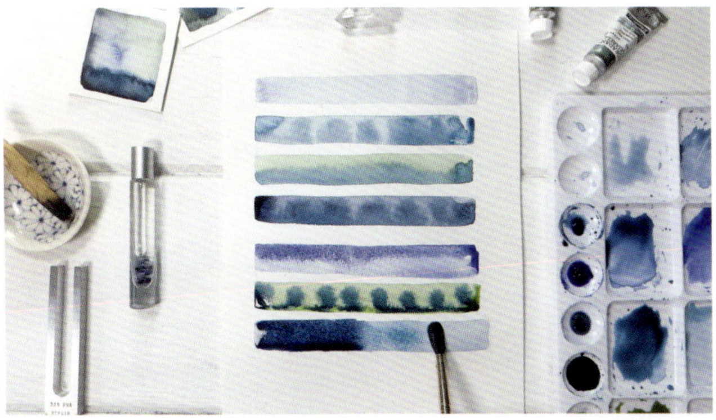

STEP FIVE: STAY WITH THE WATER

Keep the lines wet and let them move. Don't be afraid of water or blooms. Trust that the paper and pigment will settle into beauty.

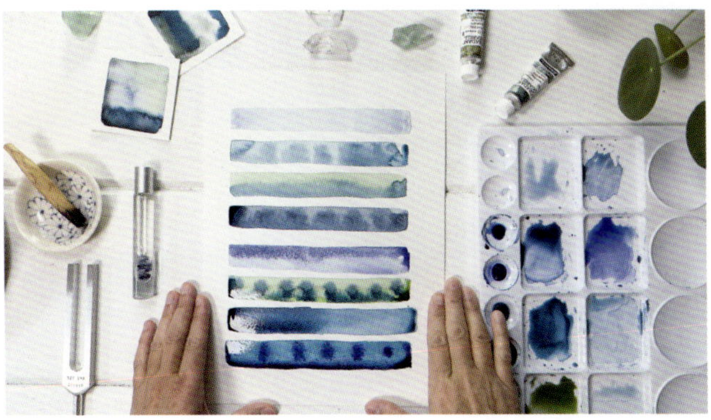

STEP SIX: PAUSE AND REFLECT

When your energy fades or the page feels complete, stop. Notice what happened where you played inside the lines.

Painting Meditation: Lines of Ease

Put on soft-frequency music. Before you begin, take a moment to look around your space. Name three things you can see. Name a color, a texture, a bit of light. Let your eyes soften. Feel your body supported and return your gaze to the page.

Between lines, pause for a moment. Notice your breath, your shoulders, and your grip on the brush. Loosen them all a little more each time. Let your curiosity lead instead of perfection. Continue line by line until your energy softens or the page feels complete.

When you finish, rest with your painting. Watch how each line dried in its own way. Notice the delicate edges, the blooms, and the quiet transitions. Let the beauty of what unfolded remind you: When you stay present and open, calm finds its way to you.

Integration

Sit with your painting. Notice how the lines dried, how the colors met, and how water shaped the space within each band. Observe the quiet beauty that came from simple play. Take one easy exhale, then write a few lines about how it felt to let the water lead.

Journal Prompts

- Which line felt most calming to paint, and why?
- Where did the water surprise you?
- How did your body feel as you slowed your pace and released control?

Gentle Reminder

Slow down, and play.

thoughts

NERVOUS SYSTEM REGULATION TOOL

10

Vagal Toning

Vagal toning is a gentle practice that stimulates the *vagus nerve*, a powerful pathway that helps your body shift out of stress and into calm. When the vagus nerve is activated, your heart rate slows, your breath deepens, and your whole system gets the message that you are safe. You can tone the vagus nerve in many ways, by humming, singing, long exhales, soft chanting, or even a quiet "mmm" with your mouth closed. You don't need to be loud or musical. The goal is simply vibration and breath, not performance.

BENEFITS

- **Soothes the stress response.** Vagal toning helps the body leave fight-or-flight mode and return to rest and repair.
- **Quiets the mind.** When the body feels safe, mental chatter naturally softens.
- **Eases tension.** Gentle vibration relaxes the throat, chest, and jaw and can support emotional release.
- **Helps you stay present.** Sensations in the body become an anchor, bringing you into the moment.

HOW TO TRY IT

- Sit comfortably and soften your shoulders.
- Inhale gently through your nose.
- On the exhale, choose a soft sound that feels good to you: "mmm," "om, "vu," or a quiet hum with lips closed.
- Let the sound be relaxed, not forced.
- Notice where you feel the vibration. Can you feel it in your throat, chest, face, or head?
- Repeat for four to six easy breath cycles.

You can stay with one sound or try different tones and notice how each feels.

WHEN IT'S USEFUL

Use Vagal Toning when your chest feels tight, when you can't stop overthinking, when emotions feel stuck in the throat, or anytime you want a gentle, body-led way to return to center.

Harmonic Waves

LET SOUND MOVE THROUGH YOU AND LET YOUR BRUSH FOLLOW

Let soft humming move through your body while you paint gentle waves. As the tone vibrates through your throat and chest, your brush finds an easy rhythm to follow. You stop overthinking and let the water carry the color.

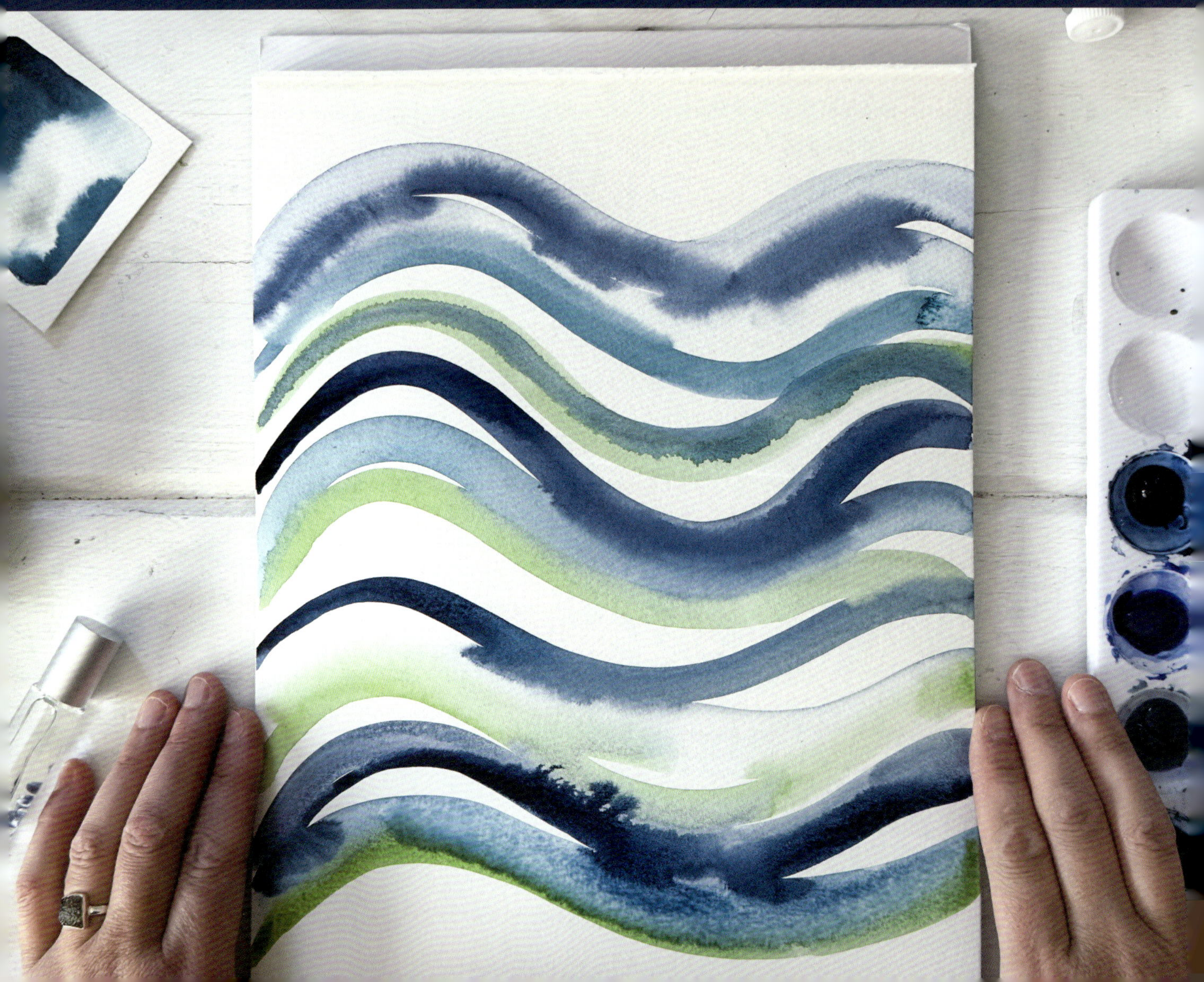

WHAT YOU'LL LEARN

- How to paint wavy lines with lots of water and simple wet-on-wet play
- How to pair humming and brushstrokes so the vibration guides your pace and helps your mind quiet down
- How to blur the lines and layer color inside the waves without chasing perfection
- How to let go of self-consciousness around toning. The louder you hum, the more vibration your body feels, and the more release you experience.

In this session, you will paint slow, flowing waves while you hum. You can try different tones ("om," "vu," "ah," "lu," "ee," a gentle "mm") and notice where you feel the vibration: throat, chest, face, head. As you tone, you lay down a wavy line with lots of water. Continue down the page, experimenting with different tones while you play with the water-filled wavy lines. As the sound takes your attention, the marks come with less effort. You feel present, grounded, and open.

WHAT YOU MIGHT FEEL

- Looser breath and softer shoulders as the vibration settles your body
- Less overthinking, as sound gives your mind a simple focus
- Curiosity and ease as the water makes quiet, unexpected patterns

HOW THIS SESSION FLOWS

Let's begin with a short technique tutorial. I'll show you how to lay a watery wave and play with color and layering. When it feels natural, move into the painting meditation. Pair the waves with gentle toning, soft background music, and an unhurried rhythm that helps you connect with your body and let the water lead.

Let the tone move through you,
then let the brush follow. Wave by wave,
the body leads and the mind rests.

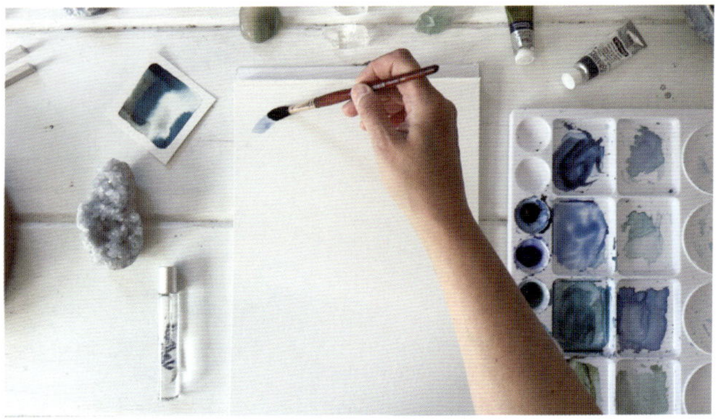

STEP ONE: PAINT THE FIRST WAVE

Mix a tea-strength wash of a color you love. Load the brush well so the line stays wet. Paint a slow, flowing wave across the page. Keep it watery. This will allow the next wavy line to blur and blend.

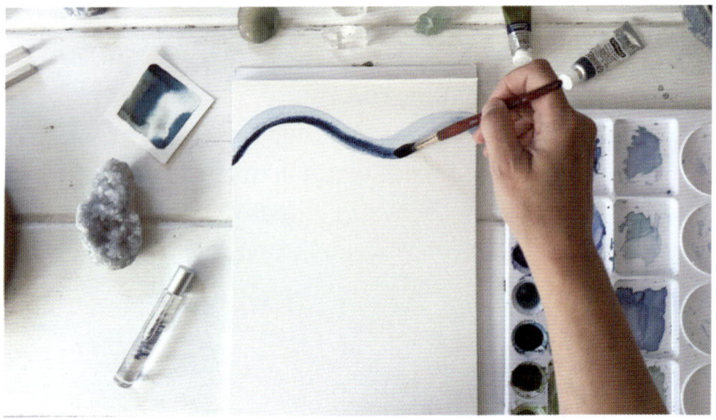

STEP TWO: ADD THE SECOND WAVE

While the first wave is still very wet, lay another watery wave at the edge of the first one. You can use a darker color for contrast. Paint it along the bottom edge, and watch it feather through the wave above.

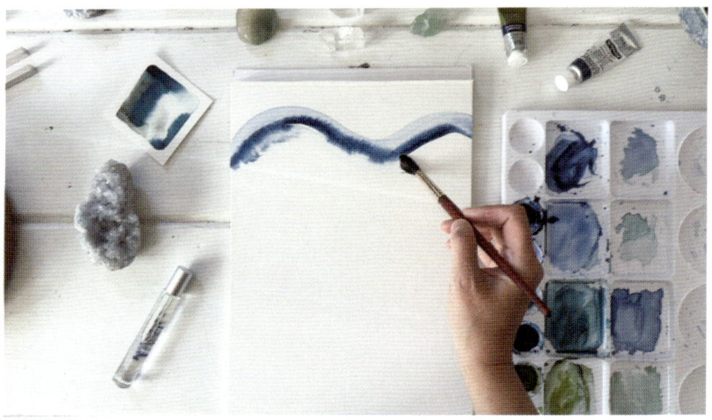

STEP THREE: PLAY WITH CLEAR WATER

For the next line, while the paint is still very wet, clean the color from your brush and kiss the line with a wave of clear water. Watch as the clear water creates magical effects. Don't try to control the outcome. Let the paint go wherever it is meant to go. The less you fuss, the more beautiful the results.

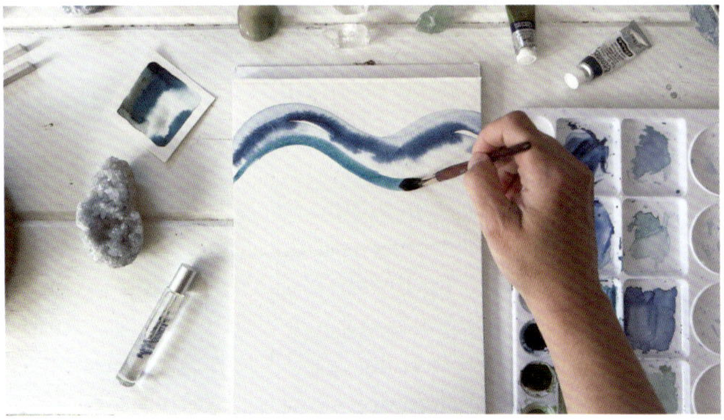

STEP FOUR: BEGIN A TONE

Once you feel comfortable with making the wavy lines, introduce a simple "om" tone. Fill your paintbrush with the next color you would like to use. Take a deep breath in, press your brush down on the paper, and as you paint the next wavy line, make the "om" sound as you paint. You may feel self-conscious or silly at first, but keep going. Let the tone out and see where you feel it in your body.

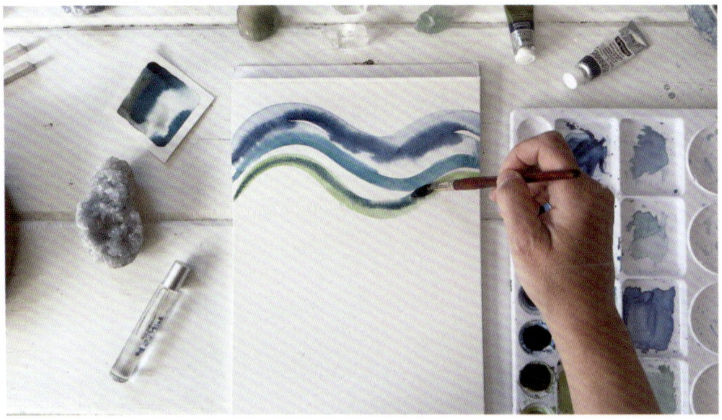

STEP FIVE: CONTINUE BUILDING

Continue wave by wave. Vary the value and play with colors. Try a blur with clean water, a dark, heavy line with saturated color, or a light layer for contrast. Let your intuition guide you. As you begin each line, choose a different sound tone and see which one feels the best to you. Try "vu" for this line.

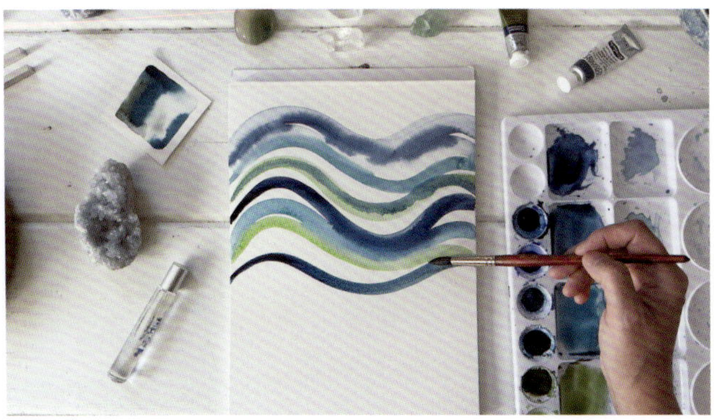

STEP SIX: STAY WITH THE WATER

Keep each band wet so the water can travel. If things feel busy, slow down, use more water, and return to a lighter value. Don't worry about making a perfect wavy line. They can all be different and touch at different places along their path. Keep your focus on the water, the wave, and the harmony. See how the "ah" sound feels.

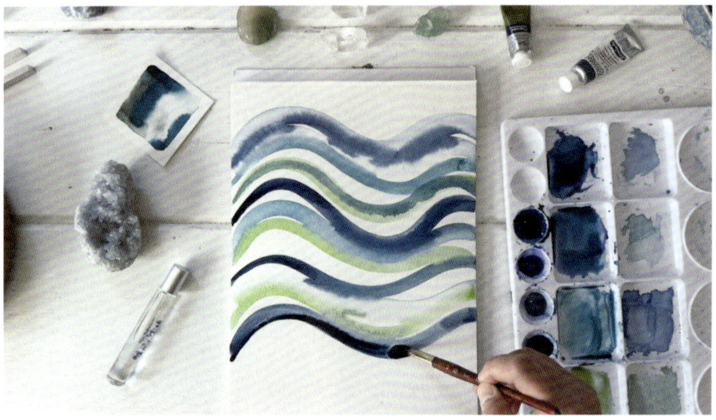

STEP SEVEN: CHECK IN WITH YOUR BODY

Between waves, notice your breath, your shoulders, and the grip on your brush. Take in a deep cleansing breath and loosen. Then paint the next wave with a different tone. Give "lu" a try. Keep going, paint each wavy line with a different tone. Try "ee," and then experiment with a simple hum, "mmmmm."

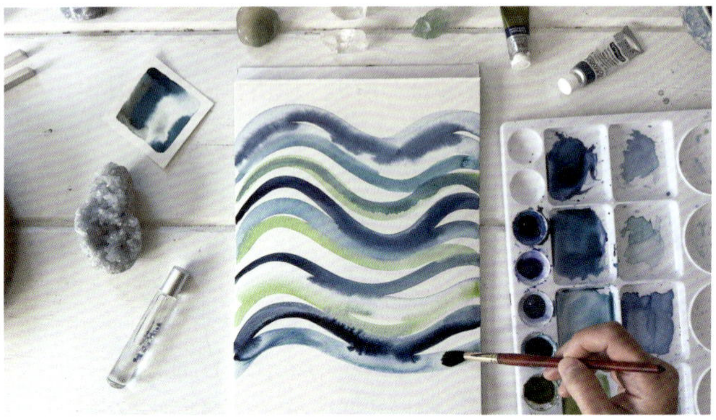

STEP EIGHT: PAUSE AND REFLECT

When your energy starts to wane or your page is complete, take a moment to look at your piece and feel your body.

Gentle Reminder

Keep the waves wet, and your grip loose.

Painting Meditation: Harmonic Waves

Put on soft-frequency music. Close your eyes for three easy breaths. Open them and begin a quiet hum that feels good to you. Let your mouth shape the tone and notice where you feel the vibration. Paint one slow, watery wave while the sound continues. On the next wave, play with the color or value. Let the water carry it. If you feel self-conscious about toning, smile, and keep going. The goal is not volume, it is vibration. If your mind starts to plan or judge, return to a gentle tone and paint the next wave. Keep your shoulders soft, your grip loose, and your pace kind. Continue until the page feels complete.

Integration

Rest with your painting. Trace the waves with your eyes. Notice where the tone was steady and how the water moved during those passes. Feel your throat and chest and take one quiet hum on the out-breath. Write a single word for how you feel now.

Journal Prompts

- Which tone felt best in your body today, and where did you feel it?
- What changed in your painting when you focused on the hum instead of the result?
- Where did you let the water lead, and what surprised you?

Energy Note

Vibration invites release. Let the hum loosen what feels tight.

thoughts

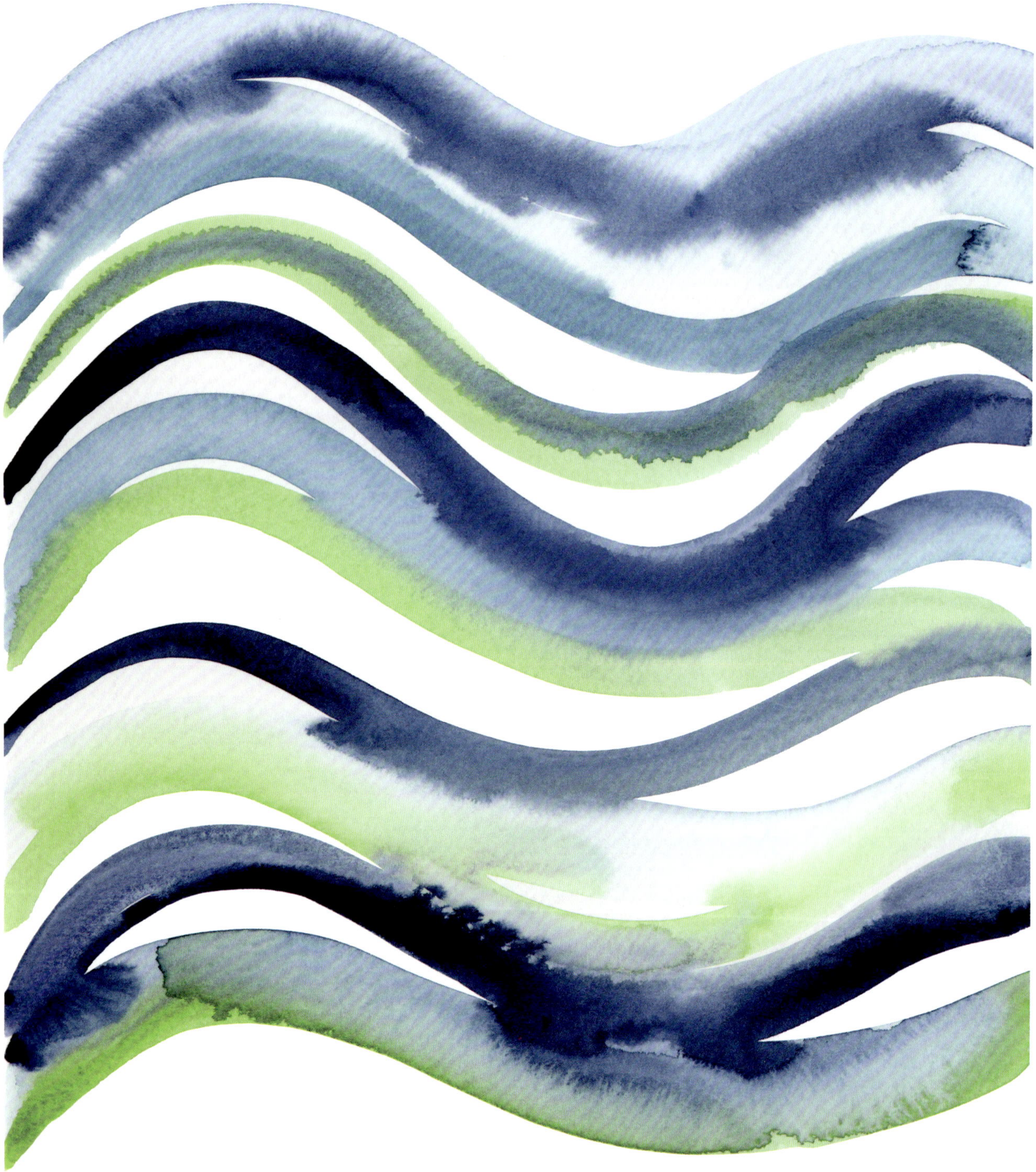

NERVOUS SYSTEM REGULATION TOOL

11

Micro-Movements

The Micro-Movements technique helps you bring gentle awareness back into your body through tiny shifts. These small movements release tension, reconnect you to the present moment, and remind your nervous system that you are safe.

BENEFITS

- **Releases tension.** Little movements soften muscles and joints before they tighten into stress or overthinking.
- **Brings you back into the body.** Feeling your feet, legs, spine, and shoulders interrupts spiraling thoughts and anchors you in the present.
- **Signals safety.** When your body moves gently and freely, your nervous system reads: "I'm okay."
- **Supports grounding.** These subtle shifts help settle you into your seat and into the moment, like placing a stone gently on the earth.

HOW TO TRY IT

- Sit comfortably with both feet on the floor.
- Feet: Wiggle your toes or move your ankles in small circles.
- Legs: Lift your knees slightly, then relax them back down.
- Hips: Tilt your pelvis forward and back in a tiny sway.
- Spine: Let your spine move softly, like seaweed in water.
- Shoulders: Roll them once or twice or let them drop with an exhale.
- Hands: Wiggle your fingers, shake out your wrists gently, then soften.

WHEN IT'S USEFUL

Use the Micro-Movements technique when you've been still for a while, when anxiety floats up into your head, when perfectionism tightens your grip, or any time you want to return to your body and the present moment.

Connect to Your Body

Holding Ground

PAINT PEACEFUL STONES AND SETTLE INTO YOUR BODY

Let simple stone shapes become your resting place. You fill each one with water and color and watch the movement inside the shape. Small, gentle micro-movements in your body help you release tension and feel supported while you paint.

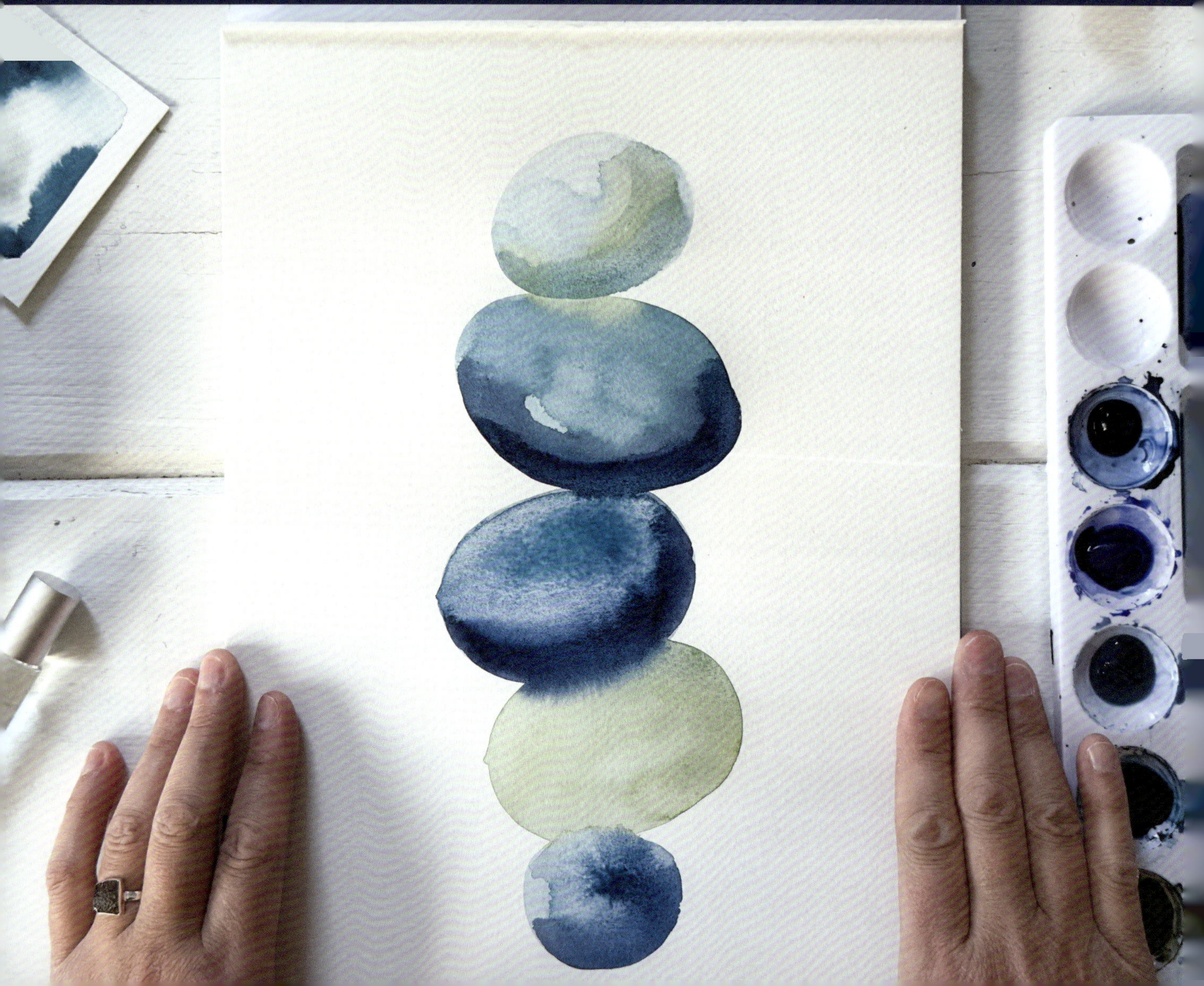

WHAT YOU'LL LEARN

- How to paint calming stone shapes with lots of water so the color can travel
- How to drip, blur, and layer inside each stone without overworking
- How to use micro-movements to reconnect with your body and keep tension low

In this session, you paint stacked, rounded, peaceful stones. You keep them wet and let the water do the work: Drip in deeper colors, blur edges with clean water, and watch the magic unfold as each shape dries. Between stones, you make tiny body movements called micro-movements. Roll your shoulders, wiggle your fingers, sway your spine, circle your ankles. These micro-movements help you stay present and grounded, like settling a real stone into place.

WHAT YOU MIGHT FEEL

- Shoulders and jaw softening as small movements release held tension
- A steadier presence as you alternate paint, pause, and micro-movement
- Ease and curiosity as the paint dries in beautiful ways inside each stone

HOW THIS SESSION FLOWS

Let's begin with a short technique tutorial. I'll show you how to shape a watery stone and play inside it with drips, blurs, lifting, and surrender. When it feels natural, move into the painting meditation. Pair the technique with micro-movements, soft background music, and an unhurried rhythm that keeps you in your body while you get lost in the process of painting.

Set a stone,
make a small shift,
breathe.
Let the water do
what water does.

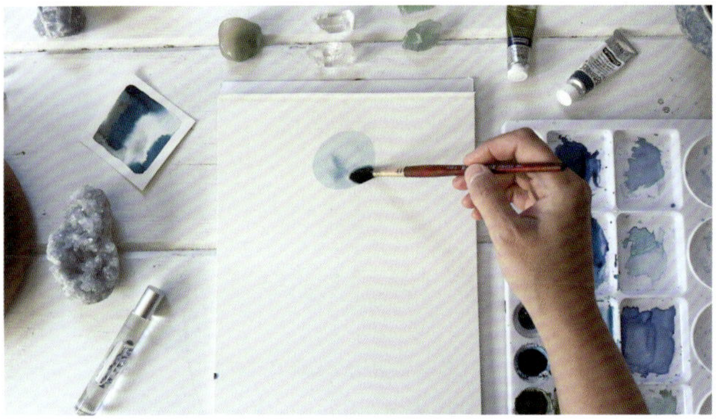

STEP ONE: DON'T BE AFRAID OF THE WATER

Mix a tea-strength wash of a color you love. Paint a relaxed, rounded stone. Load with plenty of water so the interior stays shiny and wet. As you place the color, let both of your feet settle into the ground. Feel the floor supporting you.

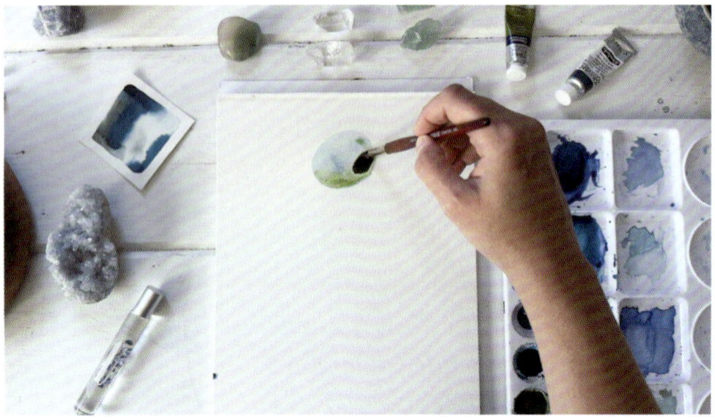

STEP TWO: WATCH THE WATER WORK

While the stone is still wet, lay a soft swash of deeper color toward the bottom. Pause and watch it spread through the water. Don't try to control it. Let the materials do what they're meant to do. Make a tiny ankle circle movement. Keep it slow and easy and notice how the body shifts into a feeling of ease.

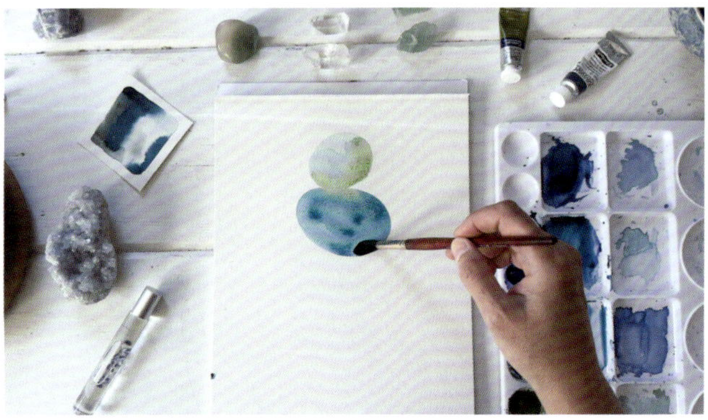

STEP THREE: STACK THE STONES

Choose another color and paint a second stone beneath the first. Make it a little bigger. It doesn't have to be perfect. Use plenty of water and watch how the colors meet and mingle on their own. Relax your knees for a moment. Let your legs soften and settle, just like the stones are settling into place.

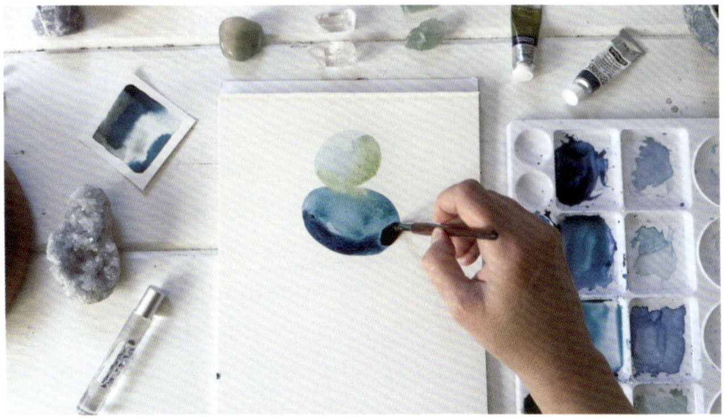

STEP FOUR: LET VALUE CREATE WEIGHT

While the stone is still wet, add a deeper line at its base. Lay down the mark and move on. The water will carry the paint beautifully. Make a tiny shift in your hips. Move just an inch forward or back in the chair. Let the movement be small and natural.

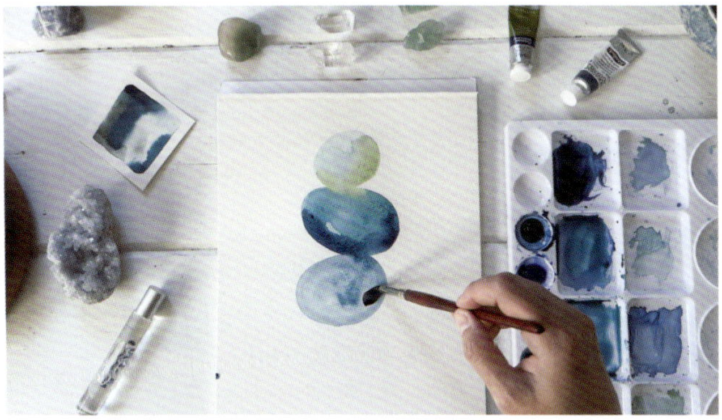

STEP FIVE: ADD ONE STONE AT A TIME

Play with the placement, shape, and size of your stones. Imagine them balancing, one on top of the other. Keep each stone wet. Drip in color or keep it light and simple. Follow your intuition. Take a moment to pause for a soft spine sway. Gently rock forward and back. Notice how a tiny movement brings ease.

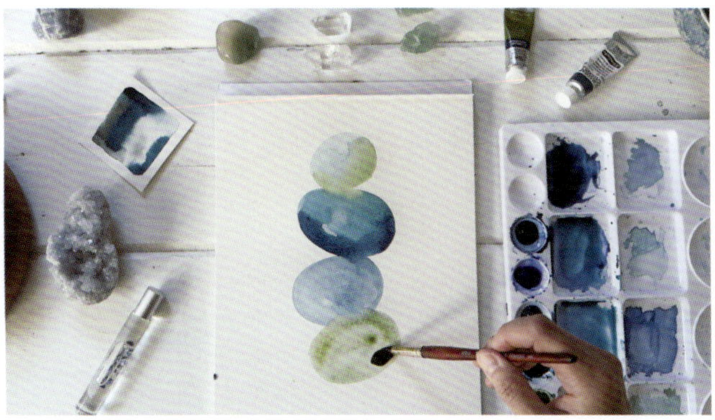

STEP SIX: FOLLOW YOUR COLOR CURIOSITY

Choose another color. I picked green to carry a thread of color down the stack. Lay the color with lots of water and move on. Don't mix or stir it. When you try to control the paint, the stones look tight. When you leave it alone, they feel alive. Roll one shoulder then the other in slow, small circles—forward, up, and back. Let the tension melt away.

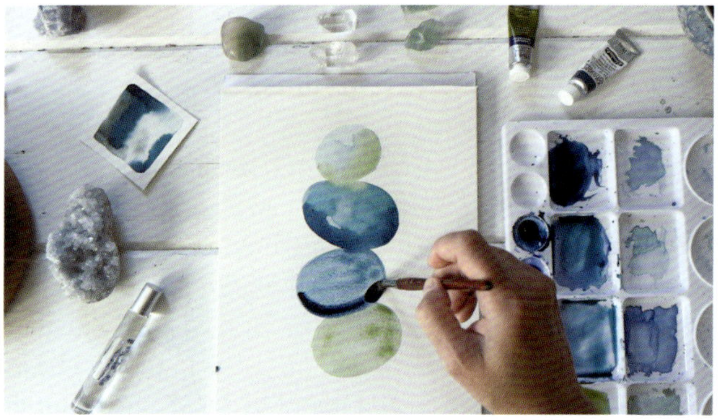

STEP SEVEN: GO BACK AND ADD MORE

As long as the stone is still wet, you can return and add color or small marks—it's okay. I added a dark line beneath this stone to gently separate it from the one below it. Lay down the color and keep going. Take a moment and soften your jaw. Let your tongue rest. Notice the shift in your body as you release the tension.

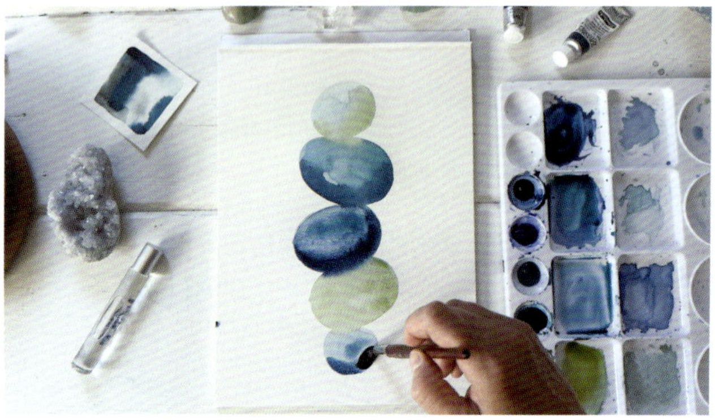

STEP EIGHT: GENTLY BALANCE

Follow whatever shape you're called to make for the bottom stone. I like making mine small like the top one, using a light wash and darkening the bottom edge. Let your shoulders drop an inch. Breathe without forcing it.

Permission Slip

Keep shapes round-ish, not perfect.

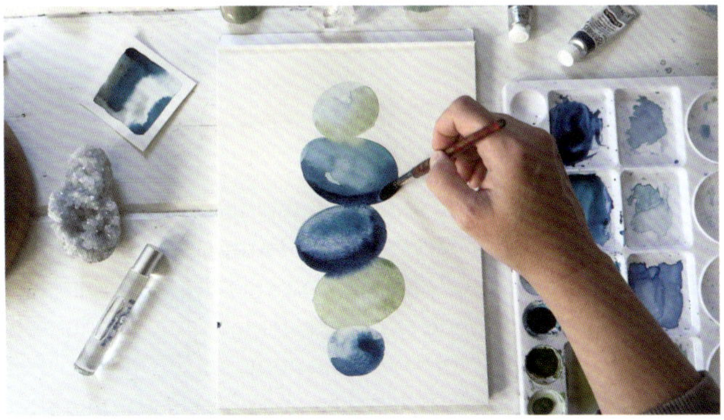

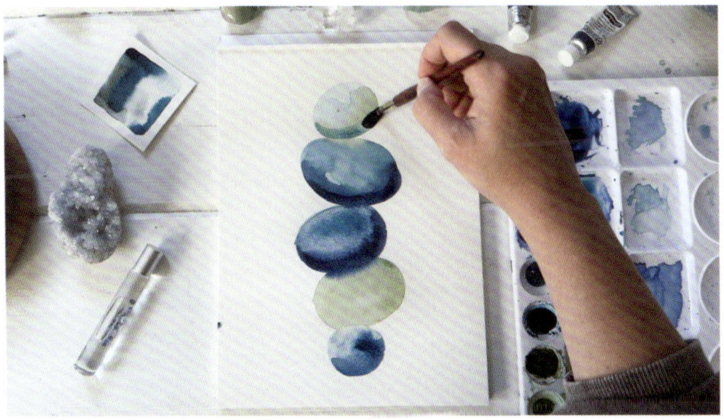

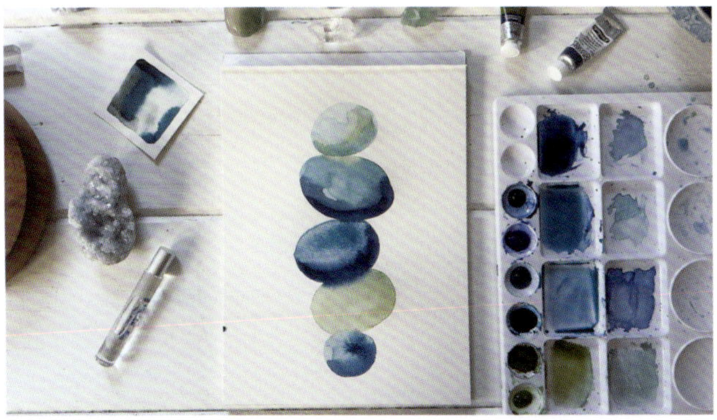

STEP NINE: MAKE A LAST QUIET PASS

Look at your stones. Do they call for more? I love the look of stones with deeper bottoms, so I went back and added a darker edge. The top stone was a little drier than the rest, so I laid down a line of color, rinsed my brush, and swept clean water through it. The pigment drifted and blended beautifully on its own without pushing or fixing. Rest your hands on your thighs for one moment. Feel the warmth, the contact, the grounding. Then let the page dry in its own time.

Energy Note

Tiny motion, big shift. Small adjustments can unlock a lot of ease.

Gentle Reminder

Let go of control.

Painting Meditation: Holding Ground

Put on soft-frequency music. Sit comfortably. Paint one watery stone, then pause for a tiny micro-movement. Roll a shoulder, wiggle your fingers, or sway your spine. Paint the next stone and shift again, small and easy. Let each stone be a moment of placing, and each micro-movement be a moment of settling. Inside the stones, keep the touch simple: a drip, a blur, a weighted line. Don't overwork. If the urge to fix rises, make one small micro-movement, soften your grip, and place the next stone. Choose ease over perfection. Continue until the page feels grounded.

Integration

Rest with your painting. Notice which stones feel most "set," which edges blurred, where more water added life. Make one small body shift and take a soft breath. Write a single word for how you feel now.

Journal Prompts

- Where in your body did a micro-movement create the most relief?
- Which stone surprised you as it dried, and why?
- What did you let go of when you stopped fixing and kept moving?

thoughts

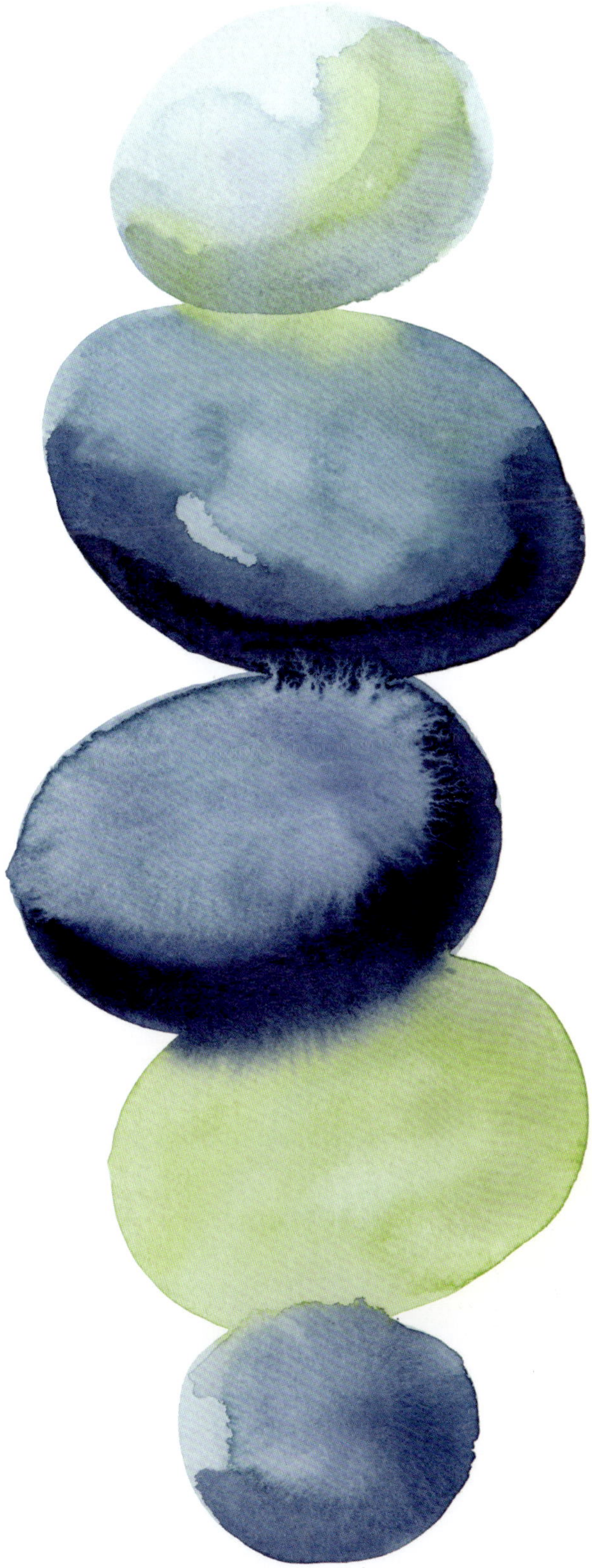

12

NERVOUS SYSTEM REGULATION TOOL

Contact Point Awareness

I love this lesson. The Contact Point Awareness technique is great for grounding and getting in touch with your body. It is a simple way to return to yourself. You gently return your attention to the body by noticing the places where it touches objects. These points of contact act like grounding anchors. They draw you out of your thoughts and back into your body.

Contact point awareness works because it gives the brain simple, reliable information: "I am here, and I am supported." That message helps the nervous system settle. Instead of scanning for what's next, your body recognizes the stability of the chair beneath you, the floor under your feet, and the brush resting in your hand. This physical steadiness signals safety. Shoulders soften. Breath deepens. The mind quiets. Take the time to try this while painting; think of it as part of the painting process.

BENEFITS

- **Anchors you in the present moment.** It brings attention to where your body is supported.
- **Signals safety.** Your nervous system feels the steadiness of the floor, chair, and brush.
- **Reduces mental overwhelm.** The technique narrows your attention to one simple sensation at a time.
- **Calms looping thoughts.** By shifting awareness from thinking to feeling, your mind settles.
- **Softens tension.** The body naturally relaxes when it feels grounded.

HOW TO TRY IT

- Begin by sitting comfortably and letting your awareness move slowly from the ground up.
- Feet: Feel the weight of your feet on the floor. Notice your heels, arches, and toes making contact.
- Legs: Notice the heaviness of your calves and the steadiness of your knees resting in place.
- Hips: Feel your hips sink into the chair. Let the chair fully support you.
- Spine: Sense your spine rising from your hips. Notice its natural curves and the way it gently holds you upright.
- Shoulders: Feel your shoulders resting over your ribs. Let them soften without forcing.
- Arms and hands: Notice your wrists, your fingers, the weight of the brush. Feel the contact between your hand and the handle.
- Jaw and face: Soften your jaw. Notice the weight of your tongue. Let the muscles around your eyes relax. Let each contact point remind your body: "I am supported. I am here."

WHEN IT'S USEFUL

Practice the Contact Point Awareness technique whenever you want to reconnect with your body and get grounded, slow your pace, or create a sense of calm. Let tiny movements guide you inward.

Grounding Anchor

FOCUS YOUR ATTENTION AND GENTLY DRAW INWARD

Let loose watercolor circles become your field of focus. You scatter them across the page in different sizes, some filled and some outlined.

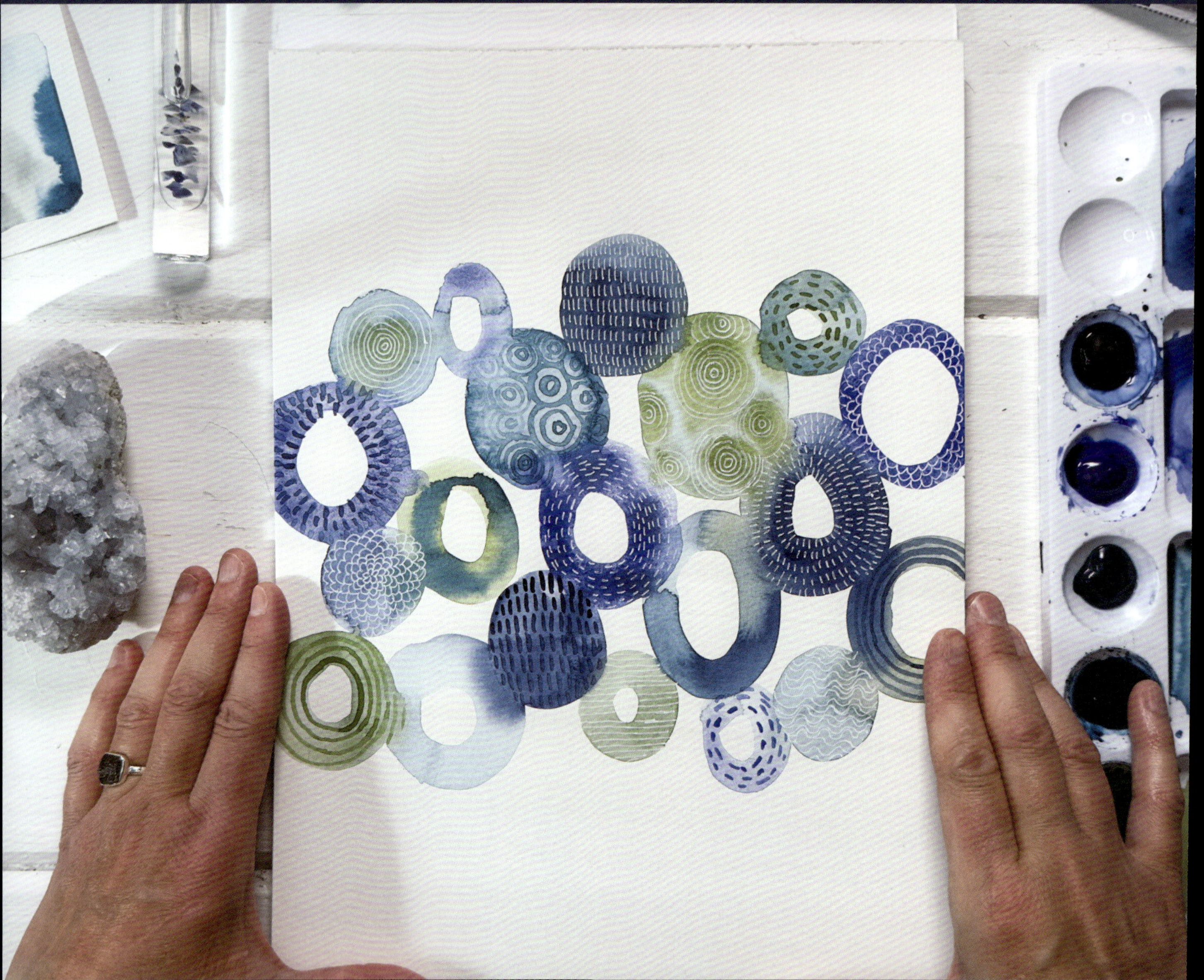

Wide, flowing movements start the session. Then, as the shapes begin to dry, you narrow your attention, shift to a waterbrush, and ease into gentle mark-making. Finally, you settle into the slow rhythm of decorating with your gel pen. Each shift brings your awareness closer inward. You move from big strokes to small touches, from a wide lens to fine details. This quiet transition naturally slows your system and helps you settle into your body.

WHAT YOU'LL LEARN

- How to paint loose circles with plenty of water so the color can travel
- How to drift between dripping, blurring, and letting the paint move on its own
- How to shift into detail work without rushing or gripping
- How contact point awareness keeps you grounded as your focus narrows

In this session, you will paint circles across the page in any size or color you feel drawn to. You keep them wet and let the water carry the paint. When you move into the details, you slow down and work with intention. Tiny dots and simple lines give your mind something easy to follow. Your breath deepens, your thoughts quiet, and you drop into a steadier rhythm.

WHAT YOU MIGHT FEEL

- A soft, steady focus as you shift into smaller movements
- A quieter mind, as the details give you a simple place to rest your attention
- Curiosity as the water creates new shapes and subtle changes

WHY THIS MATTERS

Up until now, your attention has been soft and wide. You've been painting loose shapes and letting the water flow. That kind of open focus naturally settles the nervous system. In this lesson, the focus shifts. When you move into the smaller marks with a fine brush or gel pen, your attention narrows. You're no longer following the whole composition. You're simply noticing the details in front of you. This kind of focused attention gives the brain a single, manageable task. Instead of juggling options or scanning for what's next, your mind lands on one clear point at a time.

Narrow focus is deeply regulating. The nervous system reads the shift as a cue of safety because single-task attention is something we only do when we feel secure. Repetitive detail work also has a steadying effect. When your hand repeats the same simple motion again and again, the brain begins to sync with that rhythm.

The shift from wide attention to narrow attention mirrors the way the nervous system naturally downshifts into calm. It's the same sensation as looking at a faraway horizon, then bringing your gaze down to something resting quietly in your hands. Your whole system follows that movement inward. This is why detail work matters. It's not just decoration. Each tiny mark becomes a moment of focus, a small place for the mind to rest, allowing you to drop even deeper into presence.

HOW THIS SESSION FLOWS

We'll begin with a short technique tutorial. I'll show you how to paint loose circles and let the color move through the water. When the shapes dry, you can move into the painting meditation and begin the mark-making. Pair the technique with contact point awareness, soft music, and an easy pace that keeps you present while you add gentle details.

Loose circles.
Tiny marks.
Steady breath.
Let the small details
bring you inward.

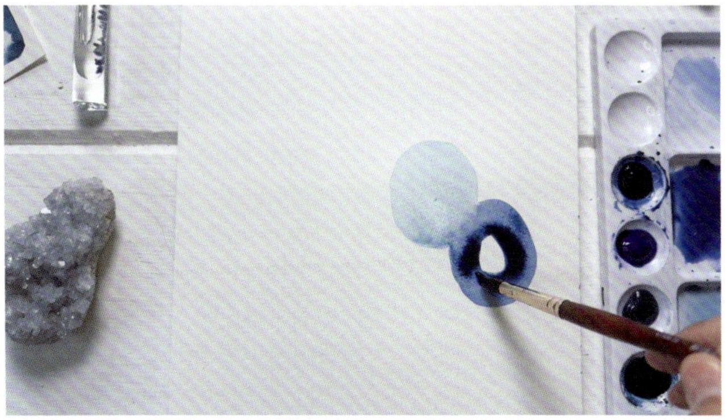

STEP ONE: PAINT PERFECTLY IMPERFECT CIRCLES

Paint your first circle with a tea-strength wash. Let it be relaxed, loose, and perfectly imperfect. Then move on to the next circle. Let this circle kiss the side of the first and see how the colors mix. Leave the center open and play with adding a darker value to the inside edge. Feel your feet on the ground. Notice the weight in your heels, arches, and toes, and let them settle fully into the floor.

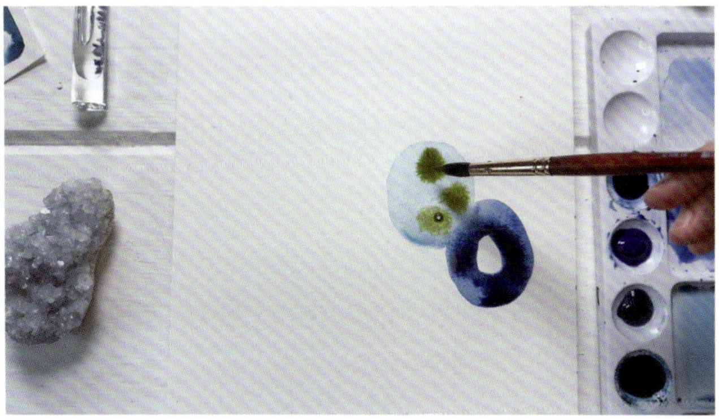

STEP TWO: PLAY WITH DRIPPING COLOR

Play with each circle. You can drip in color and watch it spread. Remember to use plenty of water; this allows the paint to flow and dry in beautiful ways. Don't try to stir the colors with your brush; let the water decide what happens. Now, take a moment to connect to your body. Bring your awareness to your ankles. Shift them and sense where they rest on your feet.

Energy Note

One moment of grounding can change your entire state.

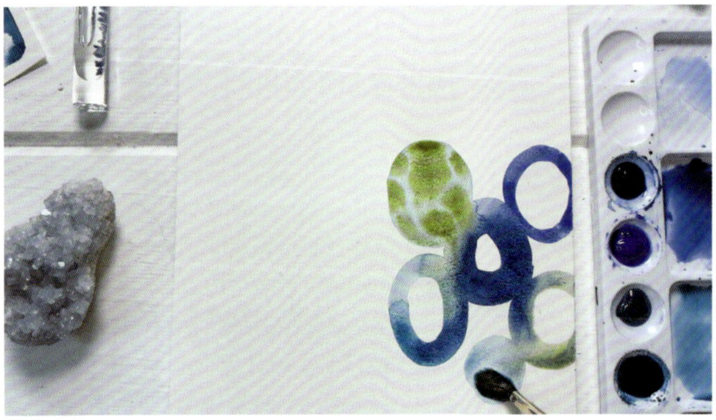

STEP THREE: KEEP GOING

Scatter more circles across the page. Vary their spacing, size, and shape. Some can be very light; others can hold a richer pool of color. Keep everything wet so you can drop in paint or water without overthinking. Treat each circle as your own little playground. Try experimenting with blending colors, dripping, and letting your imagination take over. Keep the shapes effortless and imperfect. Move your attention up your lower legs. Feel the gentle weight of your calves and the way they rest inside your clothing or against the air.

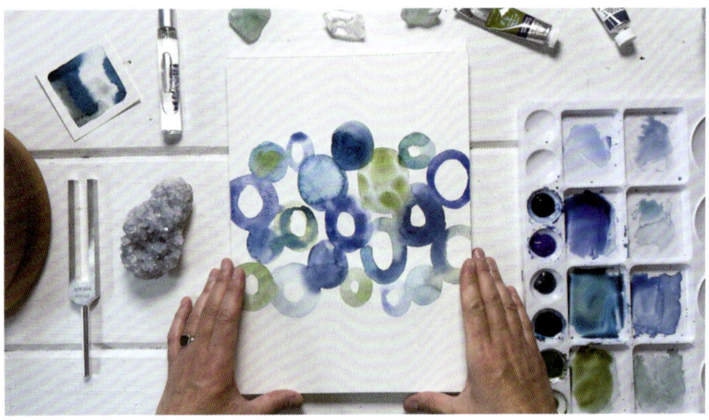

STEP FOUR: EXPLORE PLACEMENT

You can design the page however you want. I chose to make a band of circles across the middle of the page. Let your intuition guide you. Shift your awareness to your knees. Notice their bend, their shape, and the easy way they hold you without effort.

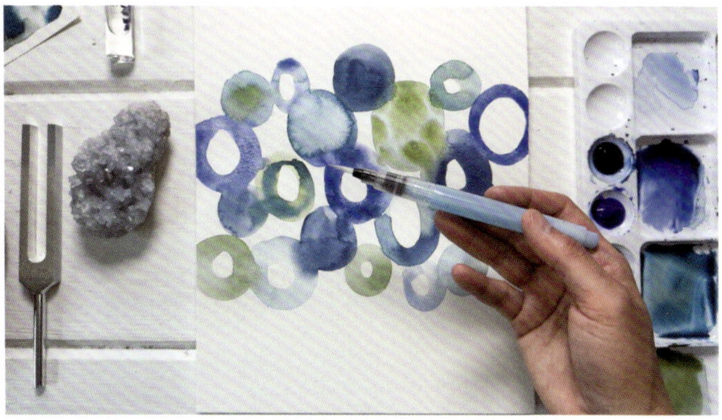

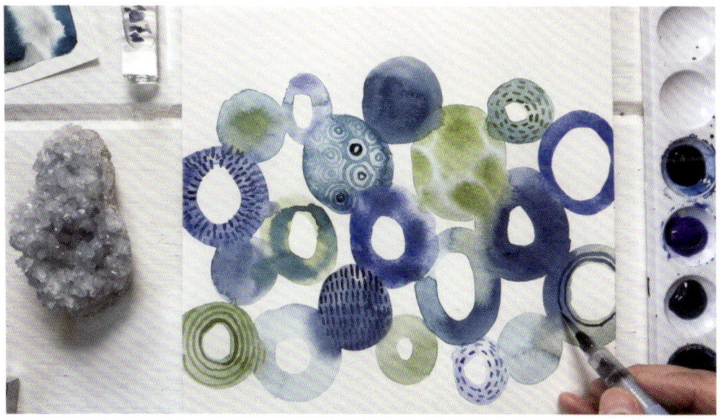

STEP FIVE: SHIFT YOUR FOCUS

It's now time to shift your focus from loose and wide to something smaller and more detailed. As the circles begin to dry, switch to the waterbrush. Its fine point makes it easy to settle into closer, more detailed work. Narrowing your focus like this quiets the mind because it gives your brain something simple to focus on. Pick the color that calls to you, and begin painting tiny strokes, short dashes, little circles, or whatever marks come to mind. Keep each stroke slow and deliberate, one small moment at a time. Feel your hips sink into the chair. Feel your spine rising from your hips. Notice its natural curves and the way it gently holds you upright.

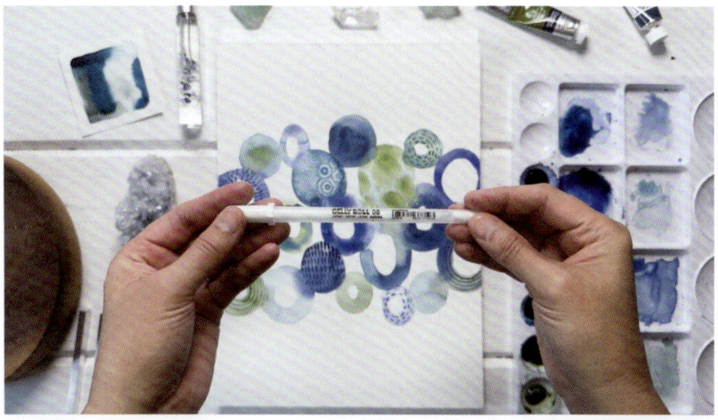

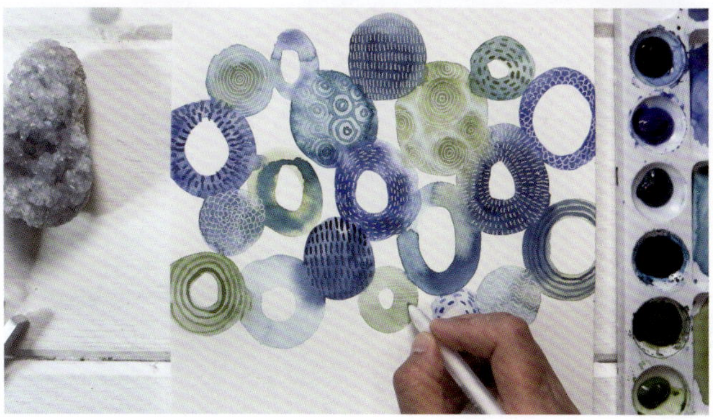

STEP SIX: SWITCH TO THE GEL PEN

When the circles and marks are dry, pick up the gel pen. Continue the same type of mark-making, but smaller and even more focused. Try playing with dot clusters, tiny lines, concentric circles, waves, or what-ever pops into your mind. This is your opportunity to play and get lost in the process. Let your pace slow naturally. The pen will guide you into a quieter rhythm. This is where contact point awareness becomes especially helpful. Feel the pen in your fingers. Feel your hand resting on the page. Notice your breath as it settles into a gentle pattern. Listen to the sound of the pen on the paper. Listen to the tick, tick, tick of the pen as you make marks. Try counting while you draw: 1, 2, 3, 4... Take a deep breath in, and release.

STEP SEVEN: FINISH WHEN IT FEELS COMPLETE

Stop when your attention begins to fade, or the page feels full. It's okay to stop when you start to feel this way. Take a slow look at what you created on your paper. Notice how the loose, watery washes and the small, focused marks balance each other out. Notice where the water pooled, where the color bloomed, where the tiniest mark changed the whole feel of a circle. Give yourself a moment to appreciate how your energy shifted as you moved from wide, open strokes into close, detailed work. Pause. Breathe. Let the calm settle in before you gently move on. Feel your shoulders resting over your ribs. Let them soften without forcing. Soften your jaw. Notice the weight of your tongue. Let the muscles around your eyes relax.

Permission Slip

Details can be messy, uneven, or incomplete.

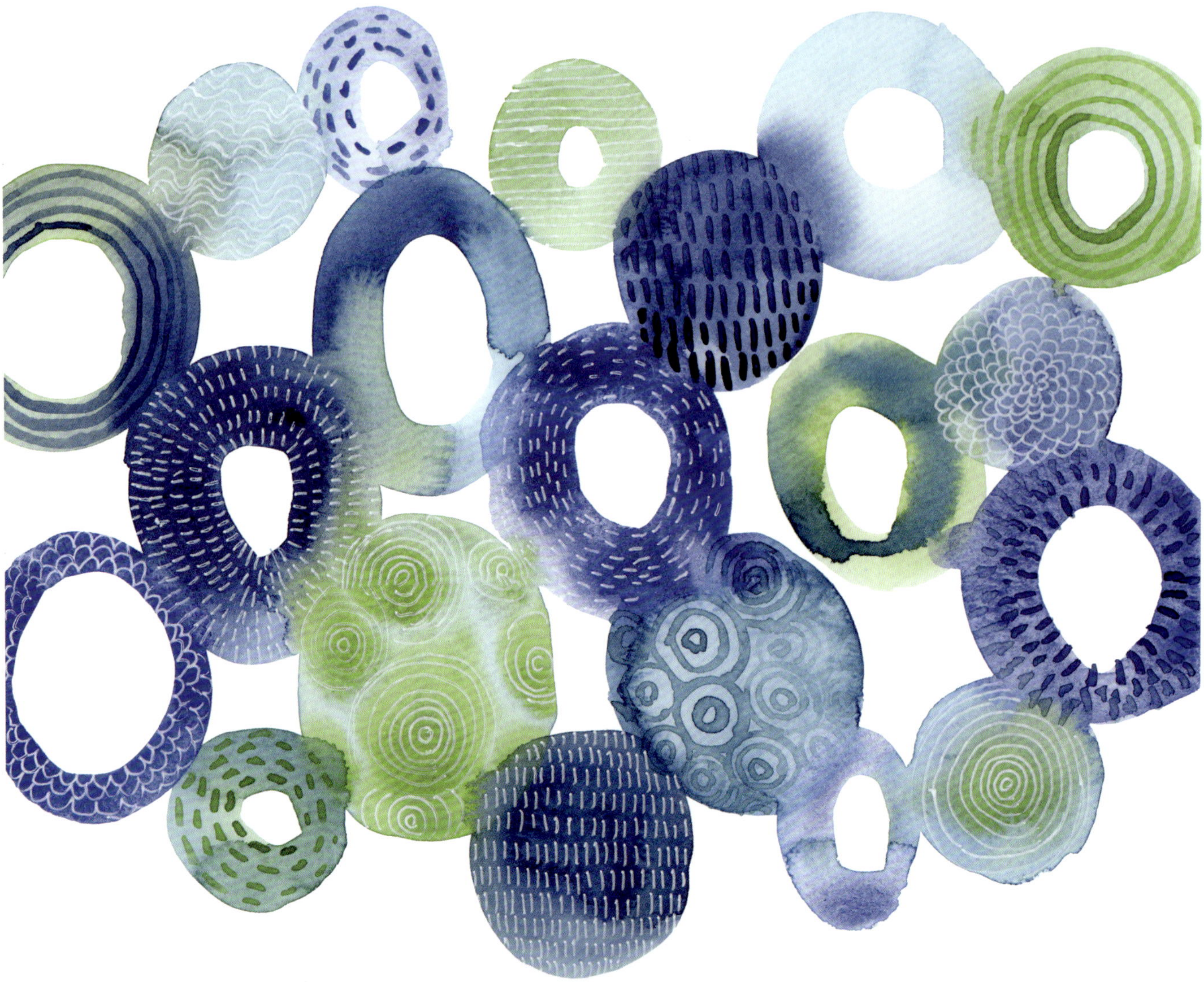

Painting Meditation: Grounding Anchor

Put on soft-frequency music and settle into your seat. Feel your feet resting on the floor. Notice the weight of them. Begin with one loose circle, letting the brush glide as you make the shape. Before moving to the next shape, pause and sense your contact points. Feel your feet pressing into the ground. Feel your seat supported by the chair. Now, paint another circle. Bring awareness to your hand holding the brush. Notice the texture of the paper beneath your fingers. Let each circle be followed by a moment of noticing. Your heels on the floor, the back of your thighs supported by the chair. These points of contact remind your body that it is supported and safe.

Inside each circle, keep the painting simple. Add a drip of color, a soft blur, a dark swash of color. Let the water move as it wants to. When the urge to fix or fuss comes up, pause and find one contact point. Feel your feet again. Feel your hand on the table. Breathe. Then gently move on to the next circle. Continue until the page feels complete and your body feels relaxed. Take a moment to reflect and breathe.

Integration

Sit with your finished page for a moment. Let your eyes move across the circles and notice where your attention naturally lands. Some shapes may feel light and effortless, others strained, or more detailed. Notice how the loose washes and tiny marks work together. There is no good or bad here, only process. This shift from wide to narrow focus mirrors a shift in the nervous

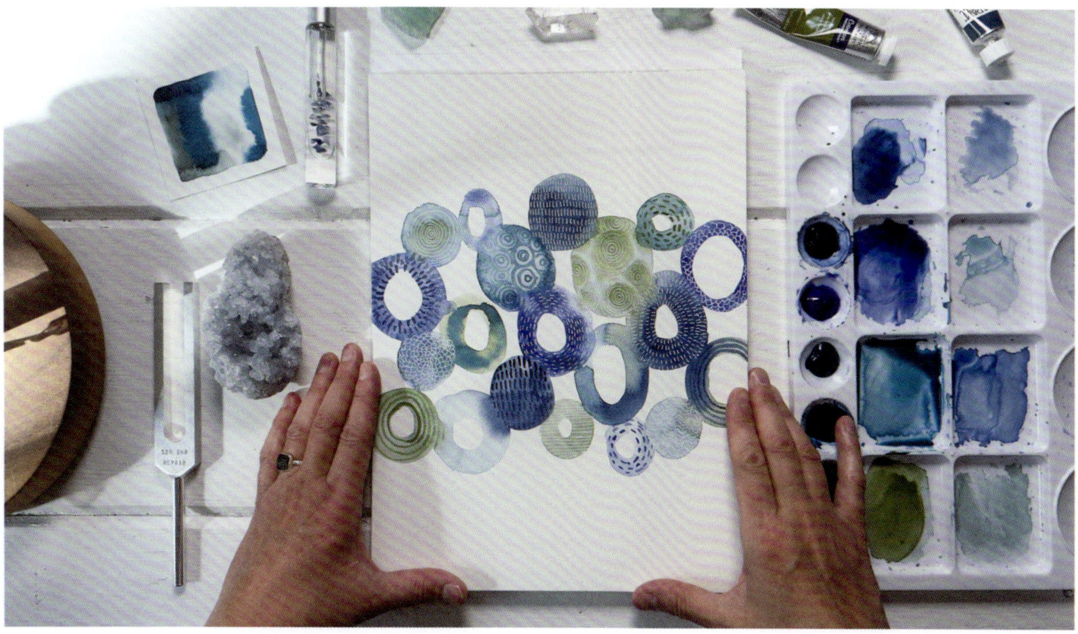

system, helping you drop into deeper presence. Take a slow breath and let the calming effects of this practice move through you.

Write a single word for how you feel right now.

Journal Prompts

- Which circle or detail drew your eye first, and why?
- Where did the Contact Point Awareness technique help you settle the most?
- Which part did you enjoy the most: the loose painting or the focused detail work?

Gentle Reminder

You don't have to be perfect at anything here.

thoughts

NERVOUS SYSTEM REGULATION TOOL

13

Progressive Muscle Relaxation

The Progressive Muscle Relaxation technique helps your nervous system calm as you gently tighten and release different areas of the body. This contrast teaches your body the feeling of relaxation and signals safety through physical release.

BENEFITS

- Helps release held tension
- Slows the stress response
- Supports deeper breathing
- Encourages body awareness

HOW TO TRY IT

- Sit comfortably. Gently tense one area of your body for a few seconds, then release it fully. Move slowly through different areas, noticing the contrast between effort and ease. Keep the movements small and kind.
- Gently tense your toes and the soles of your feet. Hold for a moment, then let them soften and relax.
- Lightly tighten your calves. Notice the effort, then release and feel them settle.
- Engage your thighs and hips just enough to feel the tension. Let go, and allow your legs to feel supported.
- Gently draw in your lower belly or pelvis. Release and feel your breath return naturally.
- Lift your shoulders slightly toward your ears. Let them drop and melt down your back.
- Tighten your hands around the paint brush or curl your fingers gently. Open them, and soften your grip.
- Clench your jaw just a little. Release, and let your tongue rest.
- Squeeze your eyes shut briefly. Open them, and allow your forehead to smooth.
- Take one slow breath, and notice how your body feels now. Stay here for a moment before beginning to paint.

WHEN IT'S USEFUL

Use the Progressive Muscle Relaxation technique when your body feels tight, when focus feels strained, or anytime you want to soften before or during creative work.

EXPLORE WHAT YOU KNOW OF WATER, COLOR, AND MARK-MAKING

Let flowing arc shapes become a playful way to explore what you already know: water first, color next, and then slow, focused mark-making.

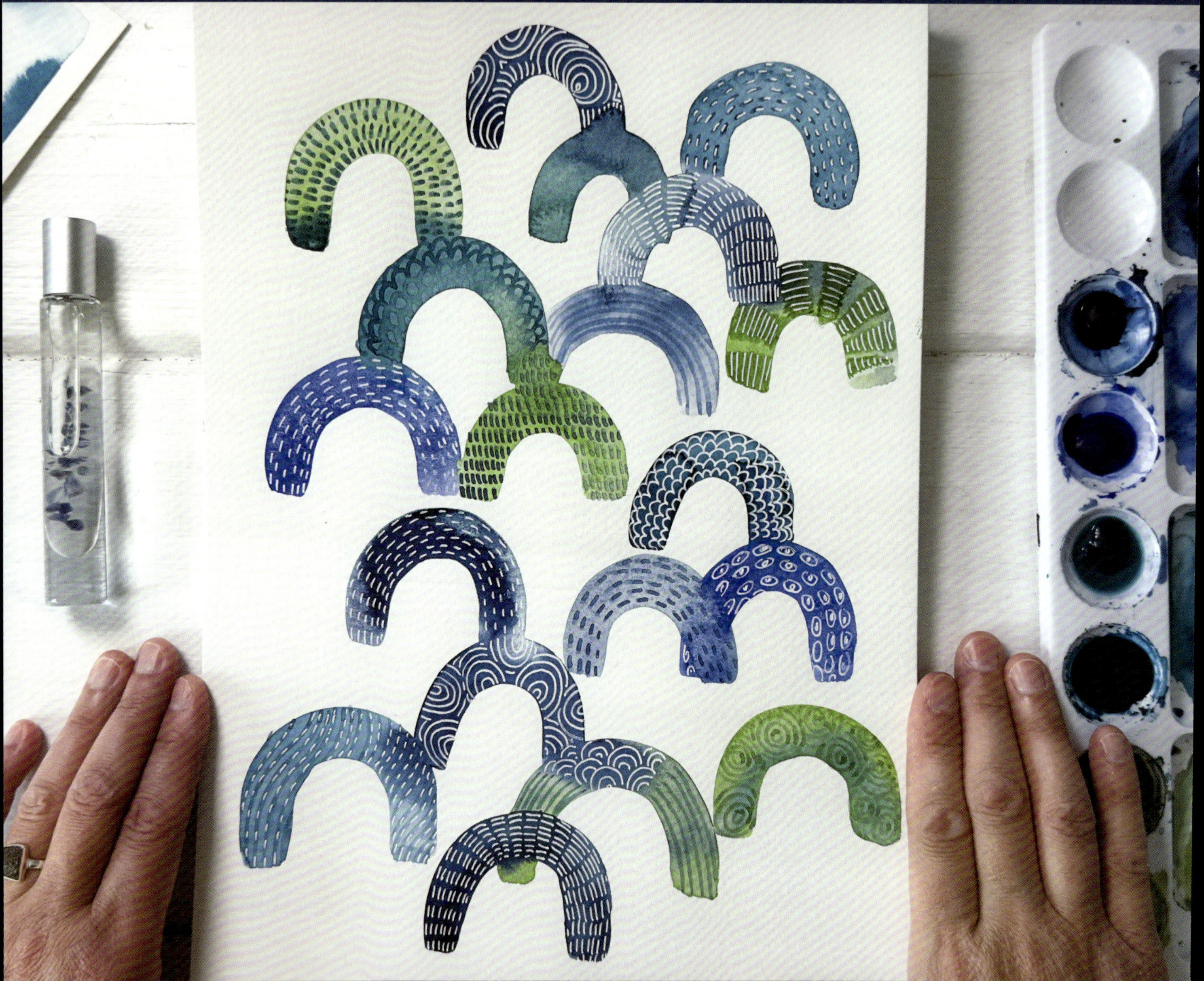

With the same gentle techniques you've practiced so far, you can turn any simple shape into a calming painting meditation. These arcs are just one idea. Your imagination can take you anywhere.

WHAT YOU'LL LEARN

- How to use a ½-inch flat brush to create relaxed, curved arc shapes
- How to drip, blend, and blur inside the arcs without overworking
- How progressive muscle relaxation helps release tension and support your nervous system while you paint

In this session, you will paint soft arc shapes across the page. Each arc is a simple, curved stroke that stays loose and watery. The shapes are uncomplicated, but they leave room to explore. You can drip color at the base, blur edges with clean water, or keep things very light and airy. As the shapes begin to dry, you narrow your focus and move into mark-making with the waterbrush, then add gentle details with the gel pen. Throughout the process, you'll practice the Progressive Muscle Relaxation technique, a nervous system tool that helps your body release held tension in small, intentional waves. This keeps your system relaxed and allows the creative process to unfold without strain.

WHAT YOU MIGHT FEEL

- Muscles softening as tension releases in small increments
- A slower, steadier rhythm in your body and breath
- A sense of ease as your focus moves between loose painting and gentle detail

HOW THIS SESSION FLOWS

Let's begin with a short technique tutorial. You'll learn how to make soft arcs with your flat brush and let the water move the color on its own. When the shapes start to dry, switch to the waterbrush and begin slow, focused mark-making. Once the page is fully dry, move to the gel pen and continue decorating at an unhurried pace. When the technique feels natural, move into the painting meditation. Pair the process with the Progressive Muscle Relaxation technique, soft music, and an easy rhythm that allows your body to soften as your imagination explores what's possible with this simple shape.

Follow the curve, trust the water,

and let your body soften as you paint.

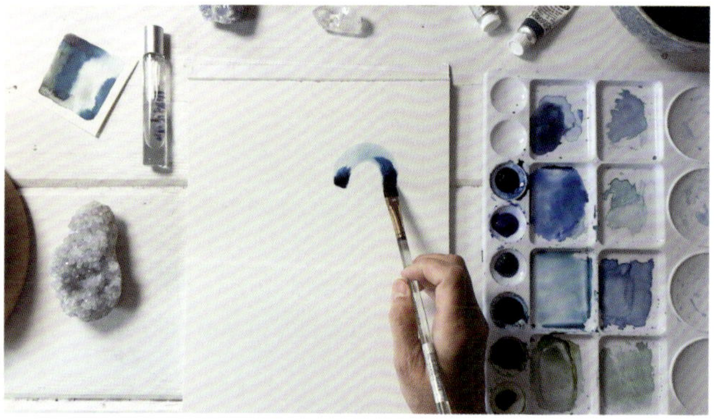

STEP ONE: PAINT YOUR FIRST SOFT ARC

With your ½-inch flat brush, mix a tea-strength wash of your chosen color. Paint a relaxed arc shape, keeping it watery so the interior stays glossy. While the arc is still wet, lay a deeper swash of color along the curve. Watch it spread on its own. As you paint, gently tense your feet for a moment, then let them relax fully. Notice the release.

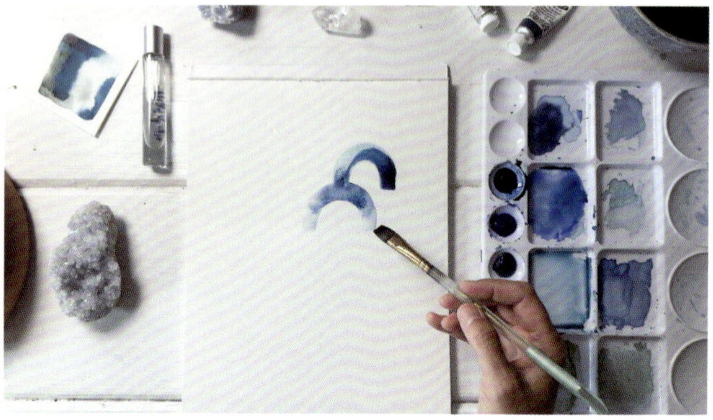

STEP TWO: LET SHAPES TOUCH

Paint another arc below the first. Let the shapes gently meet and watch the water and color blend. Keep the stroke soft and free. Lightly tighten your calves, then release. Feel how the body settles when you let go.

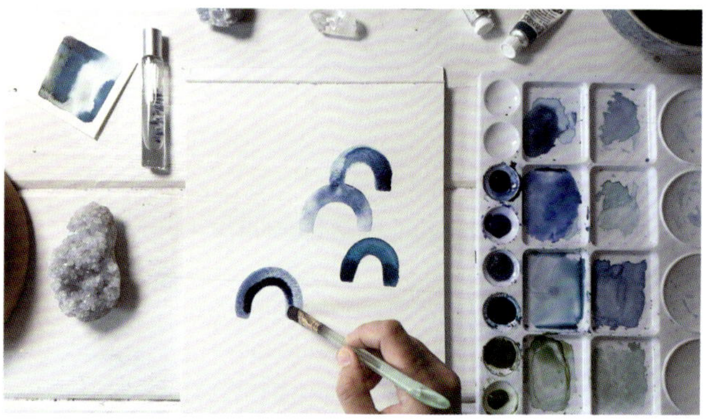

STEP THREE: PLAY WITH PLACEMENT AND VALUE

Continue adding arcs across the page. Place some close together and space others farther apart. While the arc is still wet, add a darker line near the base and step back as the water softens it. Gently tense your thighs or hips, then relax them. Let the support beneath you do the work.

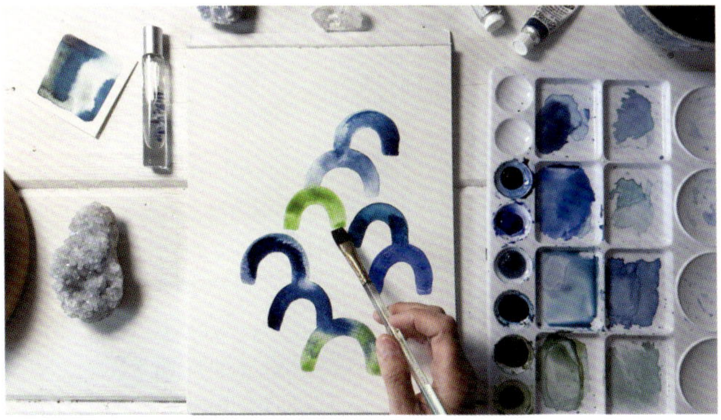

STEP FOUR: FOLLOW COLOR CURIOSITY

Choose a new color that calls to you. Lay it down with plenty of water and move on. When you don't force the paint, the shapes stay open and alive. Softly lift your shoulders toward your ears, then let them drop. Feel the shift.

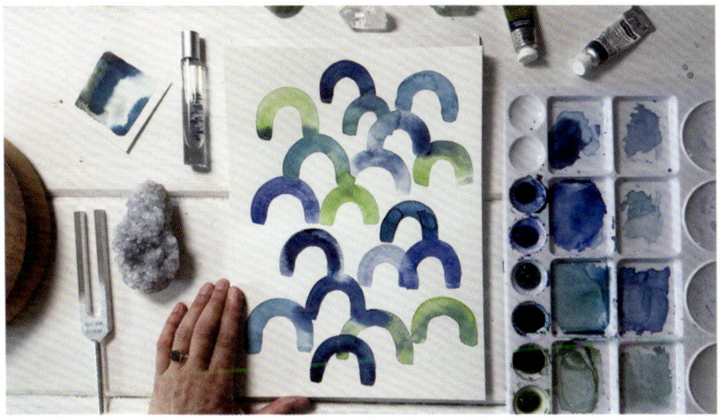

STEP FIVE: KEEP GOING UNTIL IT FEELS COMPLETE

Allow your intuition to guide you as you place more shapes around the paper. Vary the color, play with dripping, and add value with light tea washes and dark drips of paint. Feel your way through the composition; remember, there aren't any rules. Do whatever you feel called to do. Stop when the page feels complete. Gently tighten your hands around the brush, then loosen your grip. Notice how ease returns.

Gentle Reminder

Soften your body. Let the water lead.

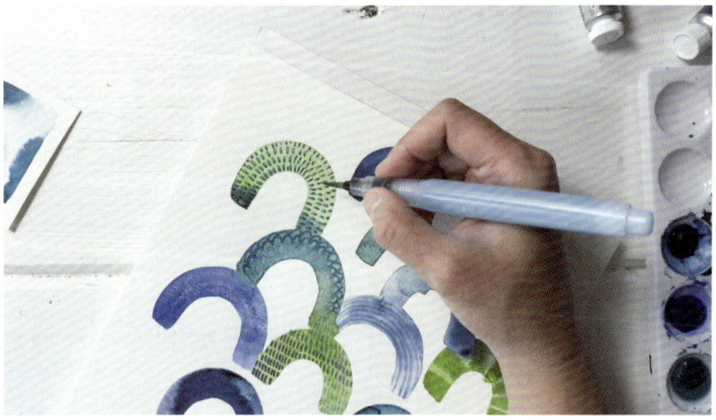

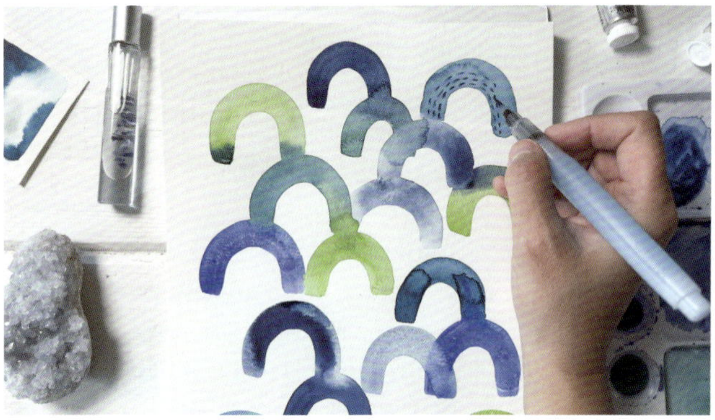

STEP SIX: BEGIN ADDING THE DETAILS

When earlier arcs begin to dry, switch to a smaller round brush or the waterbrush. Paint tiny strokes, dashes, dots, or curves inside the shapes. This narrowed focus calms the mind and slows your pace. Gently tense your jaw for a second, then release. Let your breath soften.

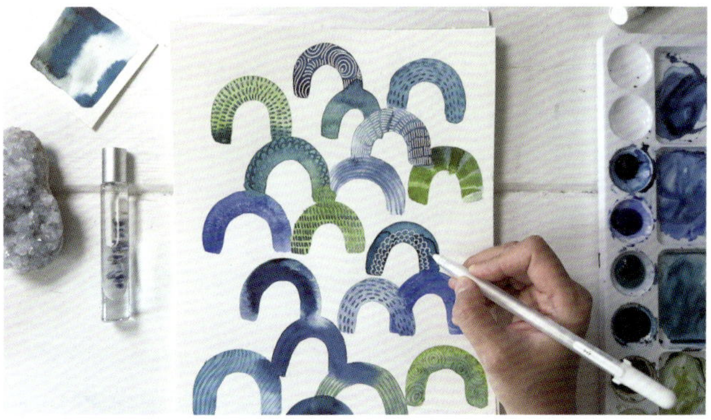

STEP SEVEN: MOVE TO THE GEL PEN

Once everything is dry, switch to your gel pen. Add simple marks: rings, lines, dots, gentle patterns. Let the details be soft and imperfect. Don't forget to breathe deeply and let your shoulders soften. Briefly tense your forehead, then relax it. Feel the quiet that follows.

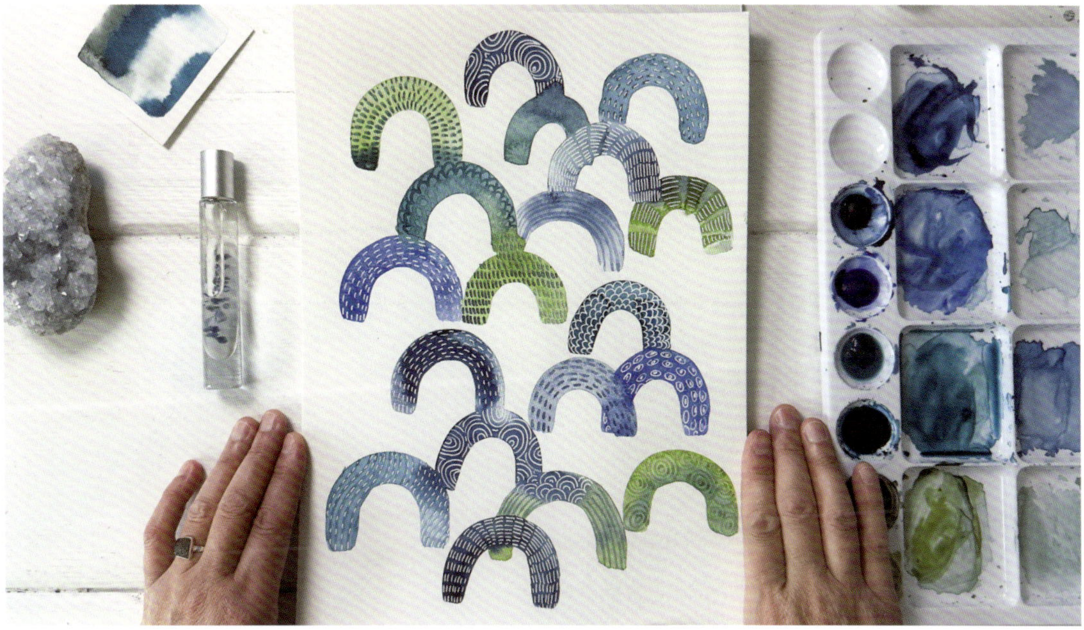

STEP EIGHT: FINISH AND FEEL

Stop when your attention naturally fades or the page feels full. Take a moment to review your painting and really look. Notice how the loose, watery washes create softness and how the tiny marks add structure and clarity. Feel the contrast. You began with wide, relaxed attention, then shifted into slow, detailed focus. That transition alone can calm the mind. As you take in the whole page, you may feel a quiet sense of satisfaction, a soft settling in your chest or shoulders, or the simple relief of seeing how everything worked together without forcing it. Let that be enough.

Energy Note

Release creates space. Space invites calm.

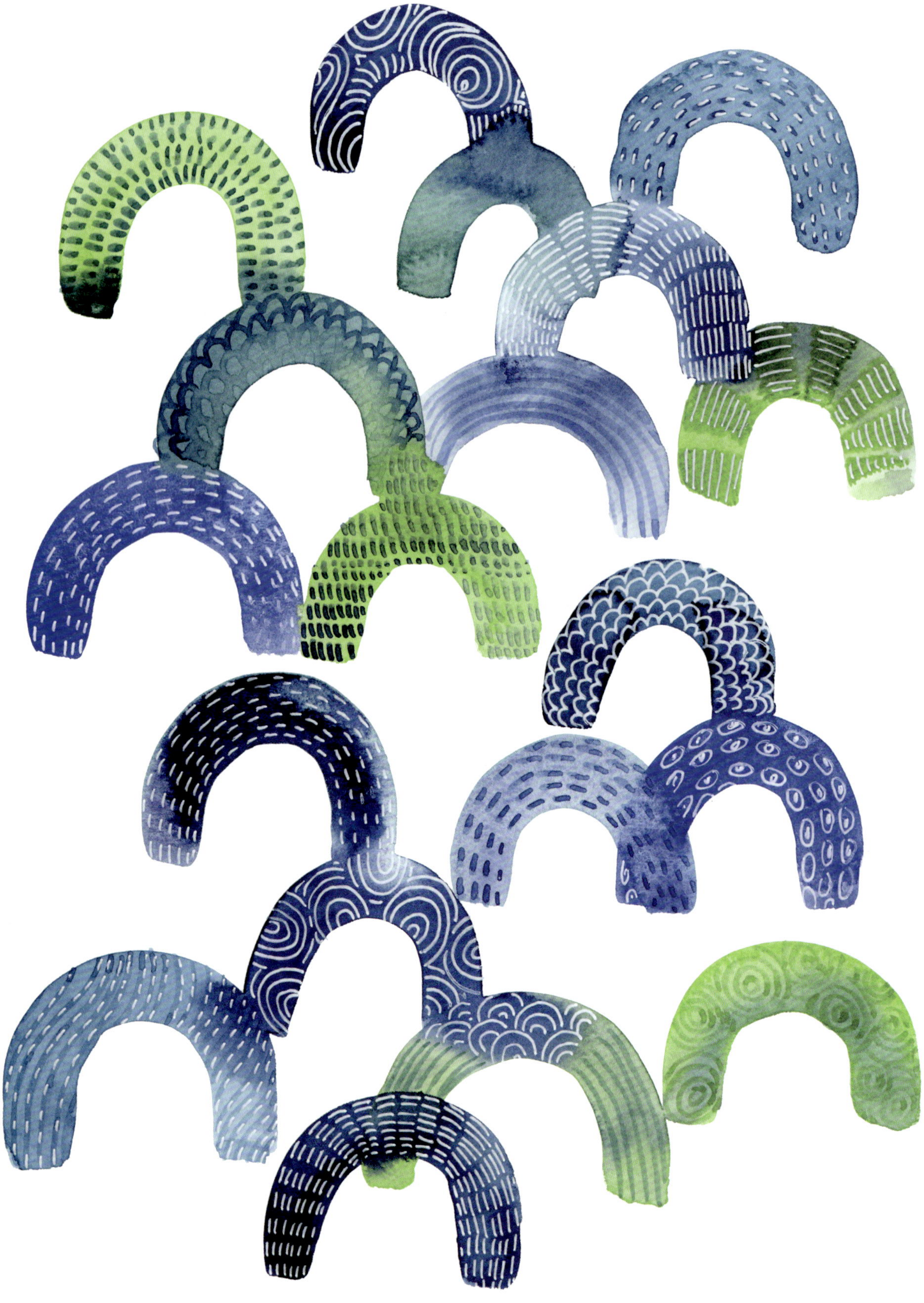

Painting Meditation: Gentle Arcs

Put on soft-frequency music. Surround yourself with things you love. Use crystals, essential oils, or flower essences if they support your practice. Paint one watery arc. Then gently tense and release a small area of your body. Paint another arc and release another place. Let each curve be followed by a soft letting go. Inside each arc, keep the details simple. Drip, blur, or add marks. If the urge to fix appears, pause and release tension somewhere in your body before continuing. Let ease guide your next move.

Integration

Sit with your painting for a moment. Notice where your body feels softer than when you began. Take one slow breath and release any remaining tension. Write one word that describes how you feel now.

Journal Prompts

- Where did you notice tension release in your body while painting?
- How did shifting between loose arcs and fine details feel?
- What surprised you as the paint dried?
- What did letting go of control allow you to experience?

thoughts

14

NERVOUS SYSTEM REGULATION TOOL

Gentle Containment

The Gentle Containment technique is the practice of offering your body a sense of support through light, intentional self-holding. Instead of looking outward for grounding, you create a feeling of steadiness from within. Using your non-dominant hand allows your body to receive support while your dominant hand remains free to paint. This is not pressure, and it is not control. It is a quiet way of letting your body know it is held.

BENEFITS

- Creates a felt sense of safety and reassurance from the inside
- Helps calm emotional overwhelm without needing movement
- Reduces mental noise by giving the nervous system a clear signal of support
- Encourages the body to soften rather than brace
- Supports focused, steady attention during creative work

HOW TO TRY IT

- Sit comfortably and keep your painting hand free.
- Place your non-dominant hand gently on one knee. Focus your attention on your hand touching your knee. Let the weight of your hand rest there, and take one slow breath.
- Move your hand to your hip. Pause, and notice the steadiness beneath your palm.
- Bring your hand to your lower stomach. Let the belly soften into the touch.
- Slide your hand up to your upper stomach. Breathe naturally, and allow the muscles to relax.
- Place your hand over your heart. Stay for a breath or two, and notice any softening.
- Move your hand to your lower throat. Keep the touch light and supportive.
- Bring your hand to the back of your neck. Let your shoulders drop as you pause here.
- Place your hand on your forehead. Notice the quieting of your thoughts.
- Rest your hand on the top of your head. Stay for one slow breath.

- Move your hand to the back of your head. Let the jaw and face relax.
- Bring your hand to the back of your shoulder. Allow the arm to feel heavy.
- Slide your hand down to your upper arm. Pause and soften.
- Finish by resting your hand on your lower arm. Let the entire arm feel supported.

You may move through these points in order or return to the place that feels most calming.

WHEN IT'S USEFUL

Use the Gentle Containment technique when you feel emotionally tender, overstimulated, or unsteady. It is especially helpful during a painting session, during moments of self-consciousness, or anytime you want to feel supported while staying engaged in your work. This practice offers reassurance without interruption, allowing creativity to unfold from a grounded, held place.

Rooted

LET YOUR BODY FEEL GROUNDED IN THE EARTH

Let this simple landscape become a place to rest. You begin with water and wide, open washes, then slowly layer color and detail.

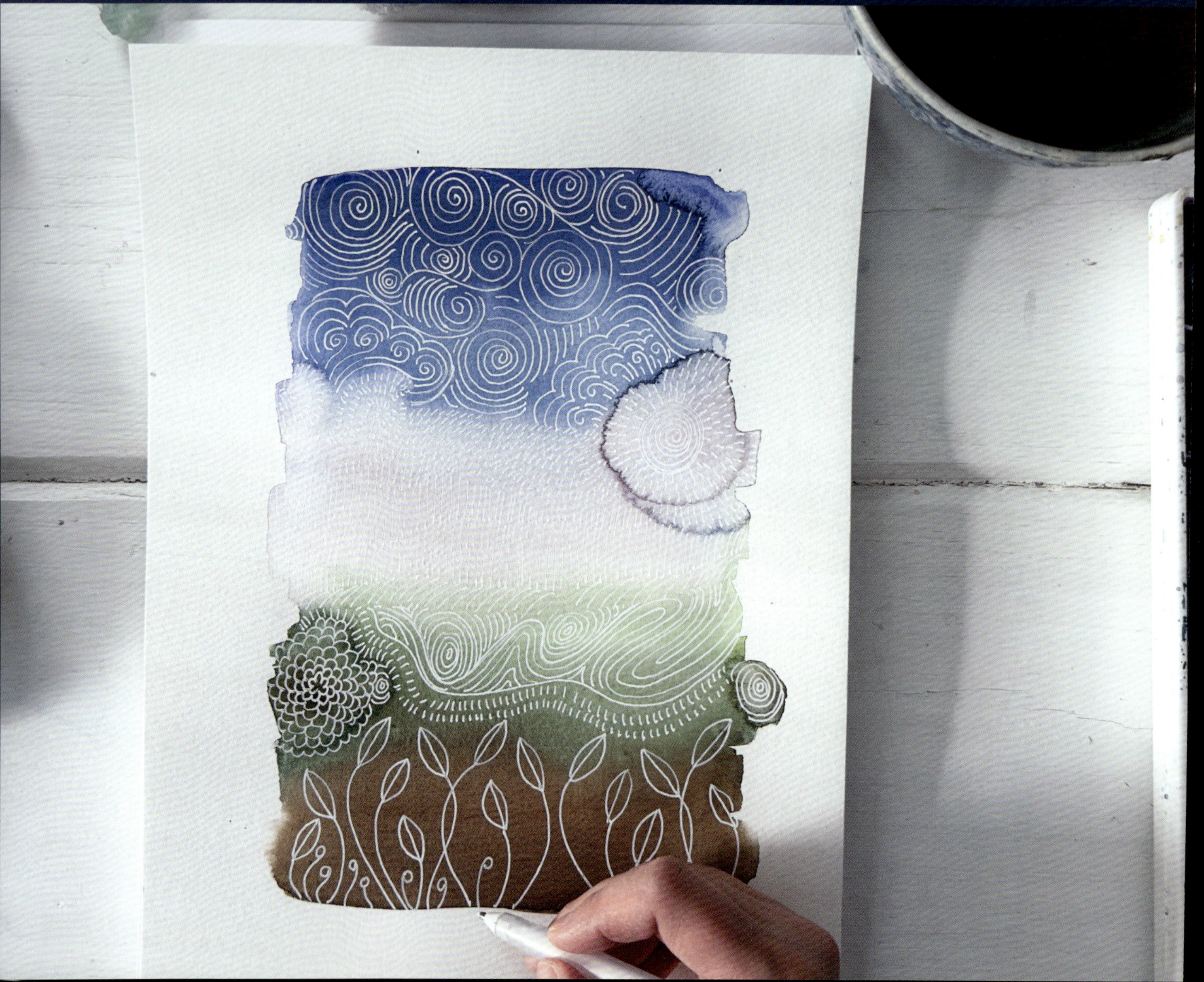

As the painting takes shape, your body is gently invited to soften and feel supported from the inside. This session is about grounding, not through effort, but through being held.

WHAT YOU'LL LEARN

- How to paint a loose, washy landscape using loose painting techniques
- How to layer color to create a sense of earth below and sky above
- How the Gentle Containment technique supports grounding and emotional steadiness while you paint

In this session, you will paint a simple landscape that feels rooted beneath you and spacious above. Begin with water, and allow color to spread naturally on the page, imagining sky, horizon, and earth. There is no need to plan or control the outcome. You are simply placing color and letting it move. As the paint dries, you shift into slower, more focused mark-making with the gel pen. Throughout the process, practice the Gentle Containment technique—a nervous system regulation tool that offers support through light self-holding. Using your non-dominant hand, you provide your body with a steady sense of reassurance while your dominant hand paints. This allows your system to stay grounded, calm, and present without breaking your creative flow.

WHAT YOU MIGHT FEEL

- A sense of steadiness as your body receives gentle support
- Deeper grounding as your attention settles into your lower body
- Ease and safety as your focus moves between loose painting and quiet detail

HOW THIS SESSION FLOWS

We'll begin with a short technique tutorial. You'll learn how to lay down water first and create a simple, flowing landscape. Add color gently and allow it to blend and settle on its own. Once the page dries, move into slow, intuitive mark-making with pen or pencil.

When the process feels familiar, move into the painting meditation. The session is paired with gentle containment, soft background music, and an unhurried pace that helps your body feel supported while your imagination explores.

Let the earth hold you as you paint.

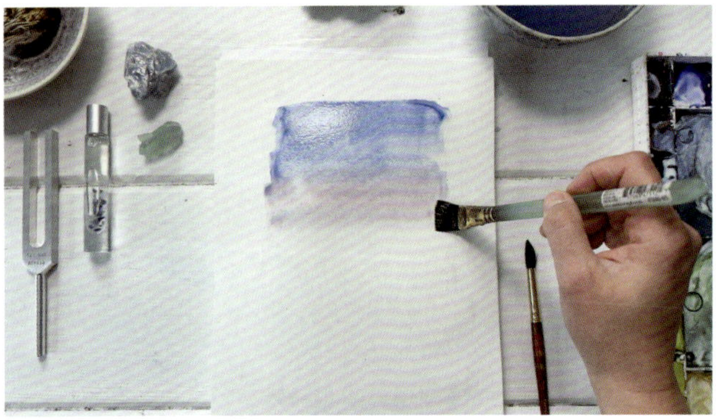

STEP ONE: INVITE THE SKY

Begin near the top of the paper. With a deep blue color, paint a line approximately 5 to 6 inches long, centering it on the paper. Use a lot of water and keep it loose. Continue painting down the page, creating a landscape horizon scene. Blues, pinks, or soft purples work beautifully here. Continue adding water and paint, blending as you go.

As you begin, place your non-dominant hand gently on one knee. Let the weight of your hand rest there. Take one slow breath.

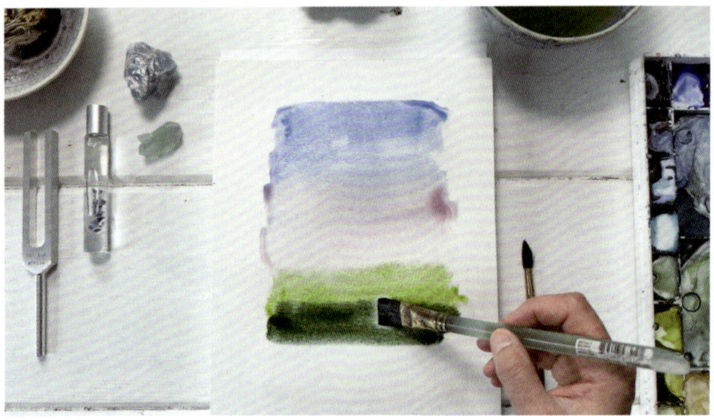

STEP TWO: LAY DOWN THE GRASS

While the page is still wet, introduce color into the middle area below the horizon line. Use light and dark greens to create a field of grass. Lay down the color while adding more water and watch the colors blend as you glide your brush across the paper.

Move your non-dominant hand to your hip. Pause and notice the steadiness beneath your palm.

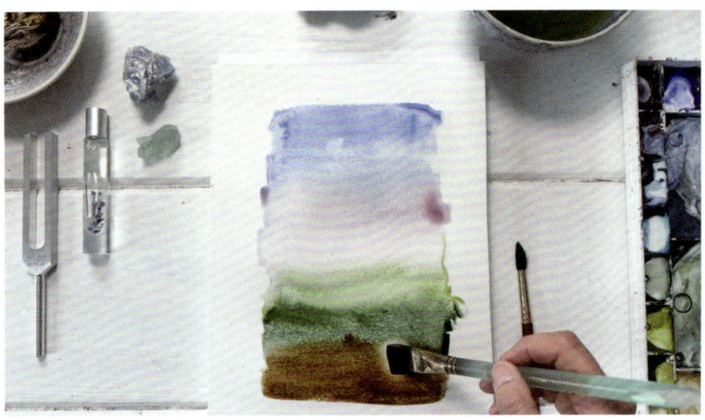

STEP THREE: FEEL THE EARTH

Add browns or earthy tones near the bottom of the page. Allow the colors to deepen as they move downward. Imagine the paint settling into the ground.

Bring your hand to your lower stomach. Let your belly soften into the touch.

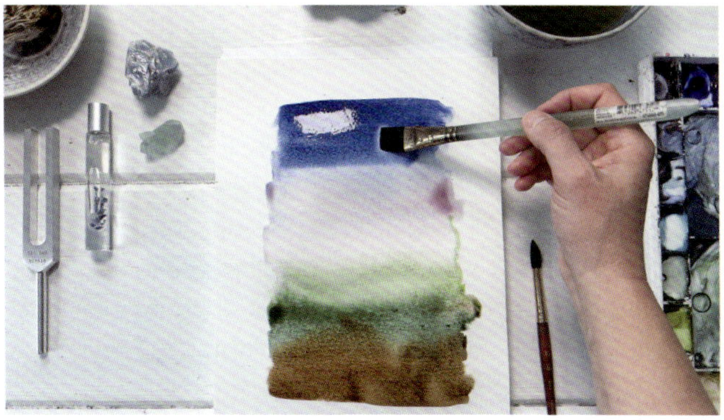

STEP FOUR: GO DEEPER

While the painting is still wet, introduce darker tones if needed. Darker blues at the top of the sky, and deeper browns at the base can suggest depth, warmth, or roots extending below the surface. Let the paint do the work. Slide your hand to your upper stomach. Notice the gentle rise and fall of your breath.

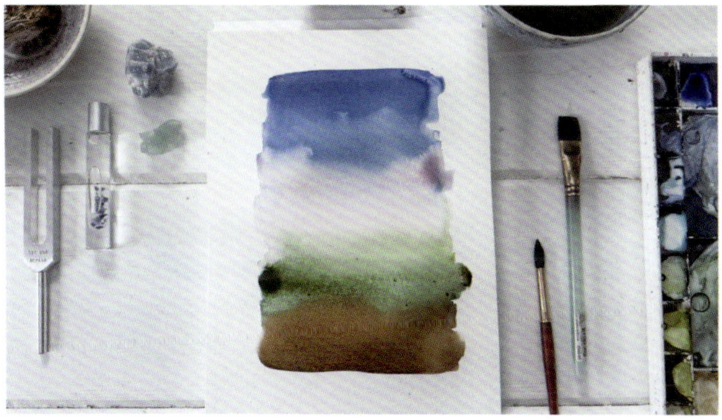

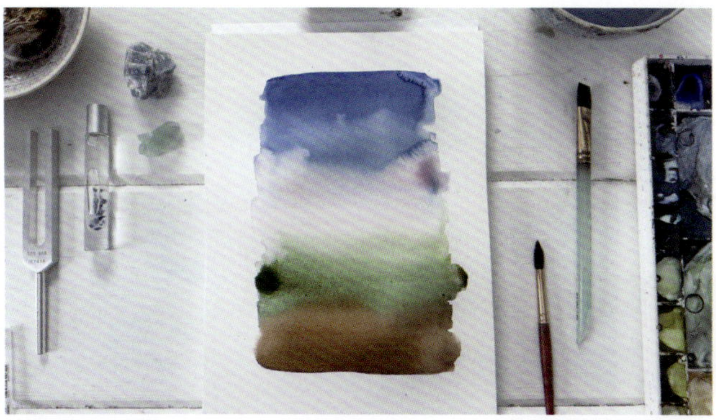

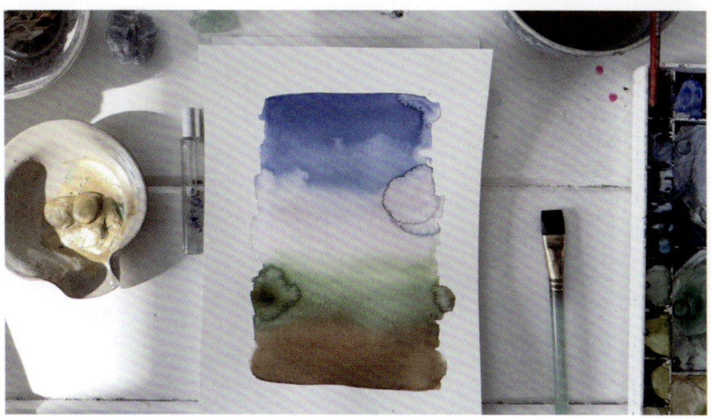

STEP FIVE: LET IT DRY

Pause to allow the painting to dry naturally. Watch the shifts in color and texture without intervening. Place your hand over your heart. Stay for a breath or two, and notice any softening.

Energy Note

Being held allows you to soften.

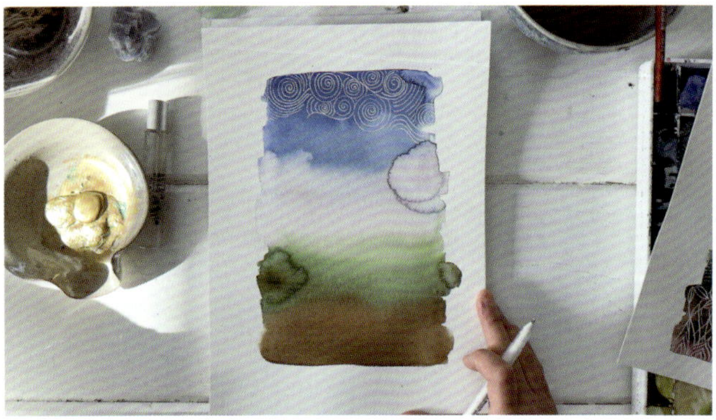

STEP SIX: BEGIN THE DETAILS

Once the page is dry, begin adding gel pen marks. Follow what you see in the paint. Spirals, dots, lines, or root-like shapes may appear. There is no plan, just play. Move your hand to the back of your neck. Let your shoulders drop.

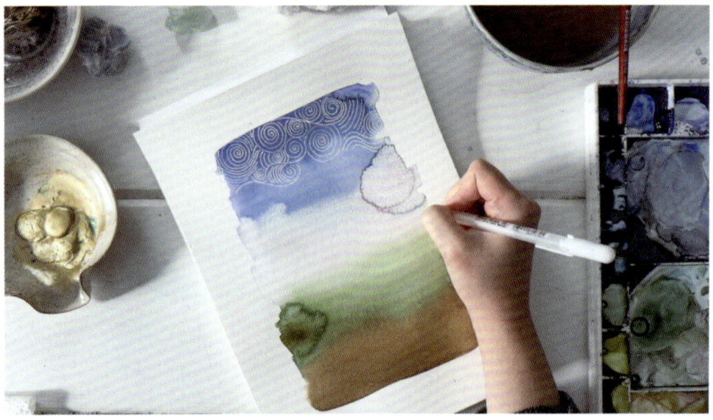

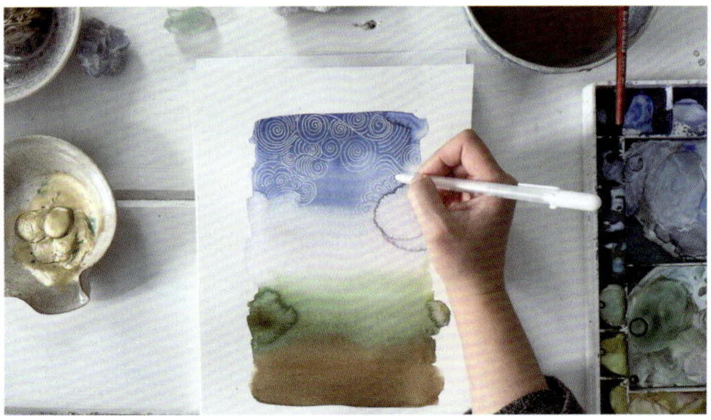

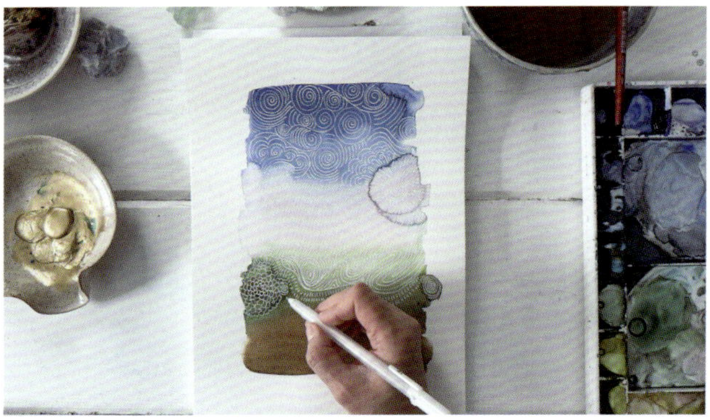

STEP SEVEN: FOLLOW WHAT EMERGES

Allow your marks to change and evolve. Some areas may remain untouched. Others may become more detailed. Let the painting guide you. Rest your hand briefly on your forehead, then the top of your head. Notice the quiet that follows.

Gentle Reminder

Let the earth do some of the holding.

STEP EIGHT: FINISH WHEN IT FEELS COMPLETE

Stop when your attention naturally fades or the page feels complete. Take time to really look at what has emerged. Notice how the wide washes and small marks work together.

You may feel a sense of grounding, a soft heaviness in your lower body, or a quiet ease in your chest or shoulders. Let that be enough.

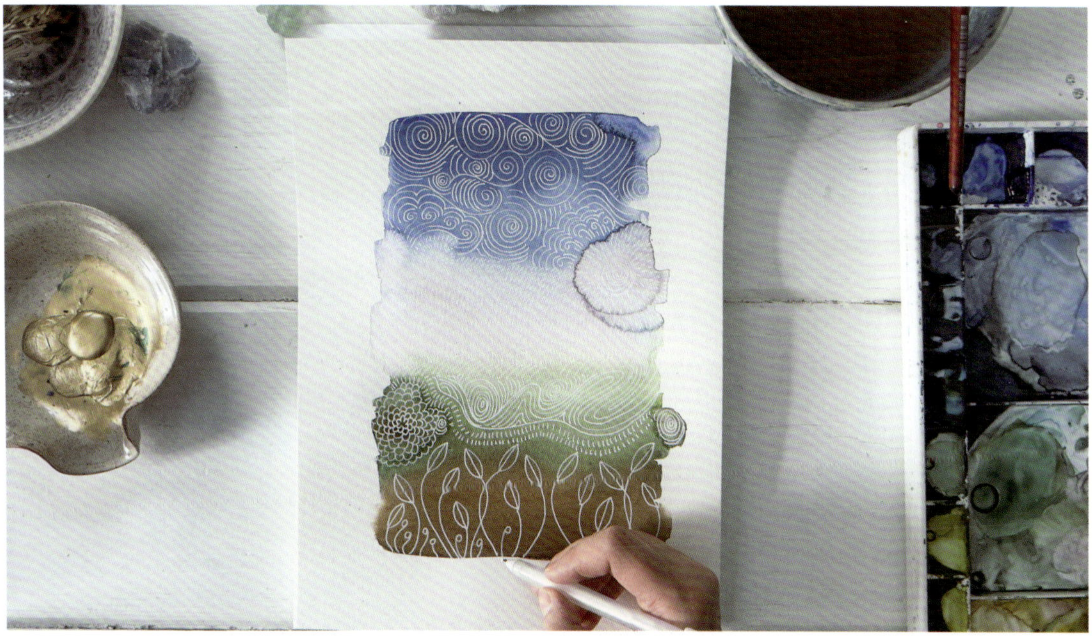

Permission Slip

You do not need to control the outcome.

Painting Meditation: Rooted

Put on soft-frequency music. Sit comfortably. Paint slowly, allowing the process to unfold without effort. Paint for a few moments, then pause to offer gentle containment somewhere in your body. Let the touch be light and supportive. Return to painting. Alternate between mark-making and moments of holding. If the urge to fix or control arises, pause. Place your hand somewhere steady. Let your body settle before continuing.

Integration

Sit with your painting. Notice where your body feels more grounded than when you began. Take one slow breath. Write one word that captures how you feel now.

Journal Prompts

- What did your body respond to during this session?
- Where did you feel the most grounding?
- What emerged when you allowed the painting to guide you?
- How did gentle support change your creative experience?

thoughts

15

NERVOUS SYSTEM REGULATION TOOL

Heart-Focused Breathing

The Heart-Focused Breathing technique gently brings your attention to the heart area while you breathe slowly and evenly. This practice is inspired by HeartMath techniques, which show that when you focus on the heart and breathe with intention, your nervous system begins to regulate and your inner world quiets down and feels more peaceful.

BENEFITS

- Calms emotional reactivity
- Slows and deepens the breath
- Supports heart-brain coherence
- Creates a sense of inner warmth and safety

HOW TO TRY IT

- Sit comfortably and soften your shoulders.
- Place one hand over your heart.
- Inhale gently through your nose.
- Exhale slowly through your mouth.
- Turn your focus to your heart and imagine the breath moving in and out through the heart area.
- Repeat for four to six easy breath cycles.

WHEN IT'S USEFUL

Use the Heart-Focused Breathing technique before heart-centered painting, when emotions feel close to the surface, or anytime you want to relax and reconnect with yourself.

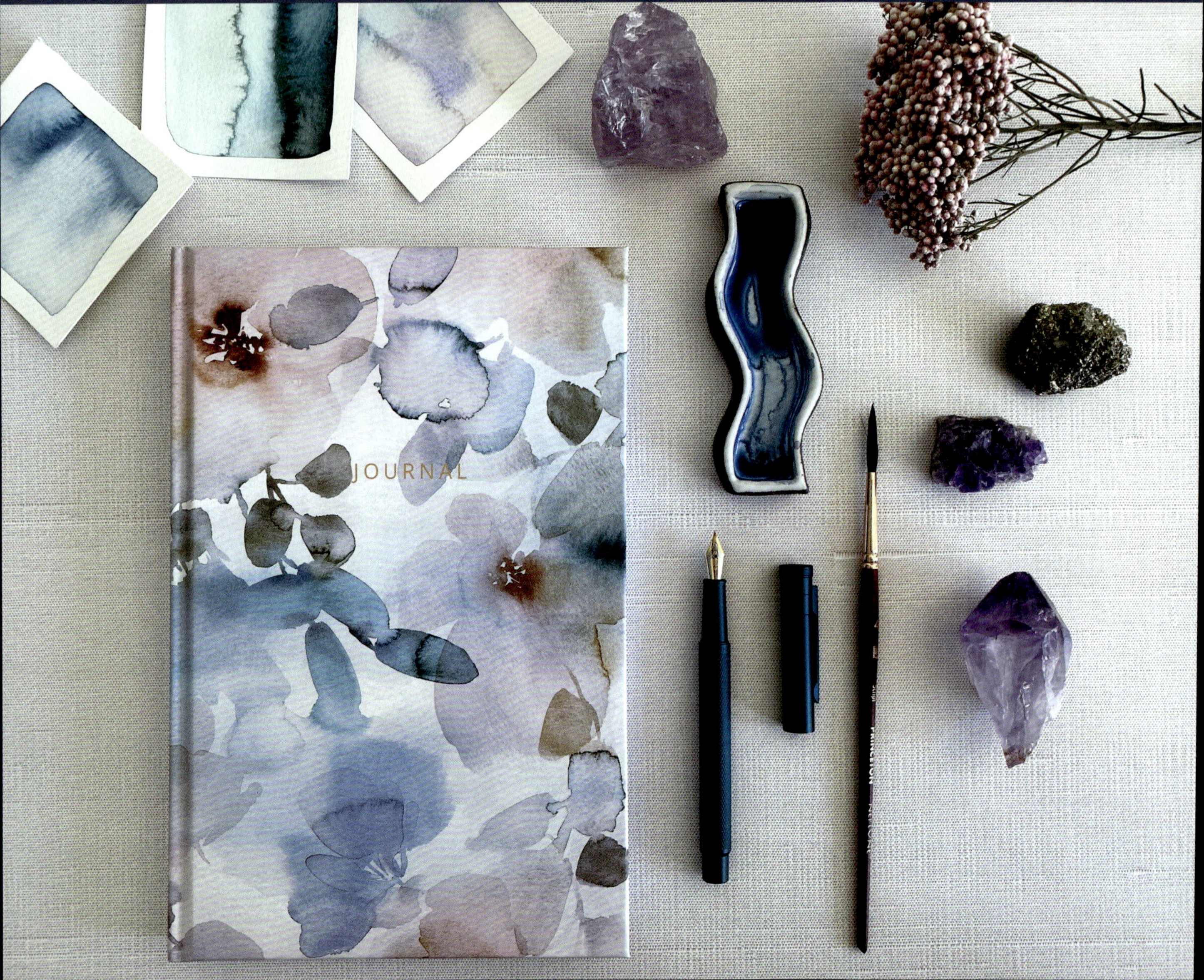
JOURNAL

When you slow down and bring your awareness to the things that you appreciate, your body begins to relax, your breath deepens, and your nervous system settles down.

WHAT YOU'LL LEARN

- How to use simple word painting as a meditative, heart-centered practice
- How to paint letters with loose, watery strokes and gentle drips
- How the Heart-Focused Breathing technique supports emotional balance and nervous system regulation
- How to infuse intention and feeling into your painting process

In this session, you will begin by journaling about all of the things you are grateful for—big or small. Make a list. These reflections gently open your heart and shift your inner state toward peace and contentment. When you are finished writing, you will paint the word "grateful" across the page. You can draw out the word first, or you can just paint as you go. Keep each letter simple and loose. Remember, nothing has to be perfect. Beauty is found in the imperfections of your paintings. Drip in color, play with the water, and let the paint move freely. As you paint, practice the Heart-Focused Breathing technique, a simple nervous system regulation tool that brings your awareness to the heart area while you breathe slowly and evenly. This creates a steady rhythm between your heart, breath, and hand, allowing your body to settle in while your emotions are gently engaged.

WHAT YOU MIGHT FEEL

- A soft opening in the chest or your heart space
- A calmer, steadier emotional tone
- A sense of warmth, ease, or tenderness
- A quiet appreciation that grows as you paint

HOW THIS SESSION FLOWS

We'll begin with short journaling to connect with gratitude, then move into a brief technique tutorial where you'll learn how to paint loose, watery letters. Once the technique feels comfortable, move into the painting meditation. You'll paint the word "gratitude" while practicing the Heart-Focused Breathing technique, keeping your pace slow and your touch gentle.

Paint the feeling first. Let the letters follow.

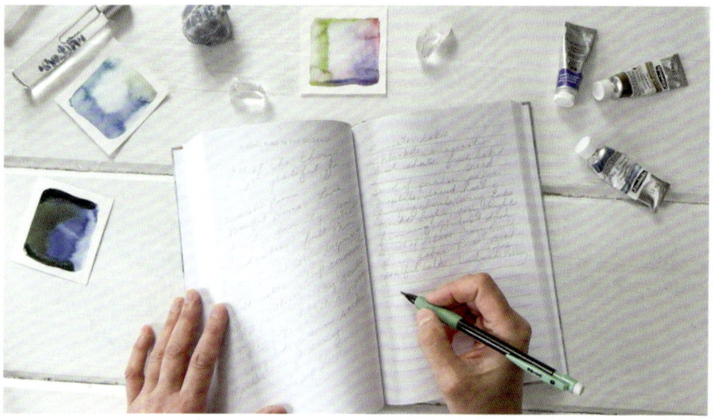

STEP ONE: JOURNAL FIRST

Take a few minutes to write a simple list of things—big or small—you feel grateful for: people, moments, comforts, parts of yourself. When it feels complete, set your journal aside.

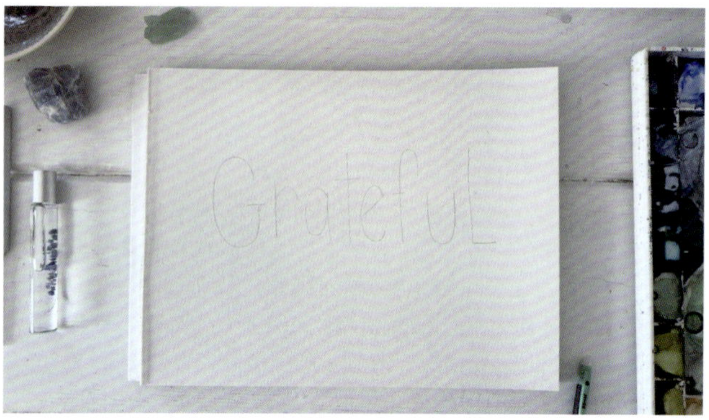

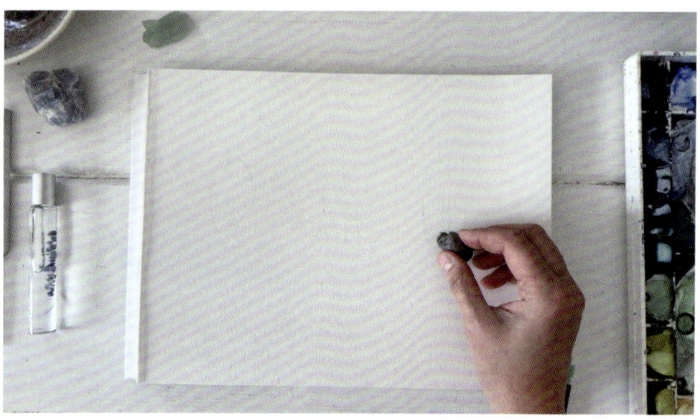

STEP TWO: DRAW THE WORD

In the center of your paper, draw out the word "grateful." Keep it super simple. I chose to use lowercase letters, but it's totally up to you how you want to draw it. Just remember, it doesn't have to be perfect. After you finish drawing, use an eraser to erase most of the pencil marks. Keep it as light as possible.

Gentle Reminder

Breathe into your heart. Let go on the exhale.

Energy Note

Gratitude heals the nervous system.

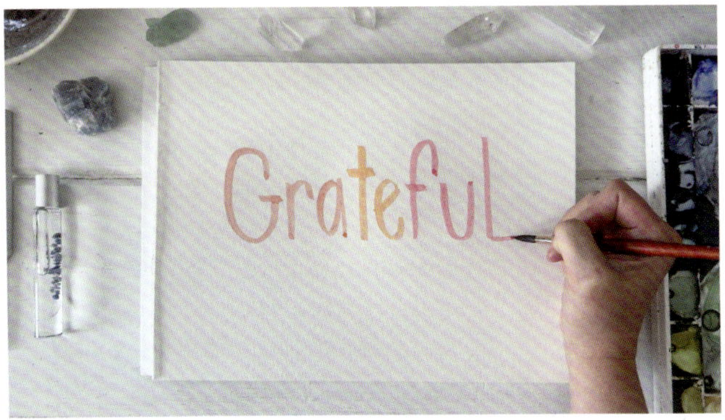

STEP THREE: PAINT IT

Fill your brush up with color and water. I decided to use a soft pinkish red to start. You can use whatever colors you like. You can change the color for each letter or every few letters; it's totally up to you. Let them be simple shapes rather than careful lettering. You don't have to oversaturate your brush with water; later you will decorate each of the letters with the waterbrush.

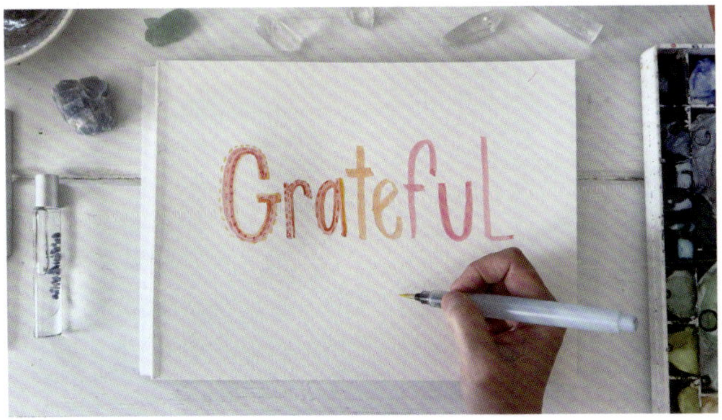

STEP FOUR: HOLD GRATITUDE AS YOU PAINT

As you paint each letter, gently bring to mind the things you feel grateful for from your list. You don't need to force any emotion. Simply feel the energy of gratitude fill your heart space as you paint.

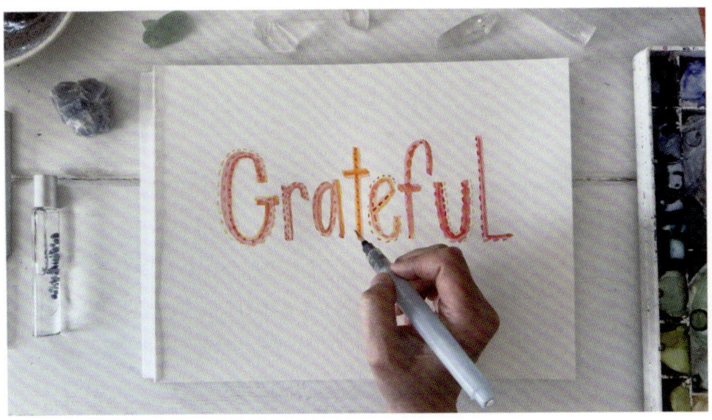

STEP FIVE: MOVE THROUGH EACH LETTER

Move letter by letter. Breathe gently through your heart. Keep your grip loose. Play with lines, tick marks, mixing up the colors, or whatever you feel called to do. Feel the feeling of gratitude wash through you with each letter.

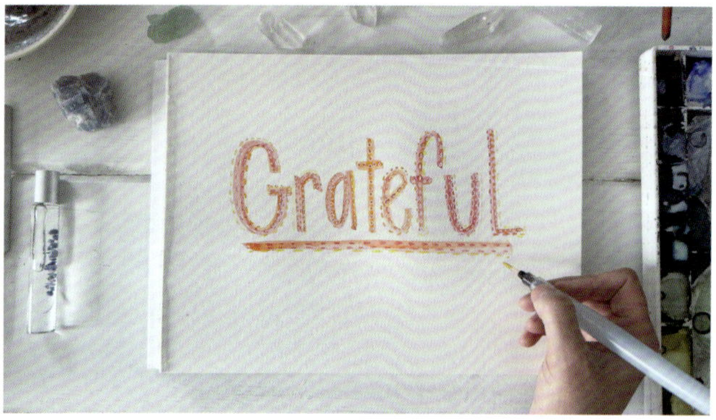

STEP SIX: PLAY WITH THE GEL PEN

When you are feeling happy with your letters, let the painting dry and grab your gel pen. Have fun making small, detailed marks in your letters. Tune into your intuition. What is it whispering to you? I decided to add a swash under my word and decorated it. As you play, get lost in the details, feel your shoulders relax, take a deep heart-centered breath, and release.

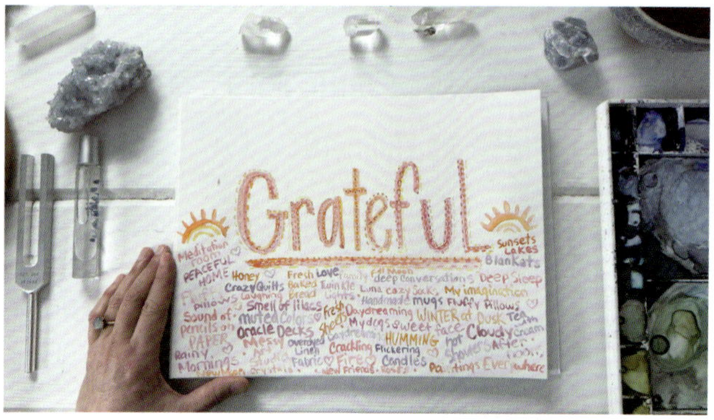

STEP SEVEN: PUT IT ALL OUT THERE

Follow your intuition and see where it takes you. I decided to write all of the things I'm grateful for on the paper. I wasn't planning on it, but it felt right. I used the waterbrush to paint the words. I kept it simple and messy. Once I painted everything that I am grateful for from the list, I decorated the paper with little suns—just because. Add whatever you feels called to add.

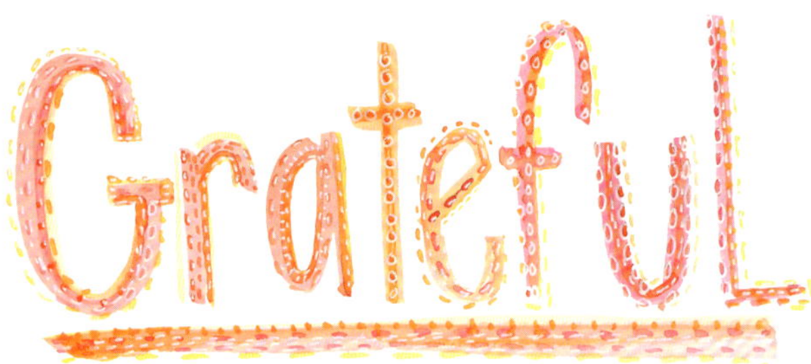

STEP EIGHT: FEEL YOUR PAINTING

Take a minute and feel the energy of your painting. You painted this word with the energy of gratitude while breathing through your heart. Your painting is now infused with that healing energy. Cool right?

Permission Slip

Your letters do not need to be perfect.

Painting Meditation: Gratitude as Practice

Put on soft-frequency music or whatever makes you feel happy. Close your eyes for three easy breaths. Place one hand on your heart. Imagine your breath moving in and out through your heart space. Try using aromatherapy. I love using rose flower essences or an uplifting essential oil. Begin painting the word "grateful." Paint one letter at a time. With each letter, think of the things you are grateful for. Let your breath set the pace. Feel the energy of gratitude as you paint. If your mind starts to plan or judge, gently return to your breath and the feeling in your heart. Continue until the painting feels complete.

Integration

Rest with your painting. Notice how the letters feel when you look at them. Place a hand on your heart and take one slow breath. Write a single word for how you feel now.

Journal Prompts

- What came up for you while painting the word "grateful?"
- Did anything surprise you about what you felt grateful for?
- How does your body feel after this practice?

thoughts

NERVOUS SYSTEM REGULATION TOOL

Heart-Centered Awareness

The Heart-Centered Awareness technique is the practice of gently placing your attention in the heart area and noticing what is present right now. Instead of trying to create a feeling, you simply listen. You allow any sense of warmth, openness, or softness to arise in its own way. For some people, self-love is easy to access. For others, it can feel distant or unfamiliar. Both are okay. You are not trying to force a big emotion. You are giving your nervous system a quiet invitation to experience even a small hint of care, tenderness, or neutrality in the heart space. Over time, this practice helps strengthen the connection between the heart, brain, and nervous system.

BENEFITS

- Supports emotional balance
- Encourages gentle self-connection
- Calms the nervous system
- Builds heart-brain coherence
- Helps access compassion without pressure

HOW TO TRY IT

- Sit comfortably and soften your shoulders.
- Place one hand over your heart or simply bring your attention to the center of your chest.
- Breathe slowly and evenly.
- Gently ask yourself: "What does the energy in my heart feel like right now?"
- Notice what feeling registers in response. You might notice warmth, heaviness, softness, numbness, or nothing at all. All responses are okay.
- If it feels difficult to sense anything for yourself, begin by thinking of a person, animal, or place that naturally brings up a feeling of love.
- Notice how that feeling registers in your heart area.
- Gently shift the focus back to yourself and see if even a small thread of that feeling remains.
- Stay with the sensation for a few slow breaths.

16

WHEN IT'S USEFUL

Use the Heart-Centered Awareness technique before heart-centered painting, when you want to connect with yourself gently, or anytime you want to soften and return to your heart.

Permission Slip

You don't have to feel anything specific. Your heart is allowed to be exactly as it is.

Heart Portrait

AN INTUITIVE HEART PAINTING

This lesson invites you to slow down and gently turn inward to your heart. You do not need to create a perfect feeling of love.

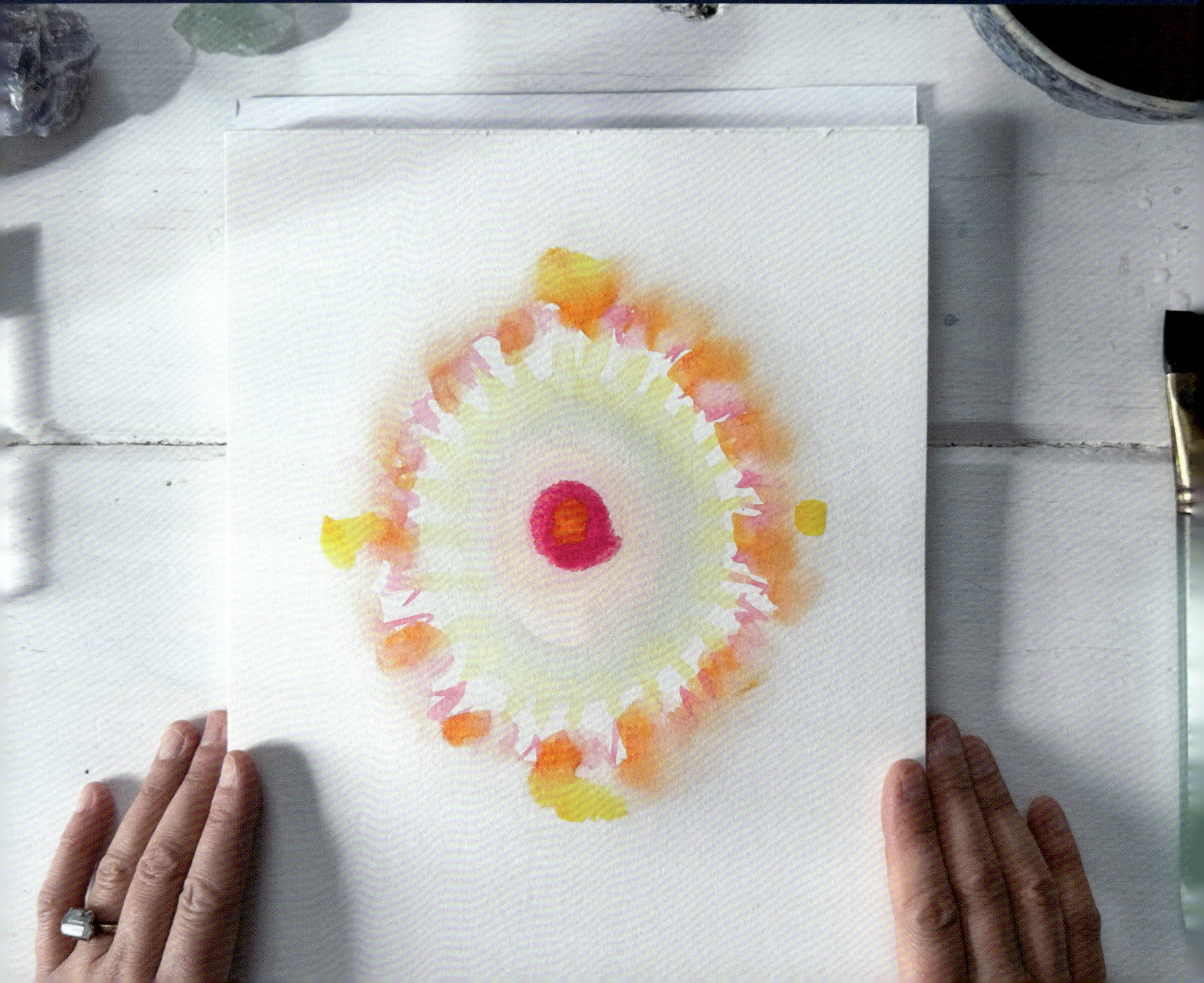

Simply meet your heart as it is, right now. You place your attention in the center of your chest and allow color, water, and marks to express what you sense. Paint from the heart space rather than the thinking mind.

WHAT YOU'LL LEARN

- How to paint what you are feeling
- How to play with color to express emotion
- How to use the Heart-Centered Awareness technique to connect with your heart in the present moment
- How to allow feelings to guide color without judgment

In this session, you will begin by quietly bringing attention to your heart center and the love in your heart for yourself. You are not trying to force a feeling. You are simply noticing what is there. You may sense warmth, heaviness, openness, tightness, or very little at all. All of these feelings are welcome. The key is to feel what is in your heart and use colors and brushstrokes to portray those feelings. Don't judge what comes out. Honor your feelings and reflect on them. Begin with water and a wash of color in the center of the page. There are no rules here. You can paint a circle, play with color, and make marks. You can let drips, blurs, and value shifts speak for you. Your heart becomes a space of listening rather than judging.

WHAT YOU MIGHT FEEL

- A softening in your chest or breath
- Unexpected emotion rising and settling
- Resistance at first, then curiosity
- A quiet sense of connection to yourself

HOW THIS SESSION FLOWS

We'll begin with a short technique tutorial. You'll learn how to paint a loose energy portrait with plenty of water and color. When the technique feels natural, move into the painting meditation. Pair the process with heart-centered awareness, soft background music, and a slow, kind pace that supports emotional regulation and self-connection.

Meet your heart gently.

Let color listen before it speaks.

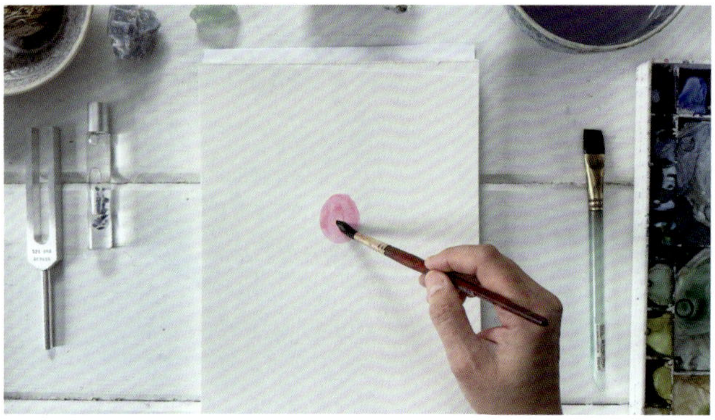

STEP ONE: BEGIN WHERE YOU ARE CALLED

Take a moment to focus on your heart. Imagine yourself in the center of your heart space. What feelings come up for you? Choose a color that matches the feeling you are experiencing. I chose a vibrant pink to start with because I felt a fullness in my heart. I felt happy. Your colors may be completely different depending on what is coming up. Place a hand on your heart for extra support. Take one slow breath. There are no right or wrong feelings. Be with them, paint them, and move on.

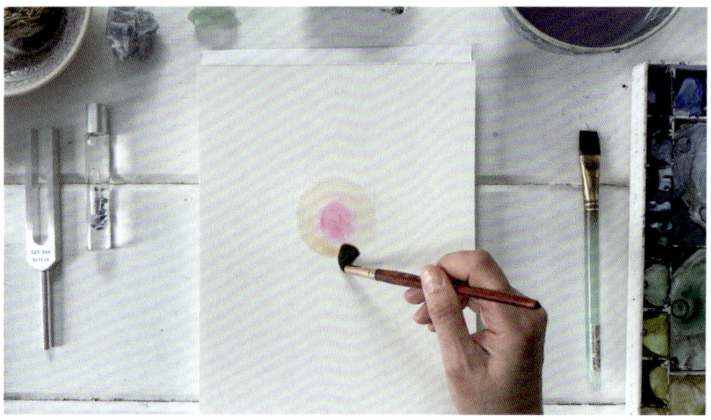

STEP TWO: CONTINUE TO FOLLOW THE ENERGY

Fill your brush up with color and water. I decided to use a soft orange next because I felt light and optimistic in the moment. What colors are calling to you? What does the energy in your heart feel like right now? If it feels hard to sense anything for yourself, gently think of someone you care about or your beloved pet. Notice how that feeling registers in your heart. Then softly return attention back to you.

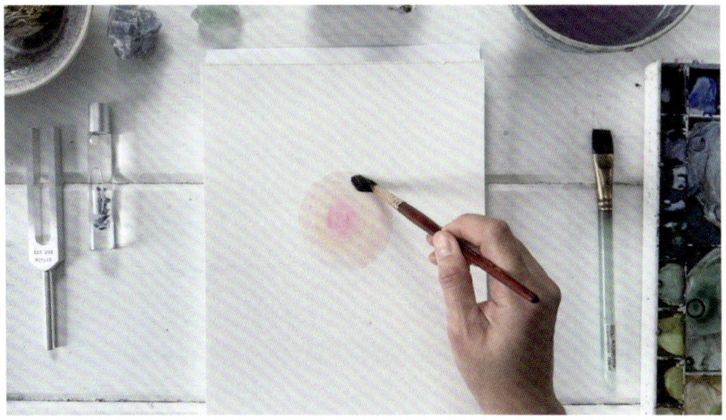

STEP THREE: PAINT HOW THE ENERGY FEELS

Connect to your heart again, without thinking, and select the color that matches the feeling that is coming up. I was still feeling the same light, happy optimism, so I grabbed some more pink. I kept plenty of water on my brush and let my brush move around my circle, blending the colors as it went.

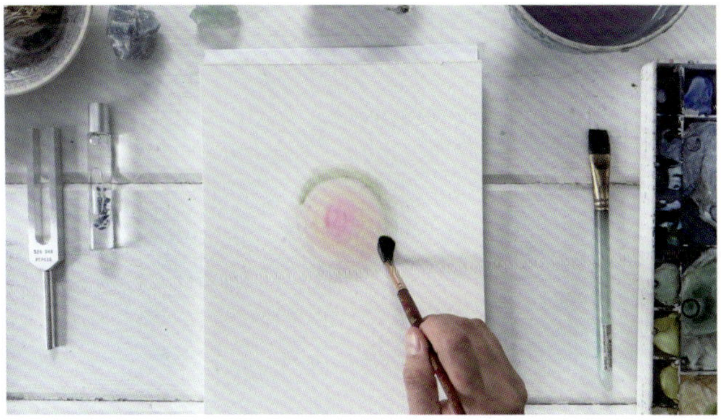

STEP FOUR: ADD GENTLE LAYERS OF COLOR

Notice if the color wants to change. Let your intuition guide your choices. I saw green in my mind's eye. Stay quiet and see how your intuition speaks to you. The green felt neutral to me. I was feeling content in the moment.

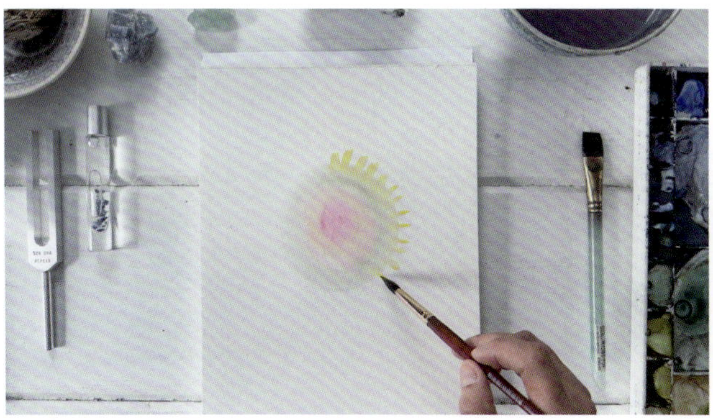

STEP FIVE: MOVE TO THE OUTSIDE EDGES

Imagine the energy of this painting. It has a center and an outer edge. Close your eyes and bring your attention to your heart center. Sense its energy. What does the outer edge look or feel like? Paint it. I closed my eyes and saw the sun, so I painted sun rays.

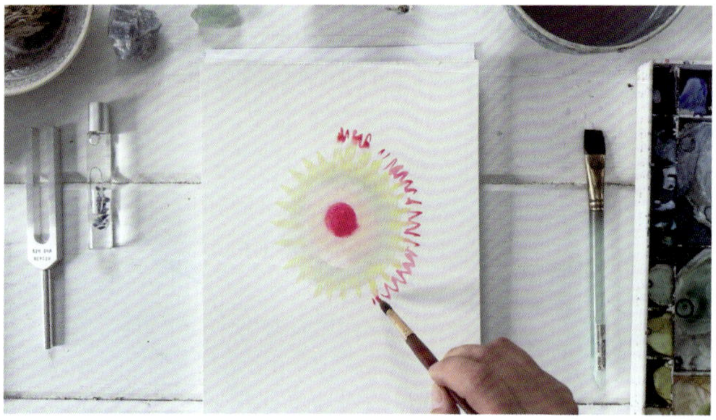

STEP SIX: LET IT EVOLVE

Close your eyes and feel the energy in your heart and around your body. Connect to you, what is it saying? I started to feel a surge of energy come in—excitement. I intuitively reached for some bright pink and painted a pop of color at the core and wavy lines on the outer edge. What are you feeling?

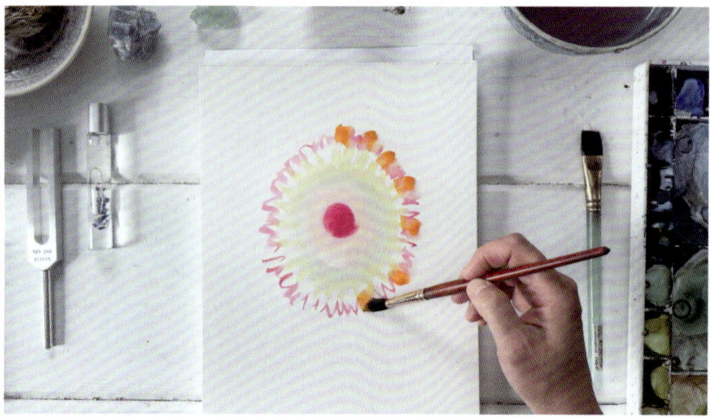

STEP SEVEN: MOVE THROUGH THE PAINTING

Continue to let the energy move through you. At this point, you are in the flow, painting feelings, following your intuition, and playing. What marks can you add that express how you are feeling in this moment?

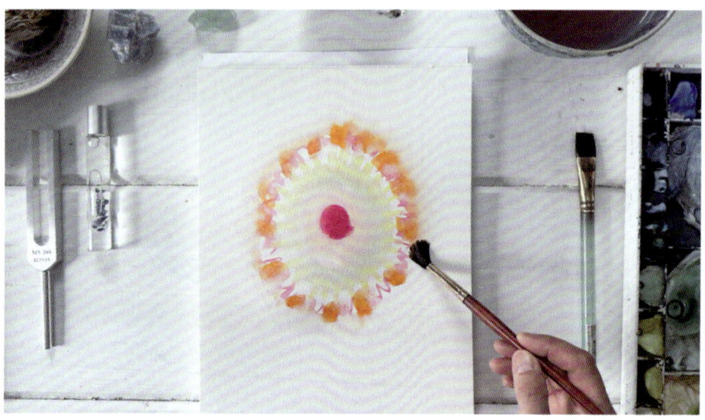

STEP EIGHT: FOLLOW THE FLOW

Continue feeling, vibing, listening, and painting. I was fully in the flow of this painting at this point. I decided to add a wash of water around the outer edge. It felt calming to me. I was settling into the painting, starting to relax, and feeling soft around the edges.

Energy Note

When you paint from the heart, the nervous system relaxes.

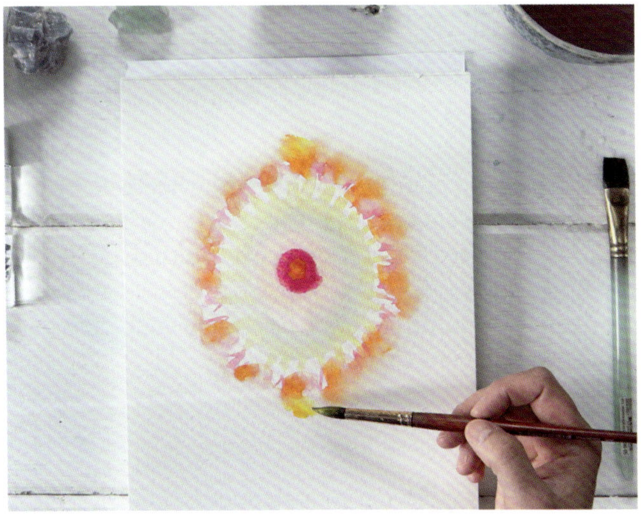

STEP NINE: TAKE IT WHEREVER IT NEEDS TO GO

Whatever comes up for you, try painting it. I saw these golden orbs and a golden center. They symbolized the four directions—north, south, east, and west—with my heart at the center. It just came to me, and I painted it. It made me feel like I was headed in the right direction. Remember, don't analyze, just paint. Keep going until it feels complete or your energy wanes.

Gentle Reminder

Let the heart lead. Let the brush listen.

Painting Meditation: Heart Portrait

Put on soft-frequency music or whatever calls to you. Sit comfortably. Place one hand over your heart or bring attention to the center of your chest. You can use aromatherapy or perhaps hold your favorite crystal and feel its subtle energy. Rose Quartz would be great for this lesson. Begin painting what you are feeling. Pause, and breathe. Notice your heart space. Lay down some color with your brush. Pause again. If self-judgment appears, return to the sensation in your chest. Noticing is enough. Continue slowly until the painting feels complete.

Integration

Take a deep breath in, and on the exhale, feel the tension leaving your shoulders. Look at your painting. How does it feel? Does the energy of the painting reflect what you were feeling in your heart? This may feel like a new way of painting. Instead of thinking about what to make, you are painting energy and your feelings. When you connect with the energy within you and the quiet presence of your heart, it naturally supports your nervous system and invites a deeper sense of calm.

Painting this way begins to shift your relationship with art. You are no longer trying to describe or explain what you are painting. You are simply expressing energy and feeling. Over time, this adds a depth to your work that the mind could never plan and words could never fully capture. The thing I love the most about this lesson is that every time I paint a heart portrait, it looks different. Some days I'm feeling great about myself, other days, not so much. The colors, brush-strokes, and feeling of the portraits are always different. Don't judge your portraits. Honor your feelings and know that they come and go.

Journal Prompts

- What did you notice in your heart as you painted?
- Did any colors surprise you?
- What felt supportive or gentle in this process?
- What would it look like to offer yourself a little more kindness today?

thoughts

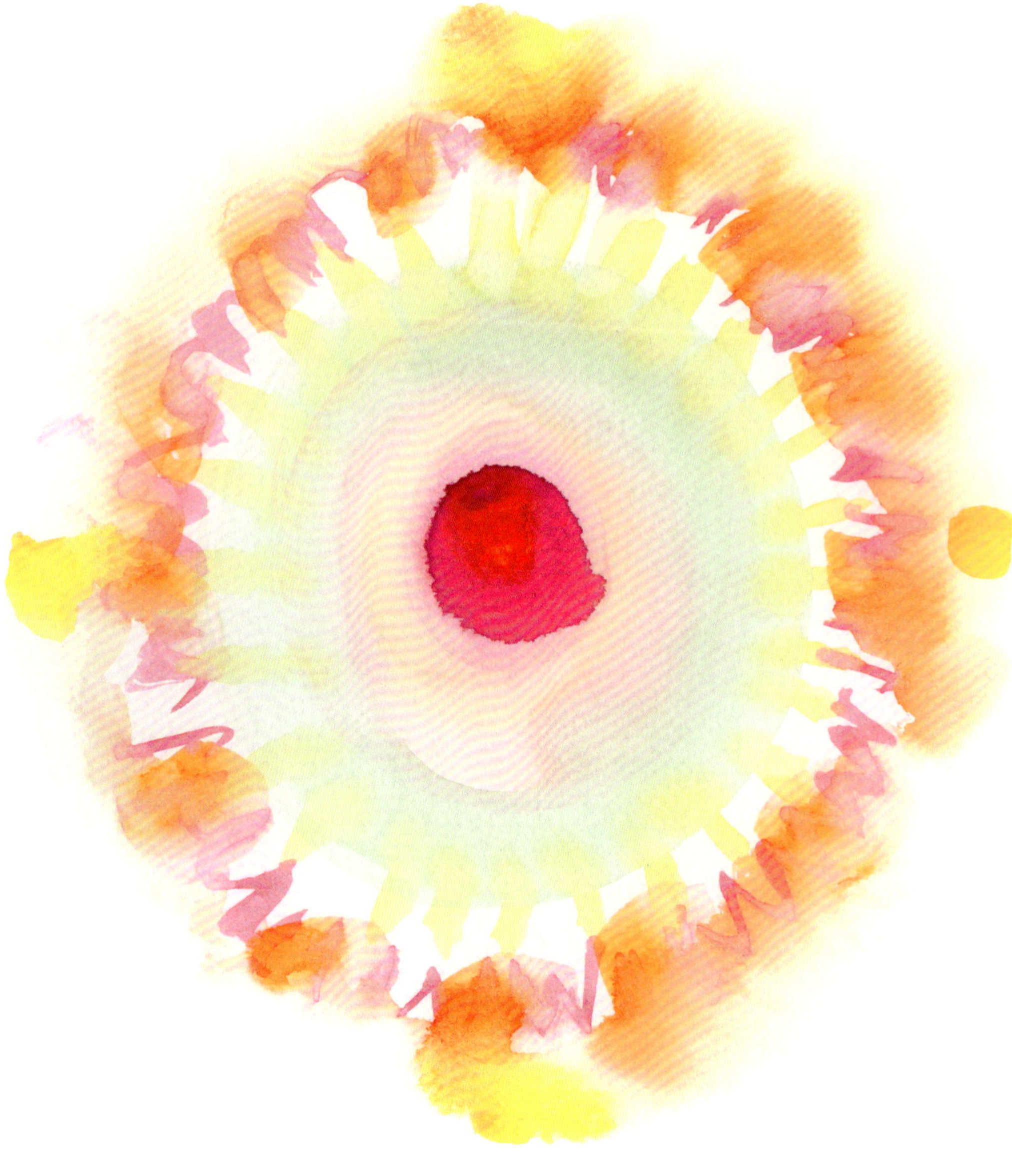

NERVOUS SYSTEM REGULATION TOOL

17

Self-Compassion Breathing

The Self-Compassion Breathing technique is a gentle way of bringing kindness directly into the body through slow, steady breaths and simple supportive phrases. Instead of pushing yourself to feel anything specific, you allow the breath to create a soft internal environment where warmth, safety, and care can slowly grow. This practice supports the heart-nervous system connection by inviting ease rather than effort.

BENEFITS

- Softens self-criticism and inner pressure
- Calms emotional intensity
- Slows and steadies the breath
- Encourages feelings of safety and support
- Helps open the heart gently at your own pace

HOW TO TRY IT

- Sit comfortably and let your shoulders relax.
- Place one hand over your heart if that feels supportive.
- Inhale slowly through your nose.
- Exhale slowly through your mouth.
- On each breath, quietly repeat one simple phrase in your mind:

"I am supported."
"I am safe."
"I am grounded."
"I am loved."
"I am understood."

You can substitute another phrase that calls to you, stay with one phrase, or let them rotate naturally.

WHEN IT'S USEFUL

Use the Self-Compassion Breathing technique when you feel tender, disconnected from yourself, or emotionally guarded, as well as when you want to approach heart-centered painting with gentleness instead of pressure.

Heart Altar

CREATE A SACRED SPACE FOR YOUR OWN HEART

This lesson invites you to honor yourself through painting a heart altar. You paint a simple altar shape and place a heart at the center. The altar becomes a container. The heart becomes the offering. You are both.

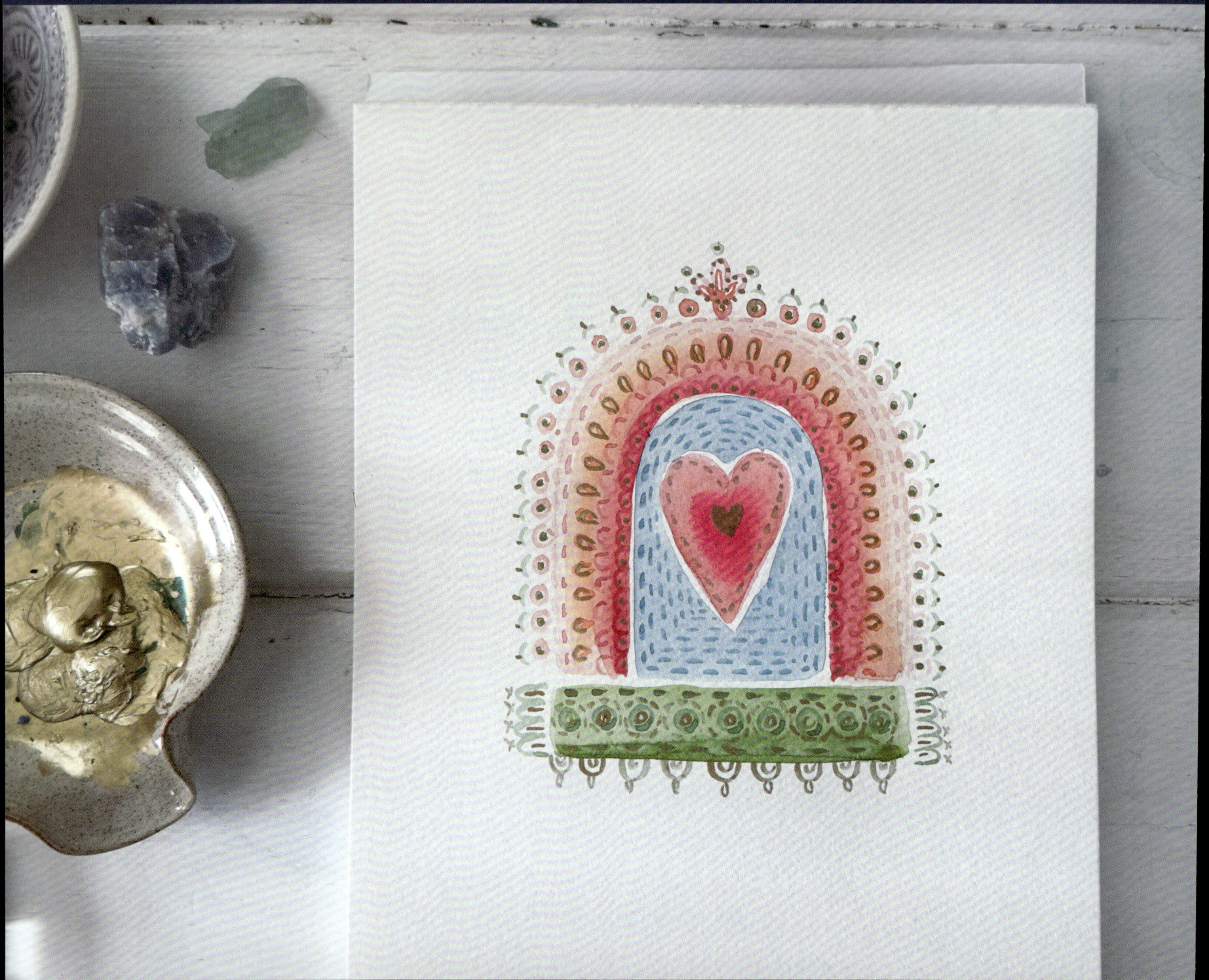

This is about choosing yourself gently, about creating space for yourself, and remembering that your heart deserves reverence, too.

WHAT YOU'LL LEARN

- How to paint a simple altar shape using watery layers and soft edges
- How to place a heart at the center and build color around it without overworking
- How to use Self-Compassion Breathing to soften inner criticism and support emotional regulation
- How to let painting become a ritual of honoring rather than performing

In this session, you will paint a heart altar. The altar represents a grounded foundation. The heart at the center represents you. You'll layer watery color to create the altar. You can drip, blur, deepen edges, or leave light spaces. As the painting dries, you will add small marks with the waterbrush and details with the gel pen. Throughout the process, you'll practice the Self-Compassion Breathing technique, a simple nervous system tool that softens the inner voice and supports emotional balance.

WHAT YOU MIGHT FEEL

- A mix of tenderness and resistance
- Softening in the chest or throat
- A quieter inner critic
- A subtle sense of steadiness or grounding

HOW THIS SESSION FLOWS

We'll begin with a short technique tutorial. You'll learn how to paint a simple heart using a light wash and plenty of water. From there, you'll gradually build an altar shape around the heart using layered color and soft edges, allowing the structure to form as you go. When the layers begin to dry, move into gentle detail work with the waterbrush and gel pen. When it feels natural, move into the painting meditation. Pair the process with self-compassion breathing, soft music, and a slow pace that allows your heart to be seen and held.

Place your heart at the center.

Let it be held.

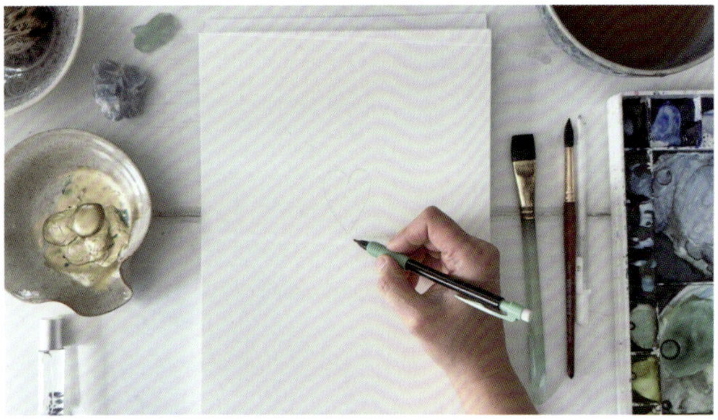

STEP ONE: DRAW A HEART AT THE CENTER

Find the center of your paper, and draw a heart there. It doesn't have to be perfect. Erase the pencil line until only a faint line remains.

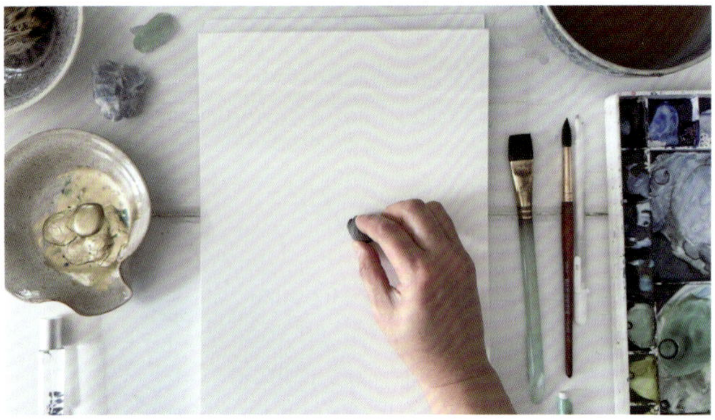

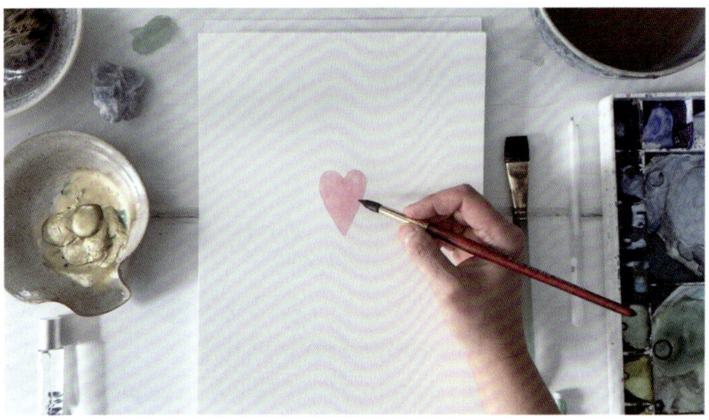

STEP TWO: FEEL YOUR HEART

Pick the color of your heart. I chose a soft pinkish red, but you can choose whatever you are feeling. Paint the heart shape. It does not need to be perfect. Let it be round, soft, uneven. As you paint, gently place your attention in the center of your chest. Notice any sensation there.

Energy Note

Reverence changes everything.

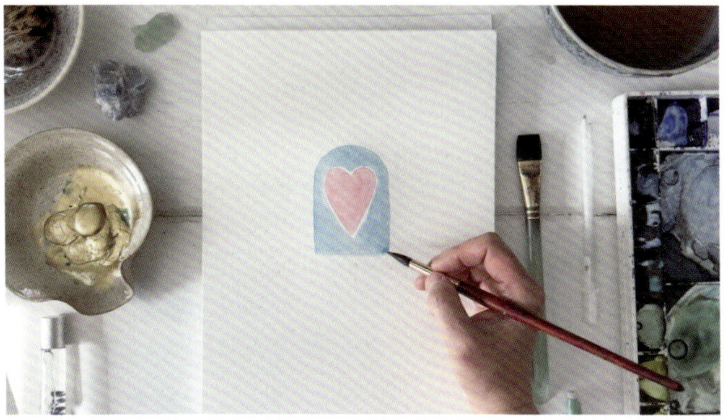

STEP THREE: MAKE THE CONTAINER

Paint an arched box around the heart. You can draw it first or paint it freehand. Let the altar hold the heart. If you notice the urge to fix or perfect the shape, pause. Take one soft inhale and one longer exhale. Return to your painting.

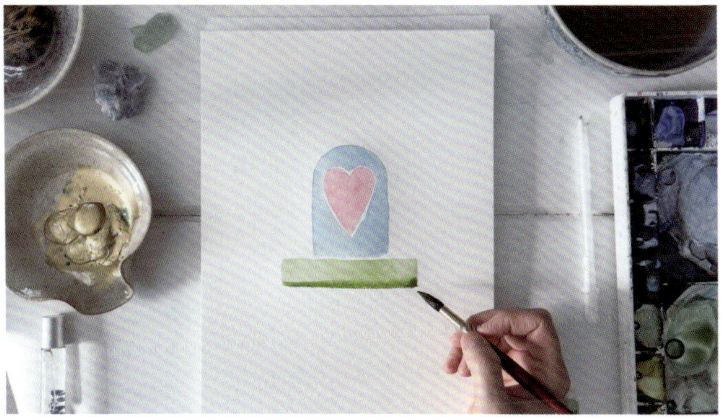

STEP FOUR: LAY THE FOUNDATION

Lay a swash of color for the base. This is your steady foundation.

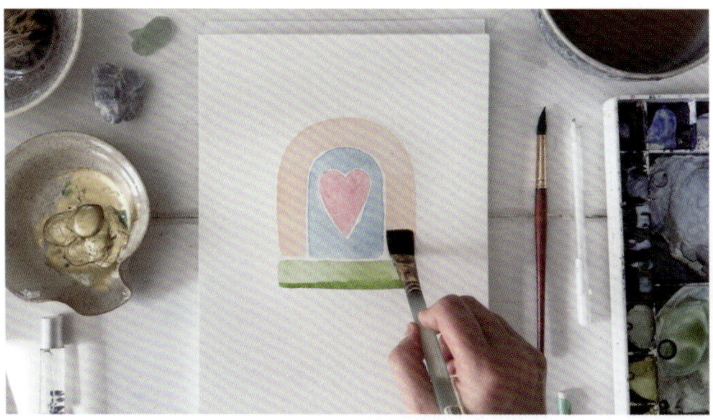

STEP FIVE: CREATE THE ARCH

Pick whatever color feels right to you based on how you feel. Create an arch shape for your altar. You can use a flat brush to make the shape easier.

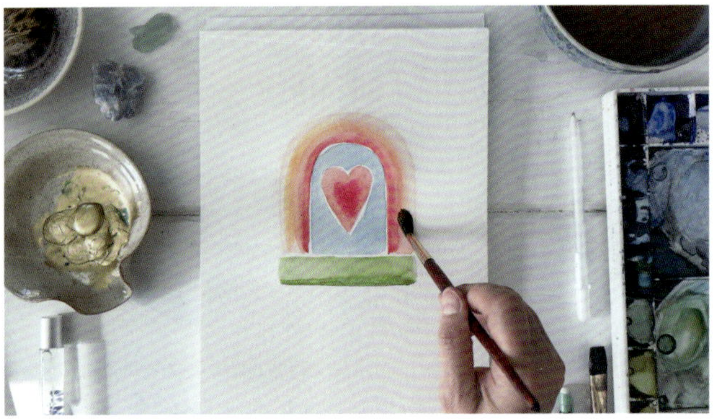

STEP SIX: PLAY

Play with color and value and add some depth with more saturated colors. Use a lot of water to soften the edges and carry the colors. Once your shape feels complete, it's time to play with mark-making.

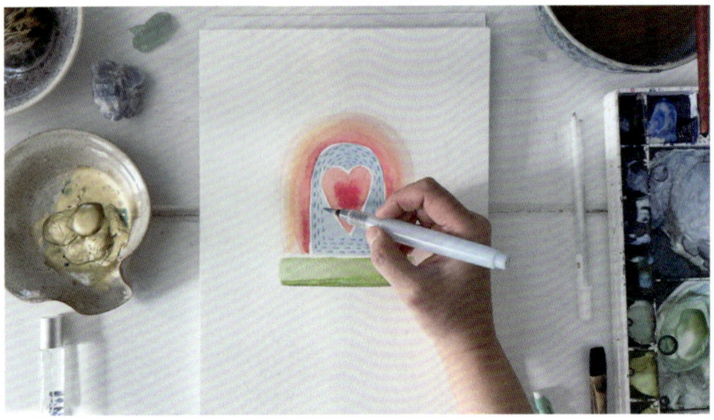

STEP SEVEN: FEEL YOUR WAY THROUGH THE PROCESS

Take a moment to center yourself, like the heart in the center of your altar, safe and supported. Connect with your intuition and begin making marks with your waterbrush. I chose to make some dashes to fill in the space and create some interest.

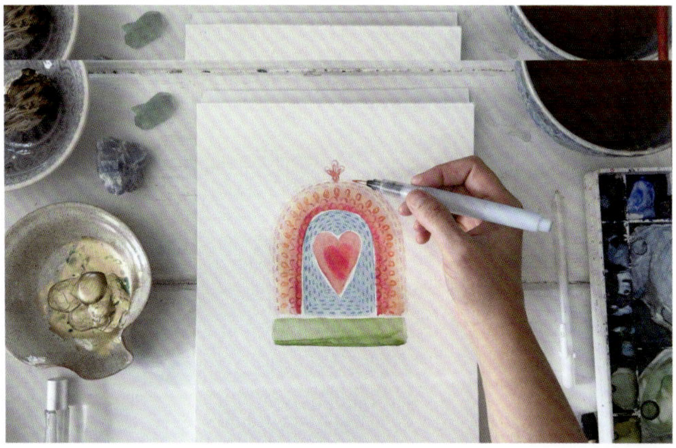

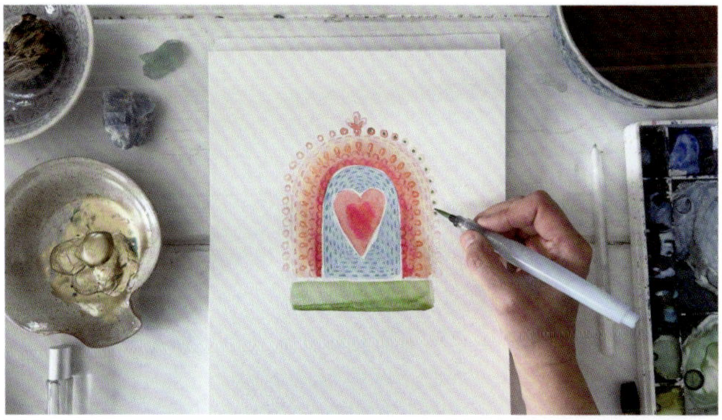

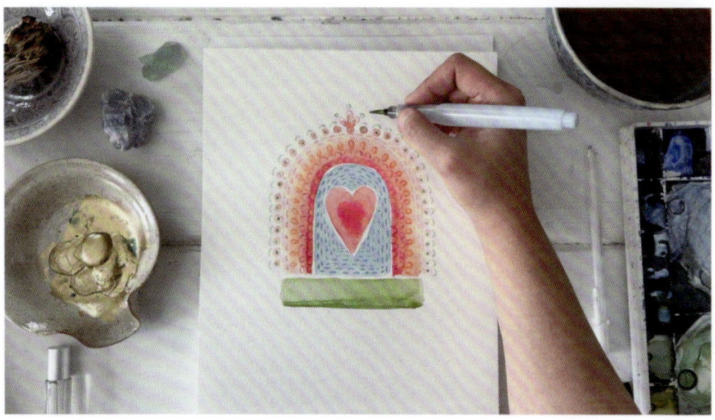

STEP EIGHT: GET LOST IN THE DETAILS

This is the time to narrow your focus and get lost in the details. Don't overthink it, lay down marks as they come to you. Don't make anything perfect. Enjoy the process, play with color, and see what happens.

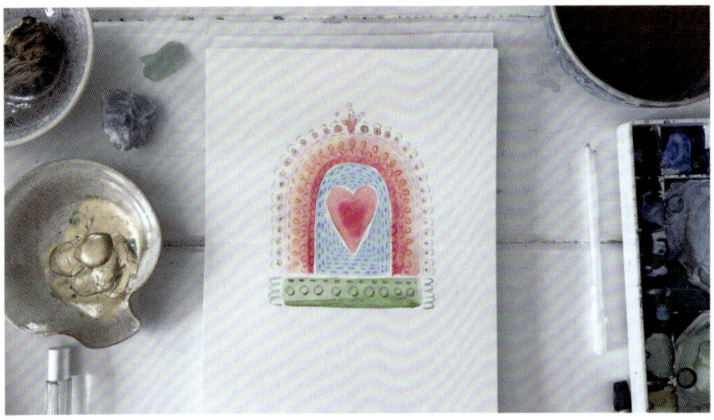

STEP NINE: GIVE ENERGY TO THE BASE

Decorate the base. This is your foundation. How do you want it to feel?

Gentle Reminder

You are worthy of your own devotion.

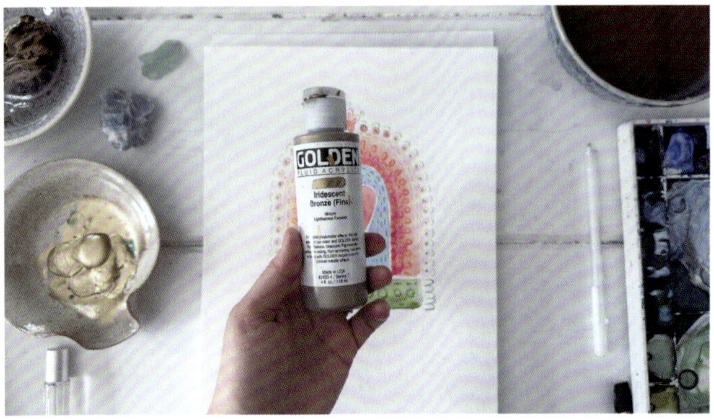

STEP TEN: MAKE IT SPECIAL

To give your altar a special look, try some bronze acrylic paint with your waterbrush. I love this paint because when it meets the wet watercolor, it naturally patinas. Some areas will shift into the most beautiful soft turquoise tones. To start, use it on dry paint, but once you feel comfortable with it, you can incorporate the bronze sooner while the paint is still wet. Let yourself be curious and playful with it. A gentle reminder, however: Acrylic paint is permanent once it dries, and it will dry on your brush. Be sure to rinse your brush in water right after using it so it stays clean and soft.

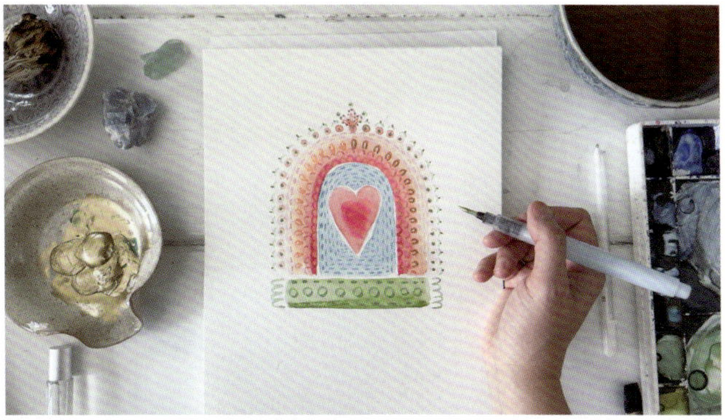

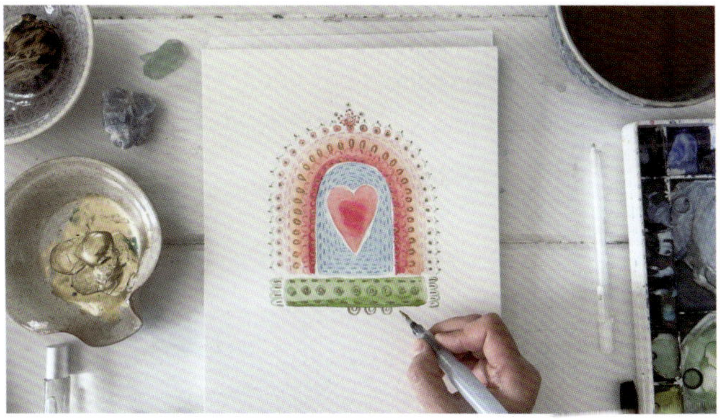

STEP ELEVEN: ADD MARKS OF DEVOTION

Something about the bronze makes the altar feel sacred. It carries a quiet, devotional quality. This becomes your offering to your heart and to yourself. Use your waterbrush to decorate your altar in whatever way feels reverent to you. Simple marks. Soft lines. Small details. Let it be slow and intentional. Continue painting until your altar feels complete or your energy naturally wanes.

Permission Slip

Nothing here needs to be perfect.

Painting Meditation: Heart Altar

Put on your favorite music. Keep it soothing, neutral, or upbeat; you want to keep the energy of your space uplifting. Frequency is very important when doing healing work. Sit comfortably. Bring your attention to the area in the middle of your chest. Not searching for a big feeling. Not trying to make anything happen. Simply noticing. Imagine a soft warmth or quiet presence there. Let color express what you feel. Paint the heart gently; pause between strokes. Breathe, and soften your grip. If thoughts arise, return to your breath and to one simple phrase: "I am supported." As layers begin to dry, you may add gentle details or keep things simple. Let your choices come from feeling rather than planning. Continue until the page feels complete. Paint the altar slowly. As you layer color, silently repeat: "I am grounded, I am safe, I am loved," or whatever feels right to you. If resistance comes up, let it. You are not forcing, you are offering space. Continue until the page feels complete.

Integration

Sit quietly with your altar for a few moments. Let your eyes rest on the heart at the center. Notice the colors, the layers, the quiet details, and the way the bronze catches the light.

Feel the devotion you placed into each mark. The care, the intention, and the reverence.

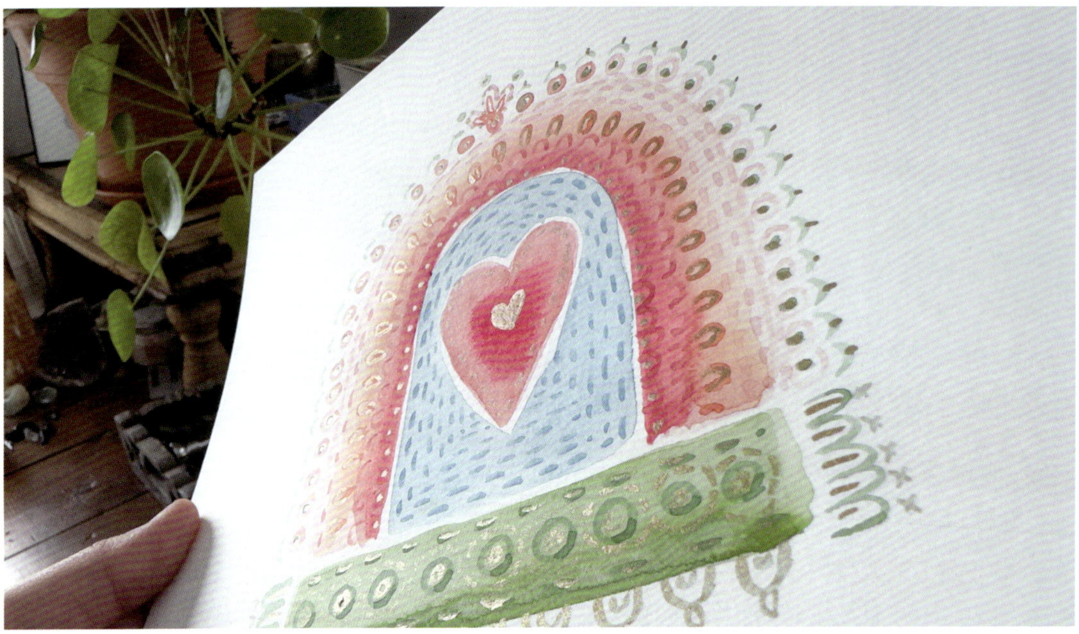

Place one hand over your heart, and take a slow breath in. On the exhale, gently acknowledge yourself for showing up. Let this painting stand as a visual prayer. A reminder that you are worthy of tenderness, of beauty, and of your own devotion. If it feels right, write one word or short phrase that captures what you are honoring within yourself today.

Journal Prompts

- Did any resistance show up while painting the heart?
- What does honoring yourself look like in daily life?
- Did the altar feel like you?

thoughts

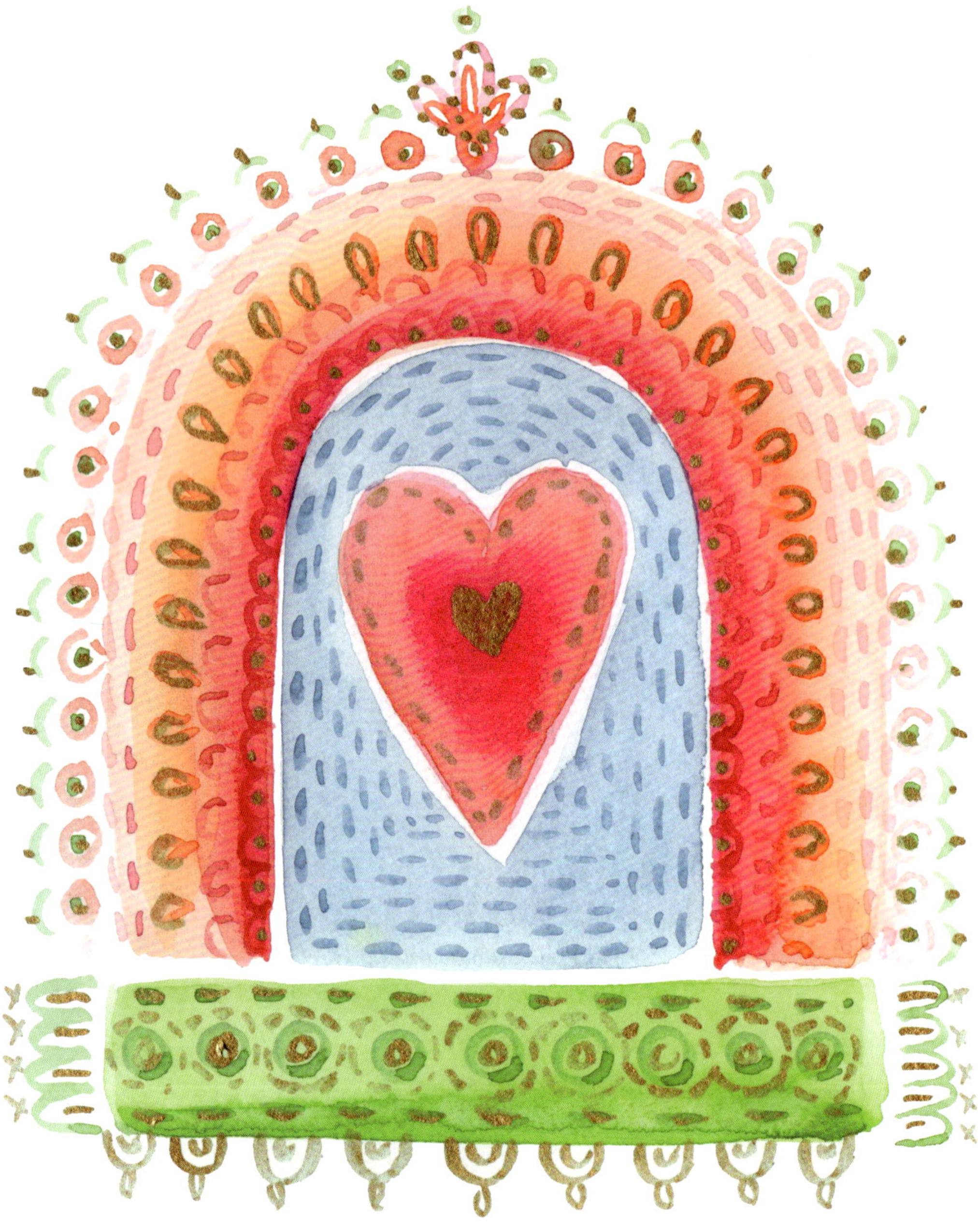

18

NERVOUS SYSTEM REGULATION TOOL

Rhythmic, Coherent Breathing

The Rhythmic, Coherent Breathing technique is the practice of breathing in a slow, even rhythm. When your inhale and exhale become steady and balanced, your heart and brain begin to communicate more smoothly. This steady rhythm encourages heart-brain coherence, meaning the heart rate, breath, and nervous system begin to synchronize into a calm, harmonious pattern. You are not trying to force the breath; you are creating a smooth, flowing, even rhythm between inhale and exhale with no holds. You are simply allowing it to become smooth and even.

BENEFITS

- Calms emotional reactivity
- Supports heart-brain coherence
- Reduces mental chatter
- Creates a steady internal rhythm
- Encourages a sense of safety and ease

HOW TO TRY IT

- Sit comfortably, and soften your shoulders.
- Inhale slowly through your nose.
- Exhale slowly through your mouth.
- Let the inhale and exhale be about the same length. If it helps, silently count four in and four out.
- Repeat for four to six easy breath cycles.

WHEN IT'S USEFUL

Use the Rhythmic, Coherent Breathing technique before heart-centered painting, when emotions feel tender, when your mind feels busy, or anytime you want to create a calm, steady inner rhythm.

They begin at the center and expand outward, just like the heart.

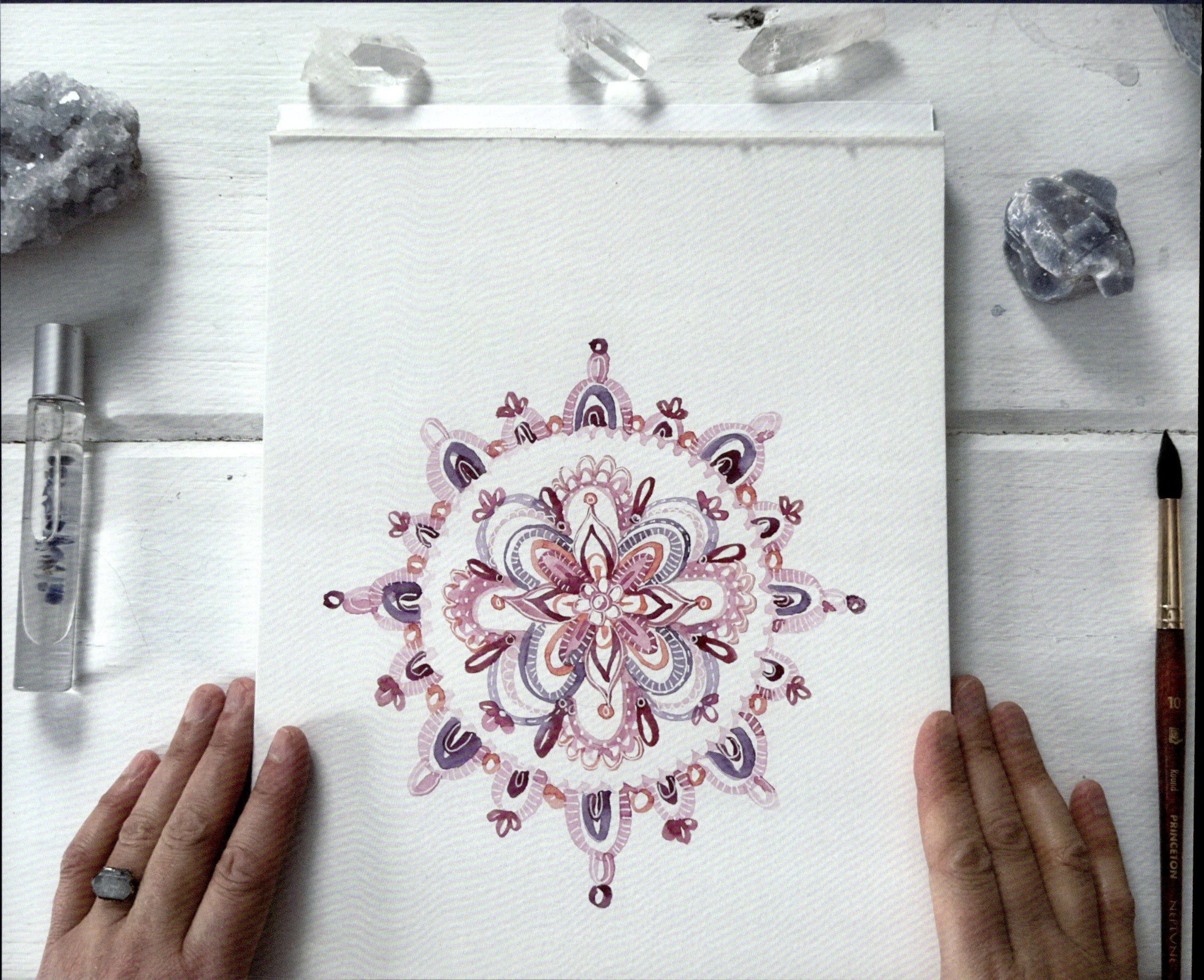

In this session, you will paint a mandala as a slow, rhythmic meditation. You will move in simple layers, using water, color, and repetition to create a feeling of steadiness and inner coherence. This is not about creating a perfect design. It is about letting rhythm, breath, and repetition guide you back to center.

WHAT YOU'LL LEARN

- How to build a mandala using simple circular layers
- How to let go of perfectionism and trust that everything will turn out in a beautiful way
- How to add gentle marks and details without overworking
- How rhythmic, even breathing supports heart–brain coherence and emotional balance

In this session, you begin with a small circle at the center of your page. From there, you slowly build outward in rings. Each ring becomes an opportunity to breathe, relax, and get lost in the process. Keep the shapes loose and watery, letting color move through the water. As layers begin to dry, you may add simple details with the gel pen. Throughout the process, you will pair your painting with the Rhythmic, Coherent Breathing technique, a nervous system regulation tool that supports a steady internal rhythm and a calm, open heart.

WHAT YOU MIGHT FEEL

- A steady, calming rhythm in your breath and body
- A sense of inner organization and clarity
- Less mental chatter as repetition calms your mind

HOW THIS SESSION FLOWS

We'll begin with a short technique tutorial. You'll learn how to create a watery center circle and build outward in soft rings, playing with color, value, and simple wet-on-wet effects.

When the technique feels comfortable, move into the painting meditation. Pair the mandala process with the Rhythmic, Coherent Breathing technique, soft background music, and a slow, even pace that helps your heart and mind settle together.

Begin at the center. Paint, breathe, and begin again.

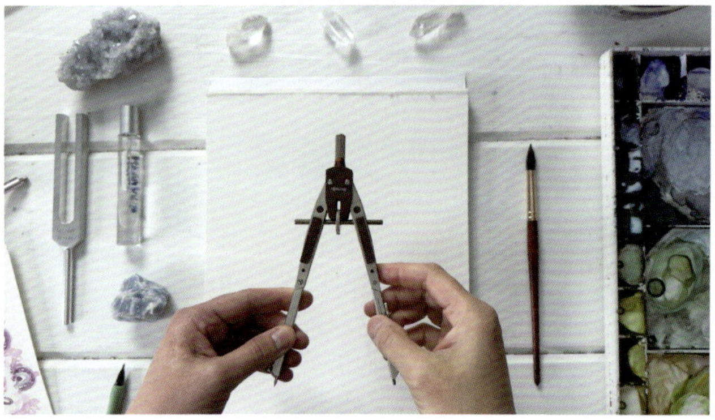

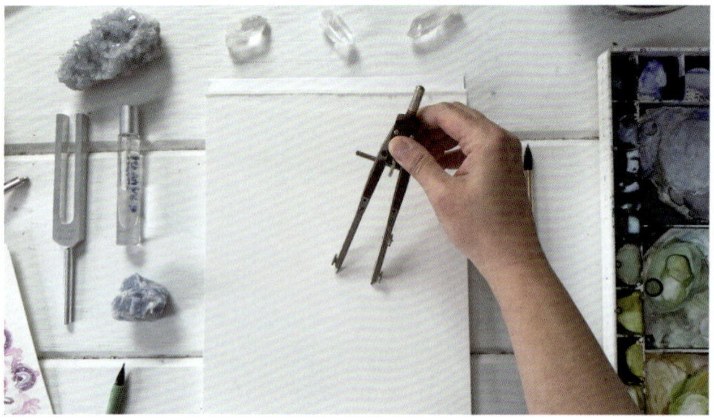

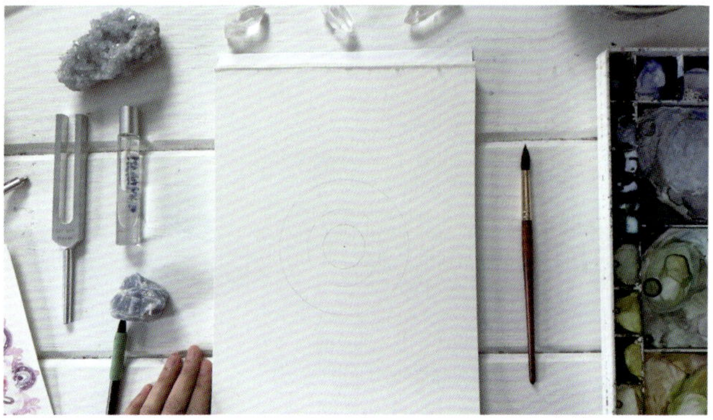

STEP ONE: CREATE THE GUIDES

Using a compass, draw three or four concentric circles centered on the paper. They can be spaced any way you want them. I decided to vary mine. These will be guides for your paintings, but you don't have to follow them perfectly. Erase most of the pencil lines, leaving just a faint line.

Permission Slip

The mandala does not need to be perfect. Move slowly and keep it simple.

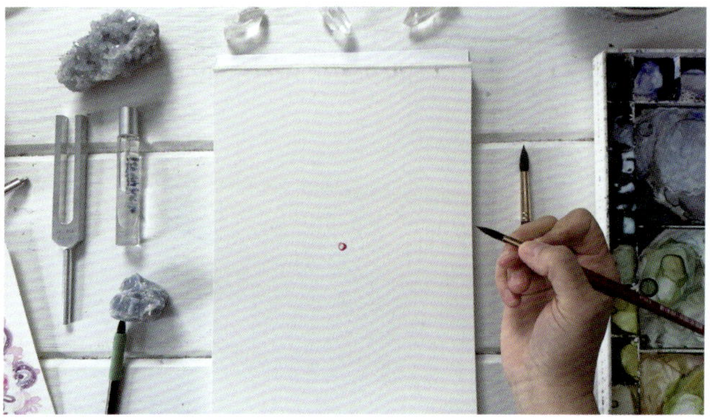

STEP TWO: START IN THE CENTER

Paint a tiny circle in the center of your mandala.

STEP THREE: CONTINUE BUILDING OUTWARD

Start working your way around the circle. I chose to start with little scalloped lines. As you finish your way around the circle, expand beyond what you painted until you feel ready to start a new line. Don't worry if you painted over your pencil line. This is an intuitive process; you aren't looking for perfection; you are following your intuition.

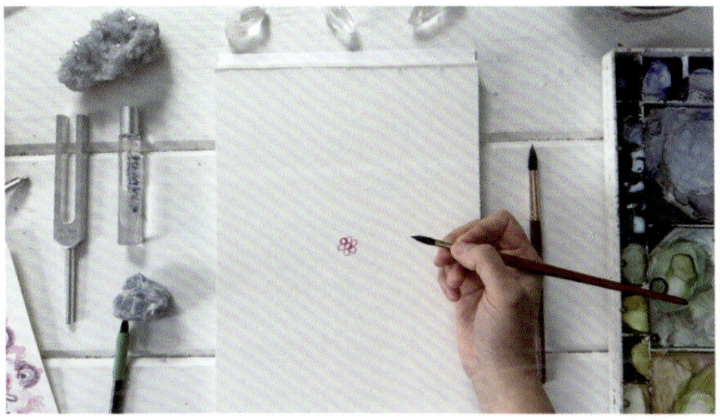

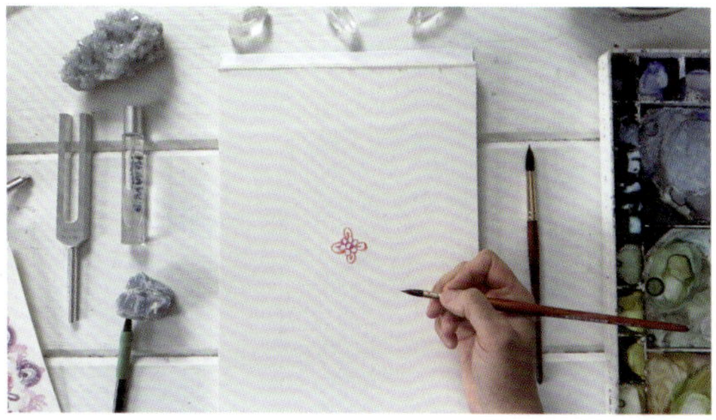

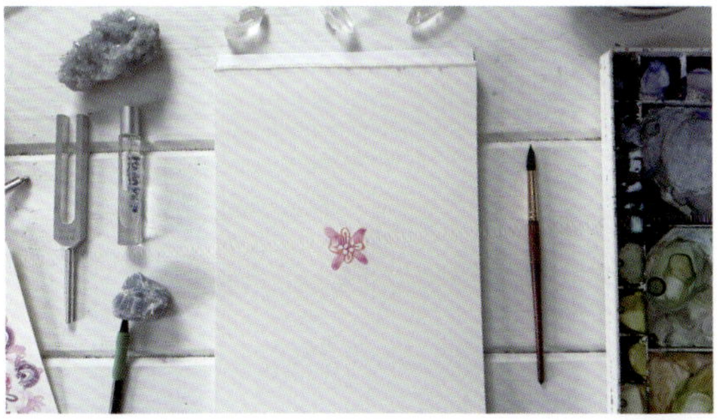

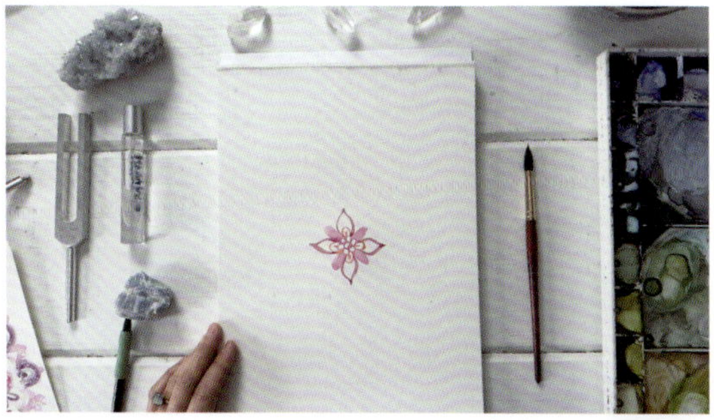

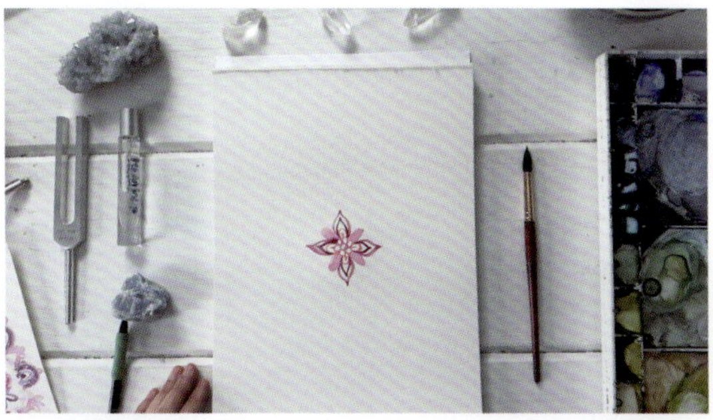

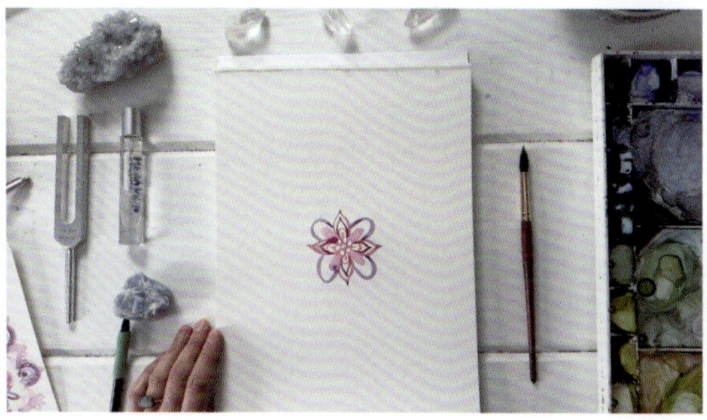

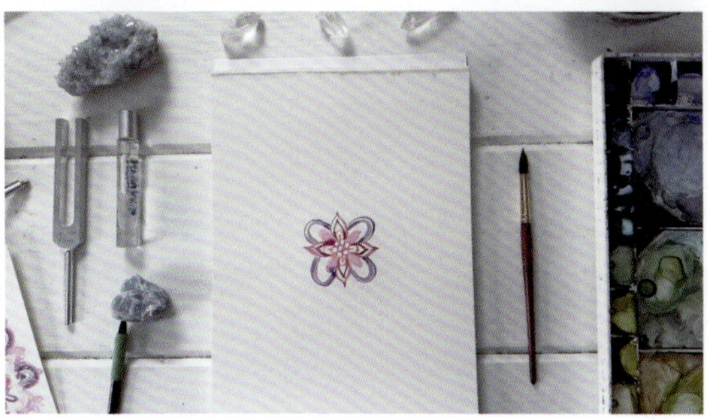

STEP FOUR: KEEP GROWING

Move your way around the circle, adding elements as you go. You can go back and add marks. Fill the space; don't judge, just play.

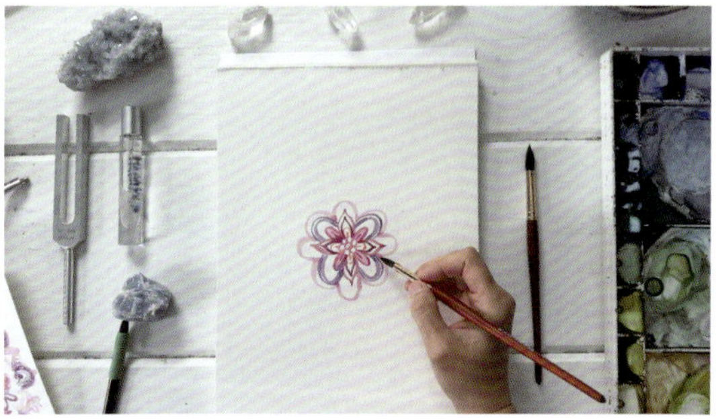

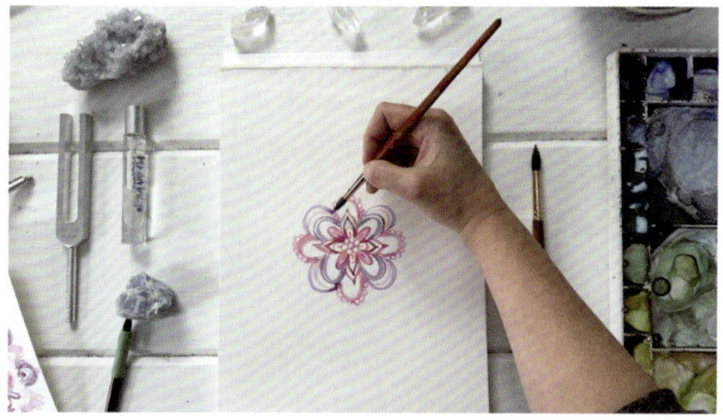

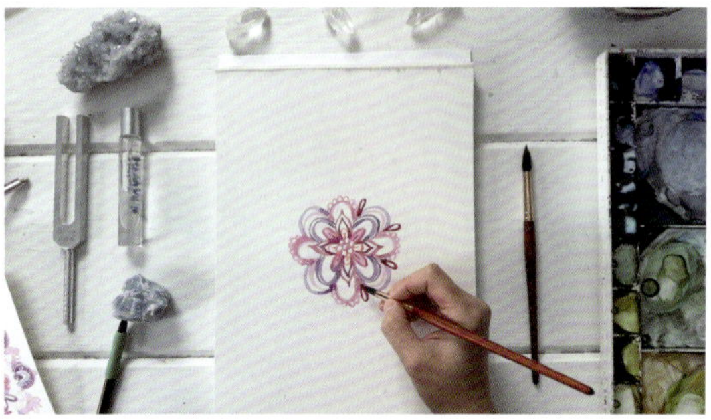

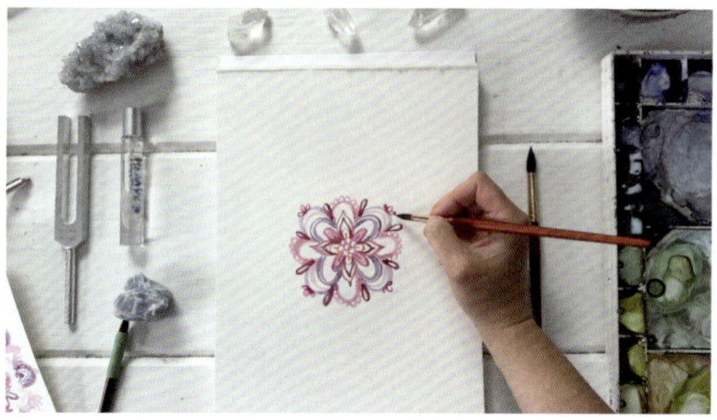

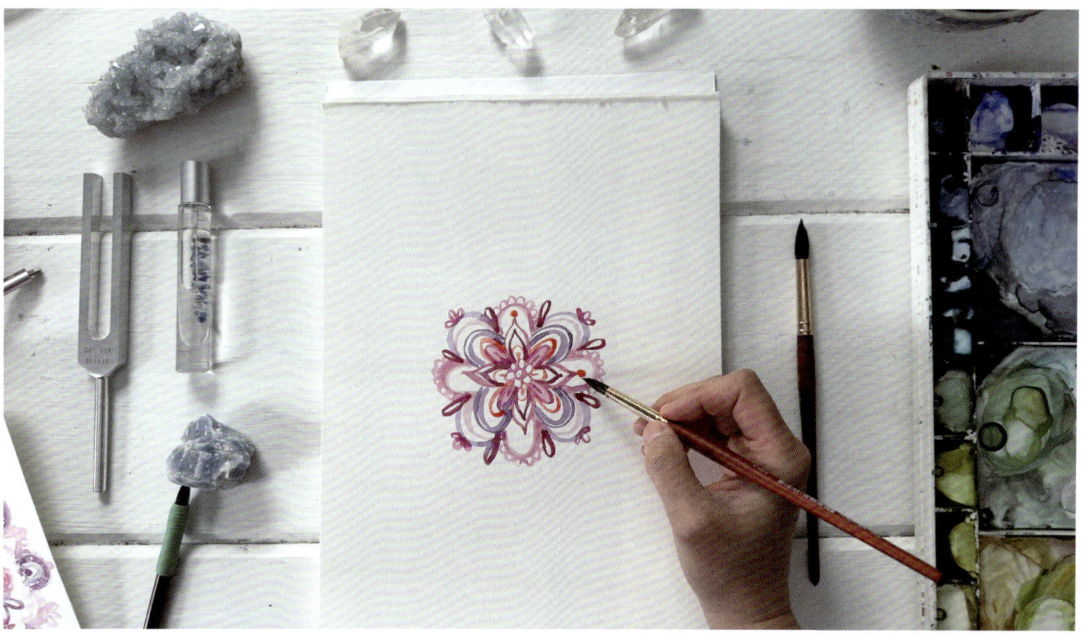

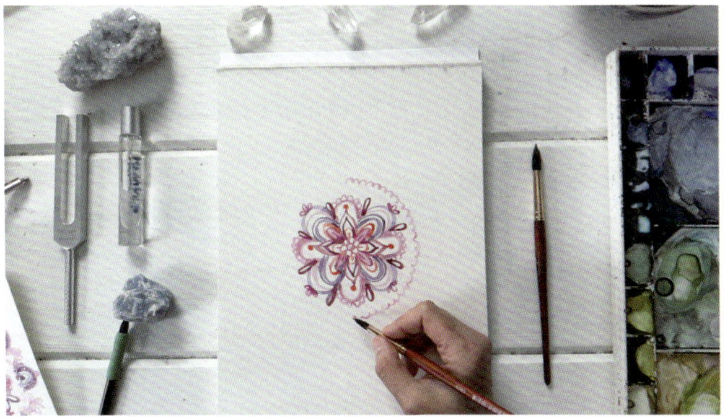

STEP FIVE: START A NEW CIRCLE

Start your next circle. I decided to add a small, scalloped line around mine. I had no plan; I made it up as I went.

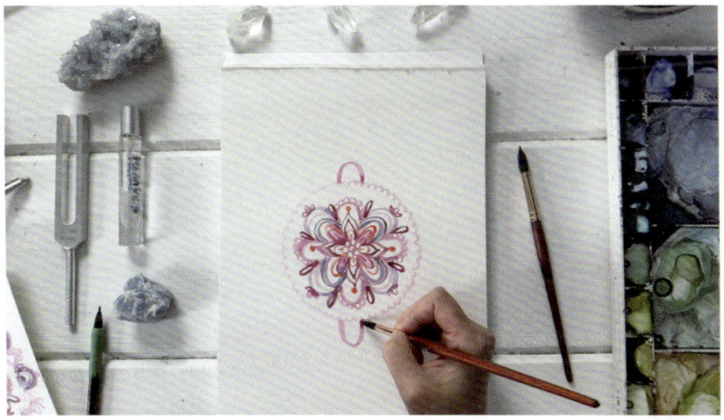

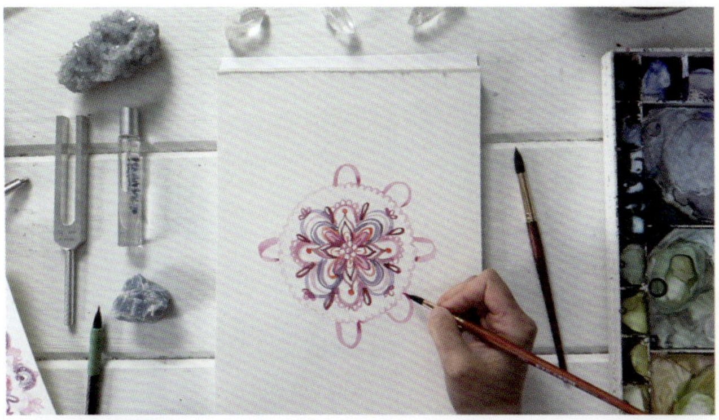

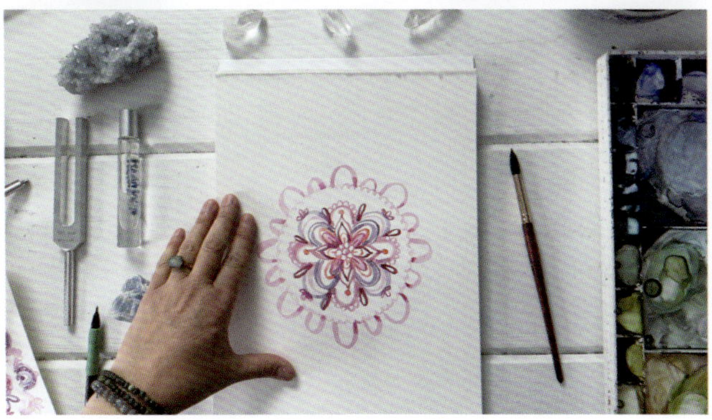

STEP SIX: BE BOLD

If you aren't sure how many arches you can fit around the circle, you can do some mirroring, to get the design to work out evenly. I placed an arch on the top and bottom of the circle, then the sides, then in between. I also made some of the shapes smaller. Remember, it's okay to change things up, not to follow the rules exactly, and to make things easier on yourself.

Energy Note

Repetition creates safety. Safety opens the heart.

STEP SEVEN: TRUST THE PROCESS

Keep playing and decorating. There is no right or wrong way to do this. Remember your steady breath, and relax into the process.

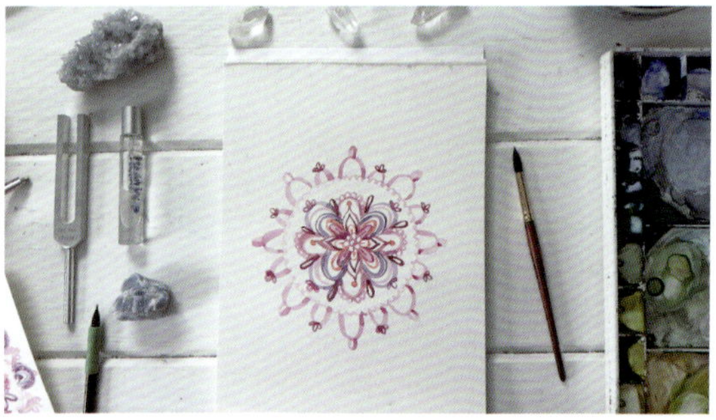

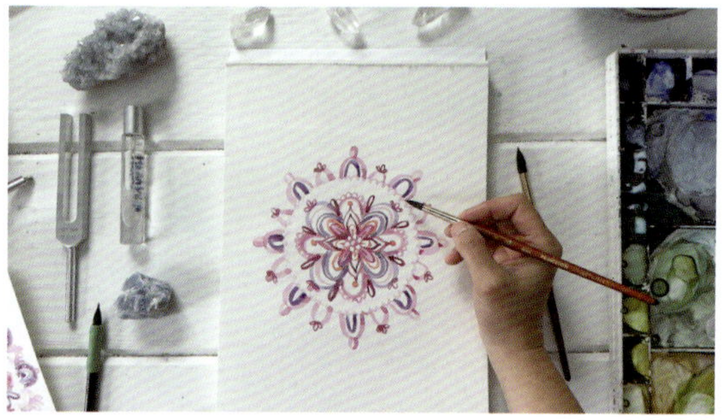

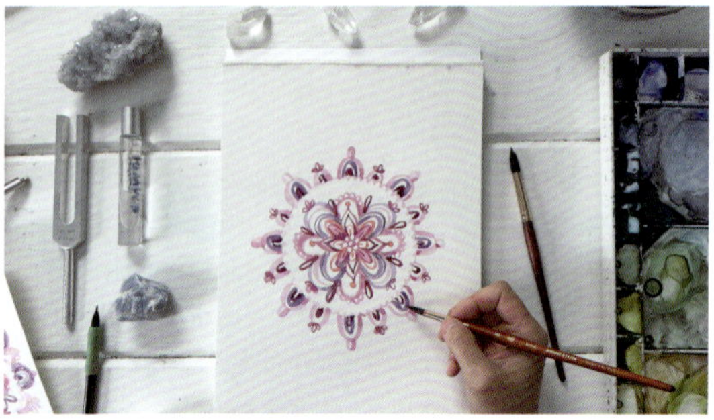

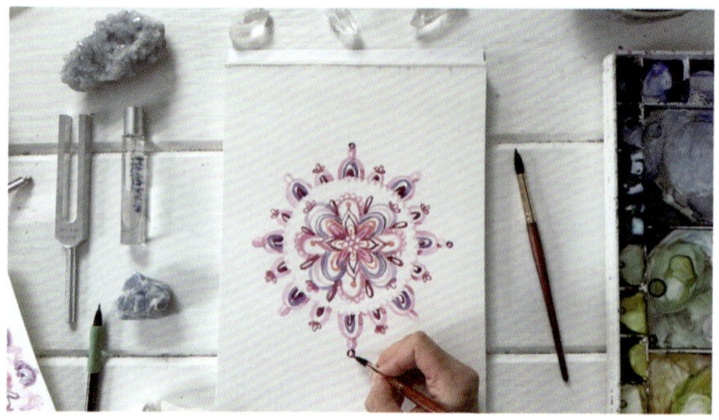

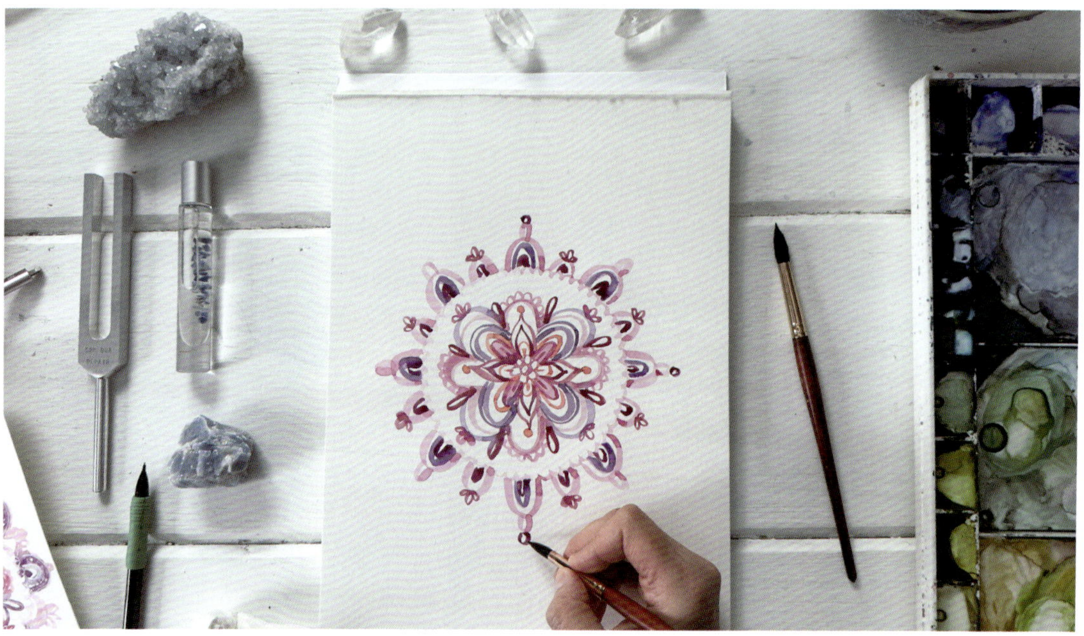

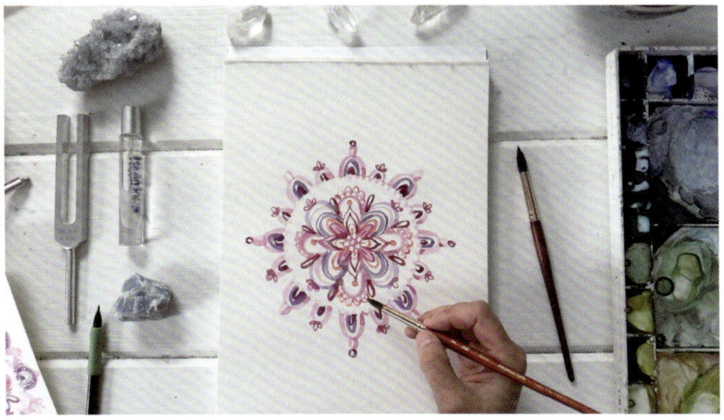

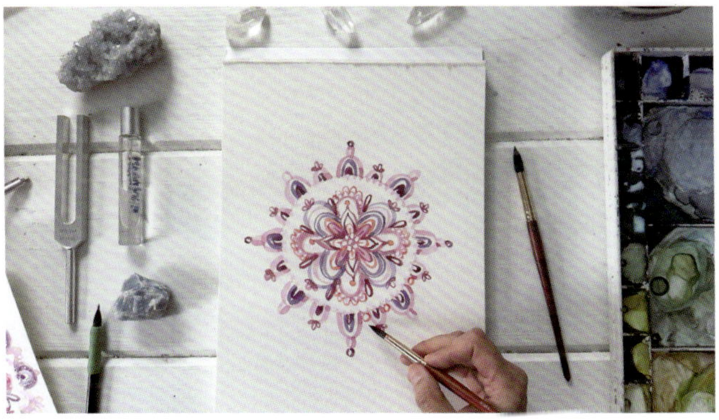

STEP EIGHT: GO BACK, OR DON'T

Go back to enhance a previous circle if you want to or don't. It's okay either way. I decided to add more scallops on lines that I had already finished, then I added some circles too—no rules, just play.

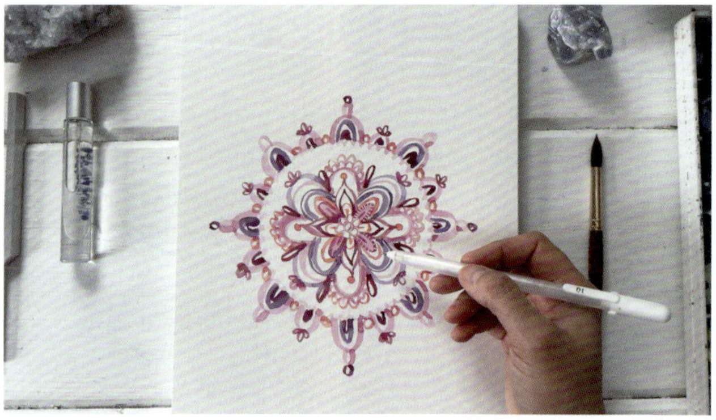

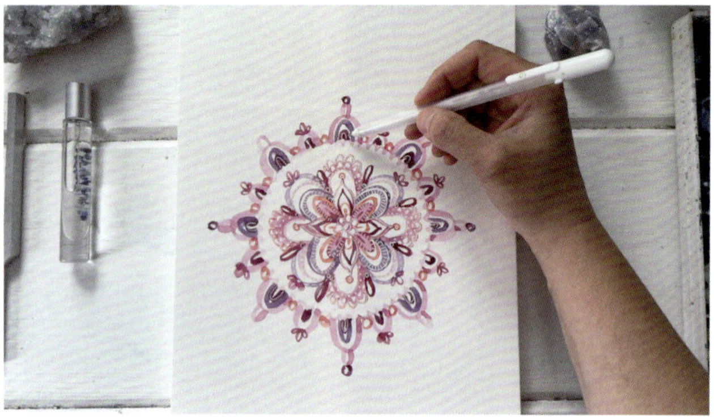

STEP NINE: FIND FUN IN THE DETAILS

It's time to play with the gel pen. Wait for your painting to dry, and start decorating!

Painting Meditation: Mandala

Put on soft-frequency music, and sit comfortably. Begin rhythmic, coherent breathing by inhaling slowly and exhaling slowly, keeping both about the same length. Paint one ring, then pause and breathe. Paint the next ring, then breathe again. If your mind begins to wander, gently return your attention to the circle and the rhythm of your breath. Let repetition carry you, moving ring by ring, breath by breath, until the mandala feels complete.

Integration

Sit quietly with your mandala, and notice where your eyes naturally come to rest. Bring gentle awareness to your breath without changing it. Place one hand over your heart, and take one slow, steady breath in and out. Then write a single word that describes how you feel in this moment.

Journal Prompts

- What did you notice as you painted in repetition around the circle?
- How did steady breathing affect your painting and your body?
- Where do you feel the mandala energy in your body?

thoughts

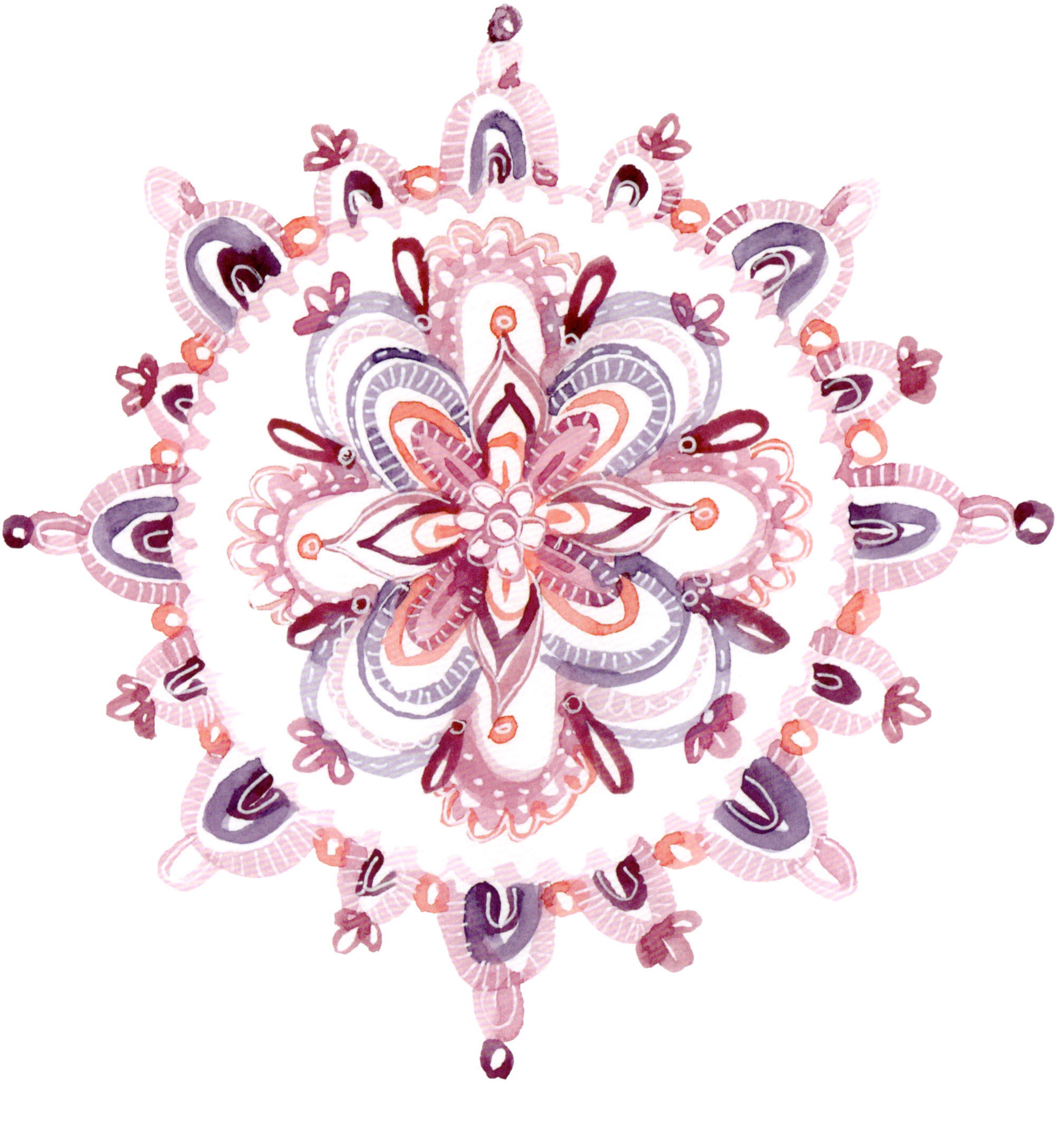

19

NERVOUS SYSTEM REGULATION TOOL

Affect Tracking

The Affect Tracking technique is the gentle practice of noticing what you feel in your body and emotions without trying to change them. You simply observe sensations, moods, and shifts with curiosity and kindness. When you allow feelings to be felt rather than pushed away, your nervous system receives the message that it is safe to experience what is present. This technique supports emotional flow, reduces resistance, and helps your system naturally move toward balance.

BENEFITS

- Builds emotional awareness without overwhelm
- Reduces the urge to suppress or fix feelings
- Supports nervous system regulation through gentle noticing
- Encourages a sense of inner spaciousness and self-trust
- Helps emotions move through rather than get stuck

HOW TO TRY IT

- Sit comfortably, and soften your shoulders.
- Bring your attention inside your body.
- Notice any sensations, emotions, or moods that are present.
  You do not need to name them perfectly. Simply notice warm or cool, heavy or light, tight or open, calm or activated.
- Let the sensations exist without trying to change them.
- If something shifts, notice that too.
- Continue to observe gently for a few slow breaths.

WHEN IT'S USEFUL

Use the Affect Tracking technique when emotions feel close to the surface, when you are unsure what you are feeling, when you want to paint from sensation rather than thought, or anytime you want to create space for feelings to move safely.

round, changing colors as you feel your way through.

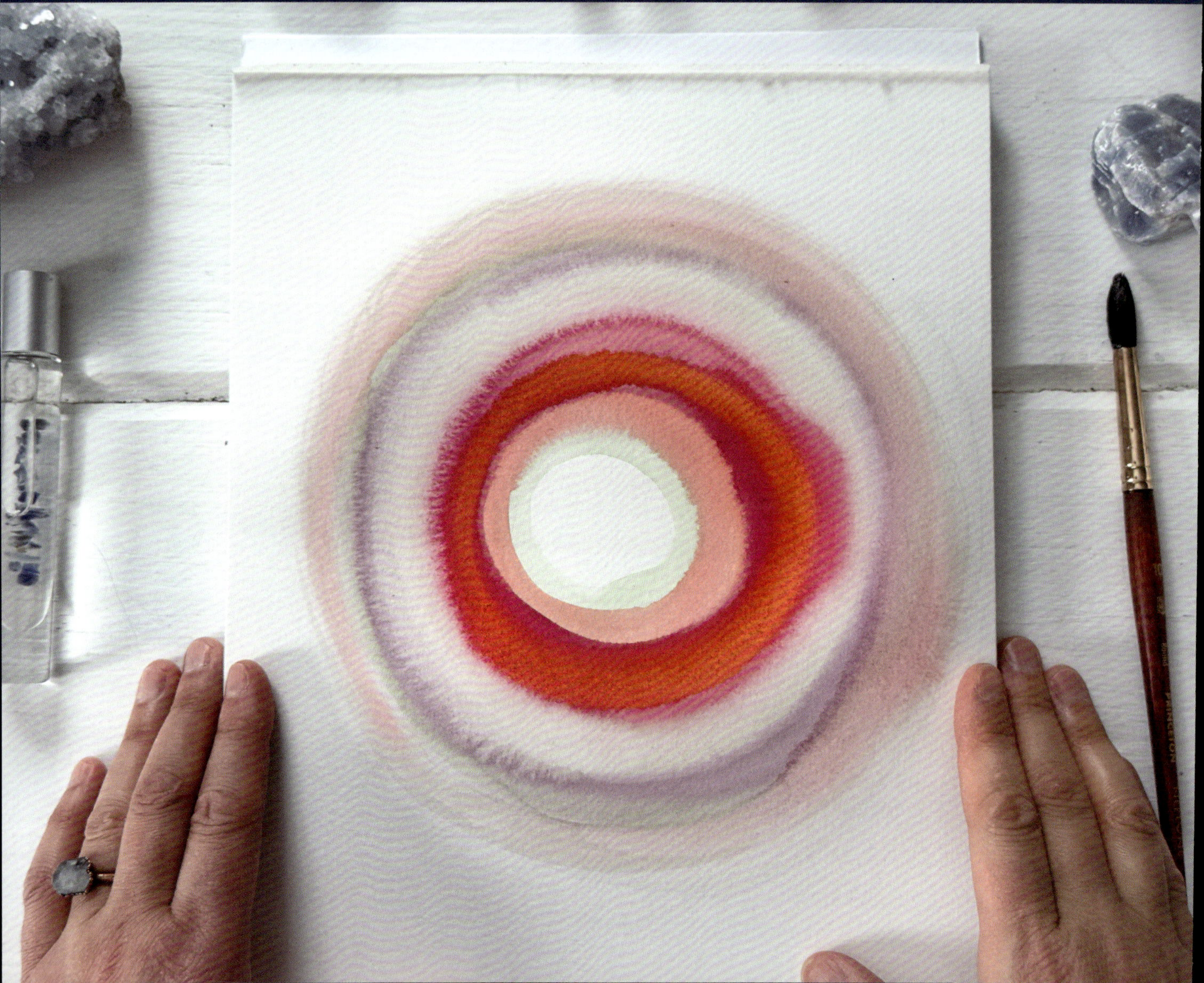

This lesson invites you to stay with your heart and allow color to speak for you. Pause, and ask yourself: "What color am I feeling right now?" Then, grab that color. As you paint, notice what shifts. Does another feeling rise up? Let that feeling have its own color too. You might feel calm, heavy, tender, open, tired, inspired, or unsure. There is no right answer; there is only noticing. This isn't about making a pretty painting. It's about giving your heart a place to be seen. Let the circle hold whatever wants to move. Through circular movement and the Affect Tracking technique, you will give your feelings a safe place to move.

WHAT YOU'LL LEARN

- How to paint a slow, continuous circle that creates a sense of containment and safety
- How to change colors based on what you are feeling in the moment
- How circular motion and repetition can soothe the nervous system
- How to let color express emotion without needing words
- How the Affect Tracking technique supports emotional awareness without overwhelm

In this session, you will paint one large circle and slowly build outward from the center with gentle circular movement. You'll move round and round, breathing steadily, letting color change as your feelings change. There is no plan or right palette. You are simply listening and seeing what happens.

The steady repetition of circular motion helps calm the body, while the freedom to shift color allows feelings to move without being forced or analyzed. I love this Sacred Circle exercise, especially when I feel stuck and don't want to paint, or I don't know what to paint. When I'm feeling off-center, I practice this exercise first. Sometimes I simply settle into the rhythm of the circle, round and round, and play with color and intensity. Other times, I let my emotions flow out of me and onto the paper. I often reach for red when I'm feeling angry or frustrated, black when I'm carrying heavy feelings, and yellows and oranges when I'm feeling light or happy. Most of the time, the colors land somewhere in between. There is no right or wrong way. There are no rules. The colors may have different meanings for you. Follow your inner guidance and trust your intuition. What meanings do the colors hold for you? Give it a try and see what happens. You don't have to analyze any of it. Just let the emotions move through you and out onto the page. The circle can hold whatever you're carrying.

WHAT YOU MIGHT FEEL

- A softening in your chest or breath
- A sense of emotional release or lightness
- Clarity about what you're feeling without needing words
- A quiet sense of being held by the process

HOW THIS SESSION FLOWS

We'll begin with a short technique tutorial. You'll learn how to paint a soft, watery circle and continue building outward in gentle rings. Once the motion feels natural, move into the painting meditation. Pair the circular rhythm with the Affect Tracking technique. Notice what you feel, and choose color from that place. Move slowly, and let repetition support you.

Let the circle hold what your heart is ready to share.

Gentle Reminder

Stay with the heart. Move slowly. You are safe to feel.

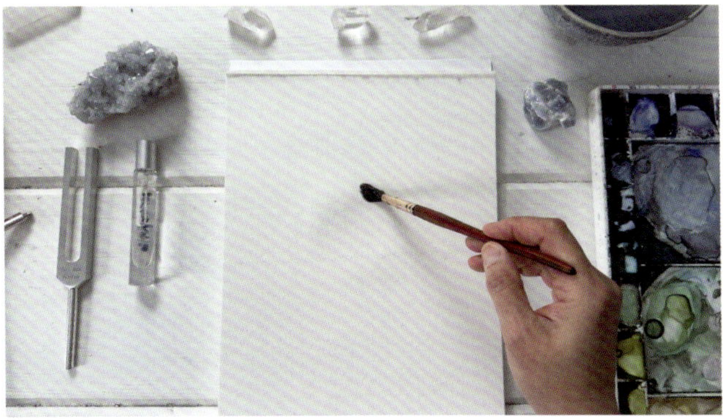

STEP ONE: BEGIN AT THE CENTER

Fill your brush with water, and begin painting in a circular motion at the center of your paper. Just clear water to start. Feel the motion of your brush on the paper. Before adding color, ask yourself: "What do I feel right now?" You don't need to analyze it. Just notice sensations or your mood. Choose a color that feels close to that experience.

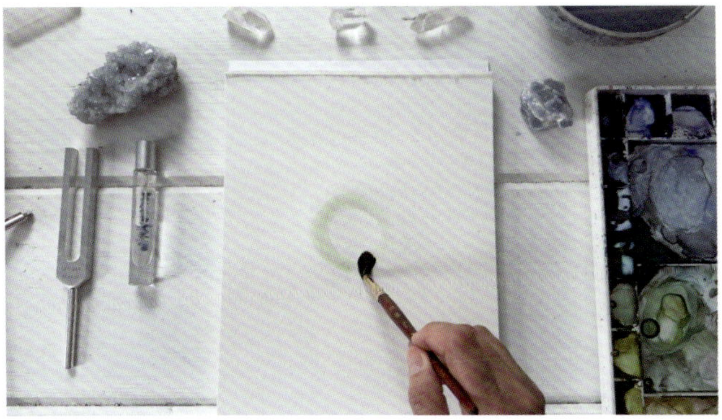

STEP TWO: PAINT THE FEELING

Begin painting with the color that matches how you are feeling. There are no wrong choices and there is nothing to follow. Simply notice what feels right. Is it a light, washy color or something more saturated and denser? Load your brush with water and color, and begin painting slowly, round and round. Let the brush move in steady circles. Stay with the motion until you naturally feel ready to shift. As you paint, continue noticing your body. Has anything changed? If so, allow the next ring to reflect that. You may paint over the same area again and again. You may layer colors and watch how they transform. If you need a pause from pigment, paint with clear water. As you move in circles, the water will soften and lift some of the color, creating space and subtle change. Let the circle become a place where feelings can move gently and safely.

STEP THREE: LET IT CHANGE

If a new feeling appears, acknowledge it gently. Choose a new color that matches the feeling, and continue. There is no right palette. There is no wrong emotion. All feelings are welcome inside the circle.

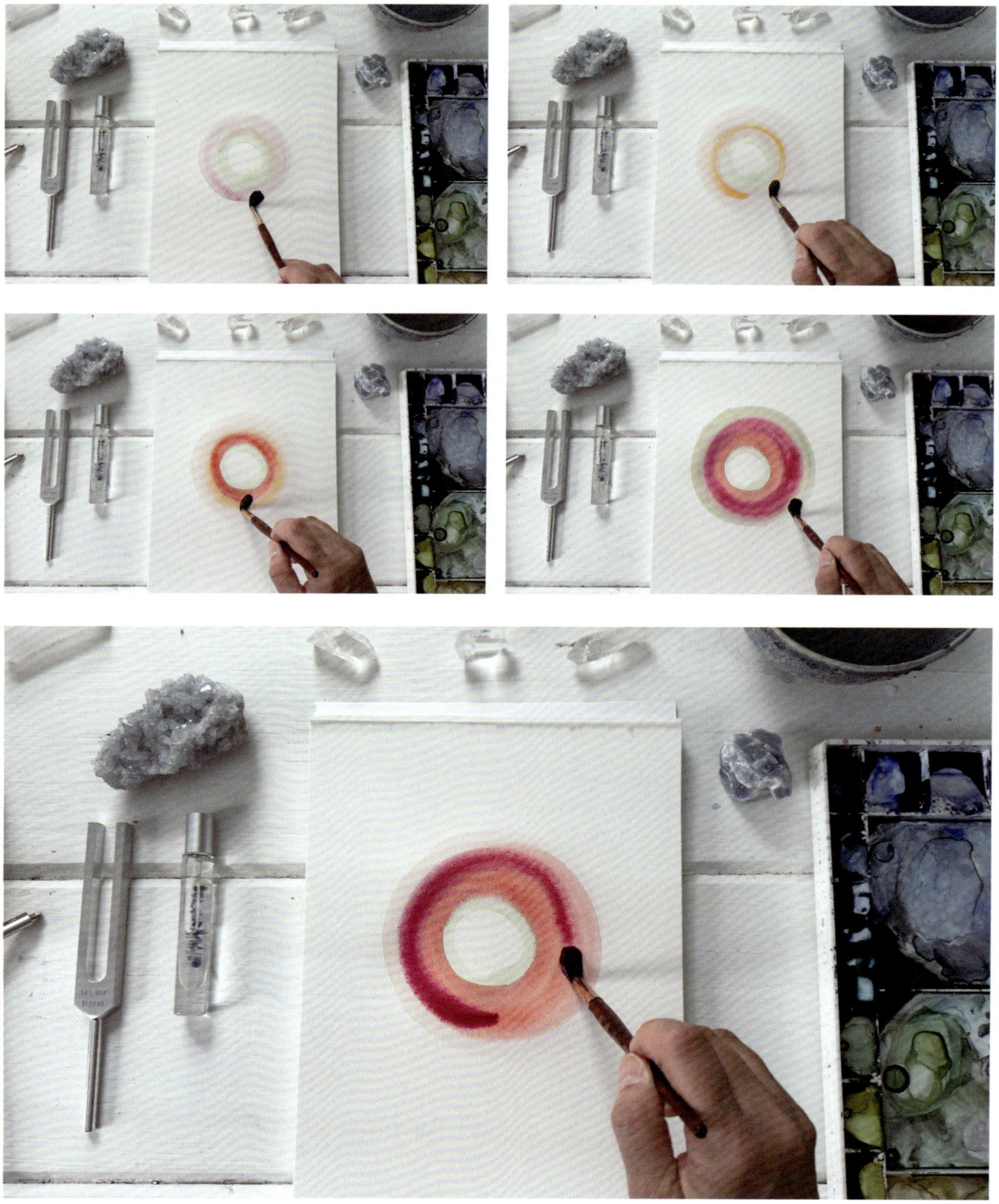

STEP FOUR: KEEP EXPANDING

Continue building outward. Keep the paint wet so colors soften and blend. Keep your mind clear and focus on your heart. If you notice tension, simply observe it—no fixing, just noticing.

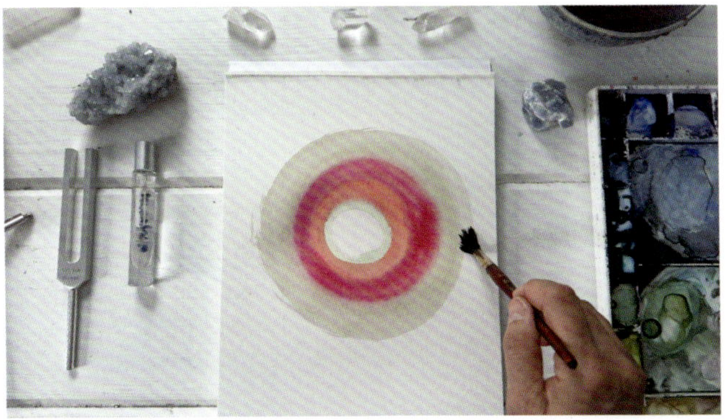

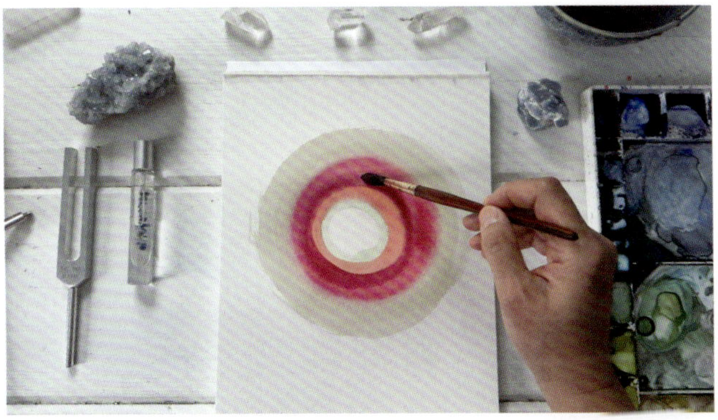

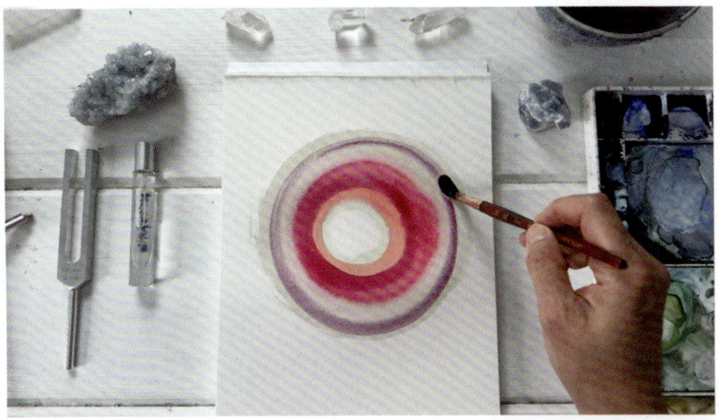

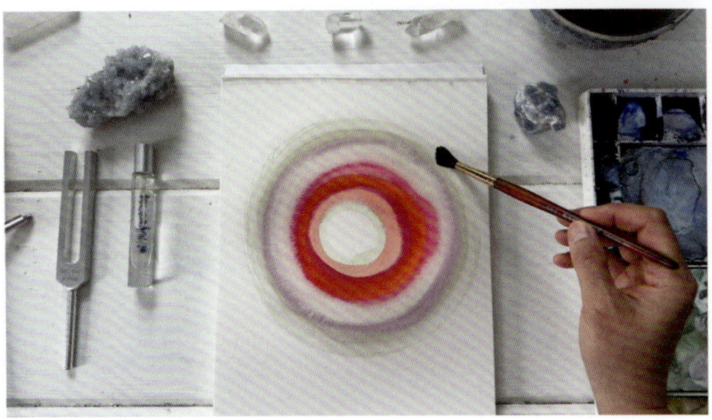

Permission Slip

You don't have to fix your feelings. You only need to notice them.

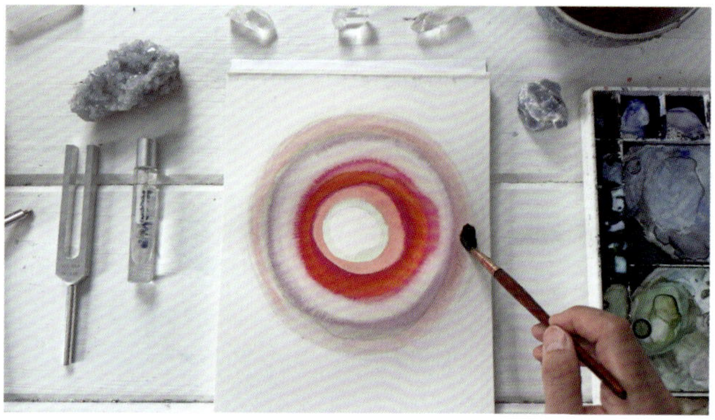

STEP FIVE: FINISH WHEN IT FEELS COMPLETE

Stop when the circle feels full or your energy wanes. Look at your painting without judgment. Notice how many small emotional moments are held inside one simple shape. Let that be enough.

Energy Note

Color gives the heart a voice.

Painting Meditation: Sacred Circle

Put on soft-frequency music, and sit comfortably. Place one hand over your heart. Take a slow breath in and a slow breath out. Begin painting a circle. As you paint, gently rest your attention in the center of your chest. Imagine the breath moving in and out through the heart area. Paint one ring, and breathe. Notice what you are feeling. Choose a color that matches that feeling. Keep going, round and round. If your mind wanders, return to the circle and the heart. Let repetition carry you. Continue until the circle feels complete.

Integration

Sit with your painting. How did releasing your feelings to the circle feel? Place one hand over your heart. Take a slow breath. Write one word that describes how you feel now.

Journal Prompts

- What colors did you choose, and what did they represent?
- Did any feelings surprise you?
- How does your heart feel after painting?
- What was it like to let color speak for you?

thoughts

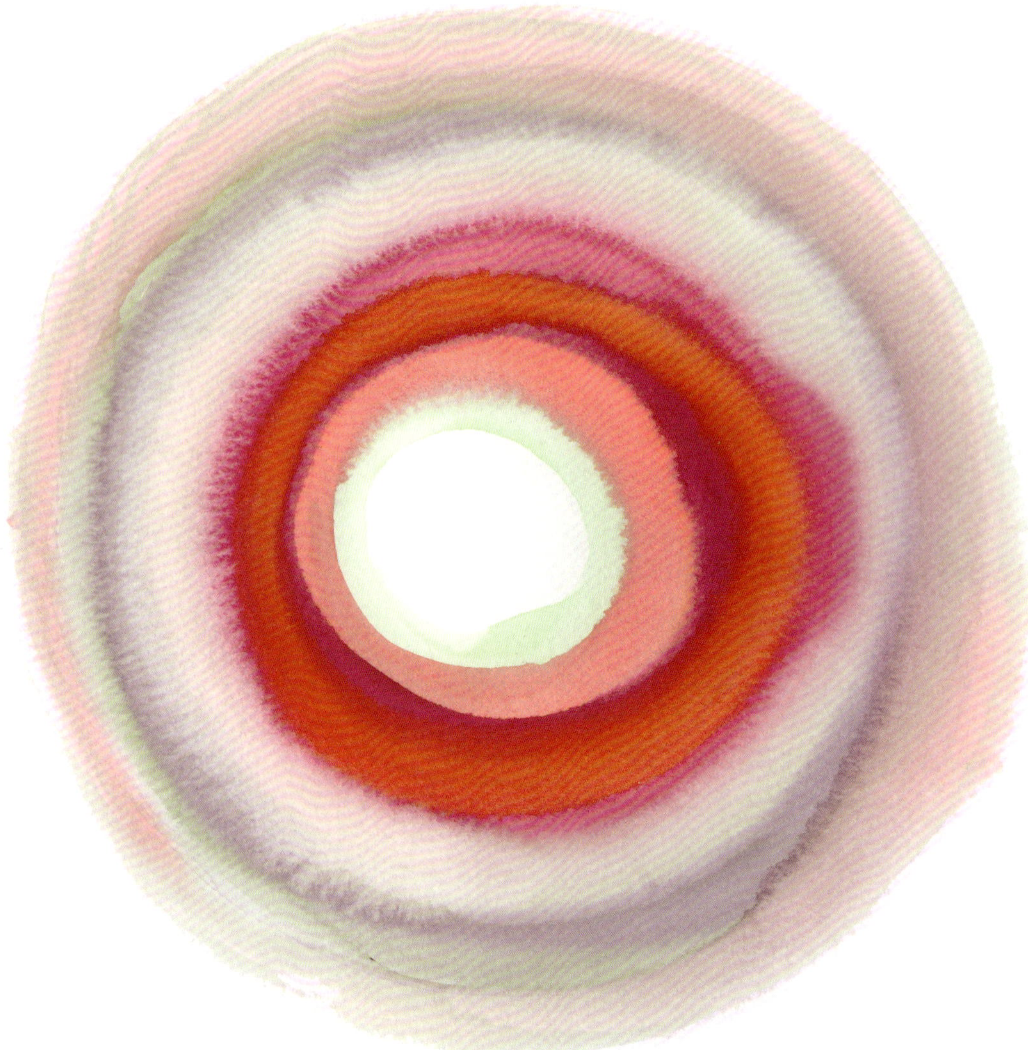

PART THREE

Creating Your Own Healing Practice

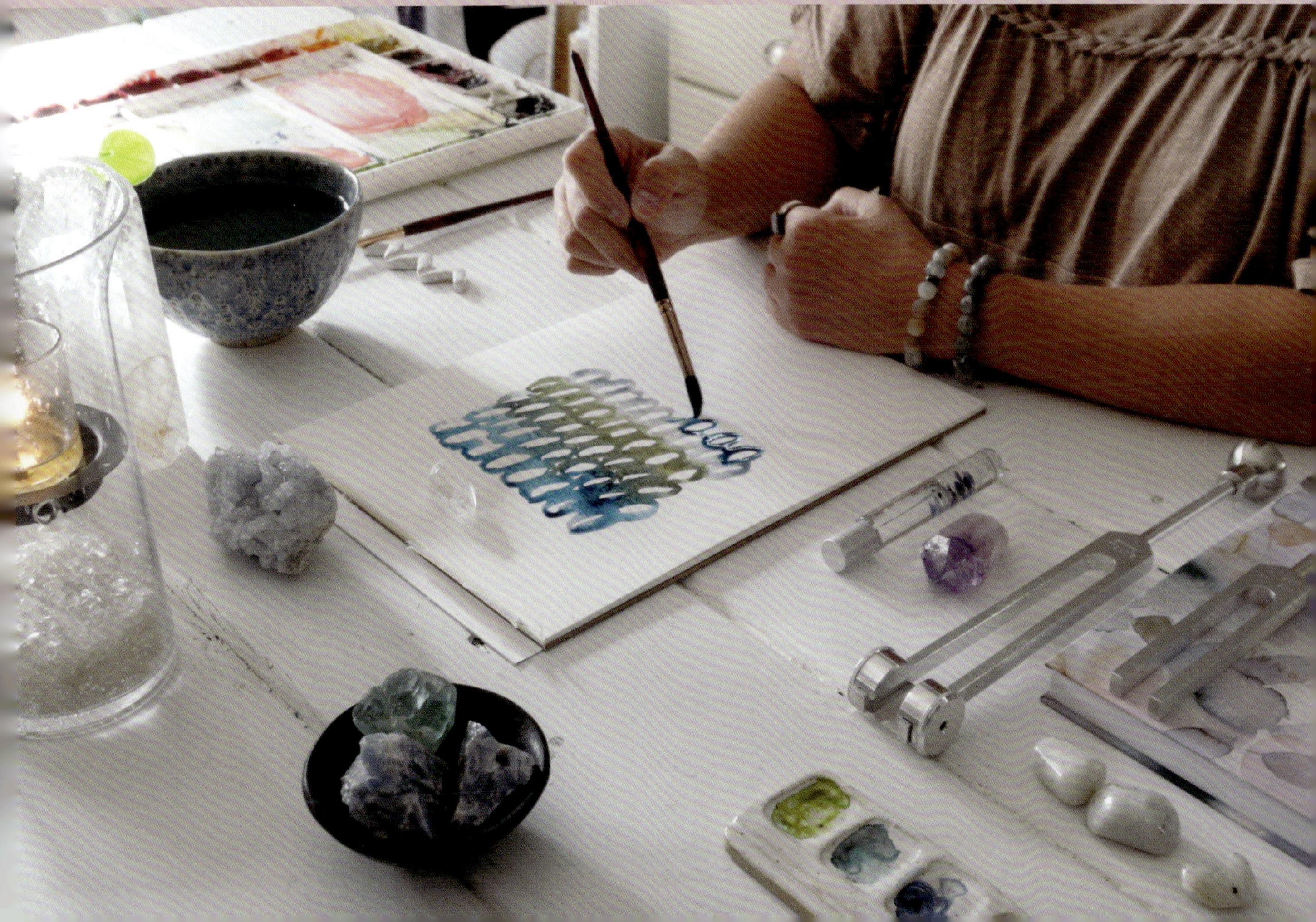

Now that you have moved through the painting lessons, you may begin to notice that the practice feels a little more familiar and natural to you. Maybe certain exercises helped quiet your mind, others helped you connect with your body, and some may have opened small moments of feeling that you didn't expect.

The lessons in this book were never meant to be something you complete once and set aside. They are simple tools you can return to again and again, especially during the moments when life feels stressful and overwhelming.

Over time, your practice will begin to shift from something you are learning into something that belongs to you and flows with ease. You may find yourself repeating the exercises that feel most supportive to you, and you may even adapt them in your own way and create your own calming practice.

In this final part of the book, we will explore how your practice can continue to grow with you, how to be kind to yourself on difficult days, and how to notice the small changes that naturally unfold as your nervous system begins to feel safe and supported.

When Things Feel Hard

Showing up on the hard days is the most important thing you can do for yourself, even if it's just for five minutes. There were many days in my own healing practice when I did not want to show up, when I would think "I don't feel like it today," or "I don't have the energy." On those days, I learned to stop trying to talk myself into doing more, and instead, I would quietly say, "Just do five minutes. Just sit down and see what happens."

Most of the time, something small would relax me, not in a big or dramatic way, but enough to feel a little different, and those five minutes would turn into more. Sometimes not so much, but either way, I had shown up for myself.

Eventually, I came to understand that this practice is not about forcing yourself into a better energetic state or waiting until you feel motivated. It is about offering yourself a safe place to land, especially on the days when things feel heavy and overwhelming.

If you have days like this, you are not alone, and you are not doing anything wrong. You are allowed to make the practice as small as you need it to be. It's okay.

What matters most is the slow building of trust with yourself, the kind that says, I am willing to meet myself where I am. That willingness, more than anything else, is what creates change over time. Small, sweet steps will get you further than any big leaps ever will.

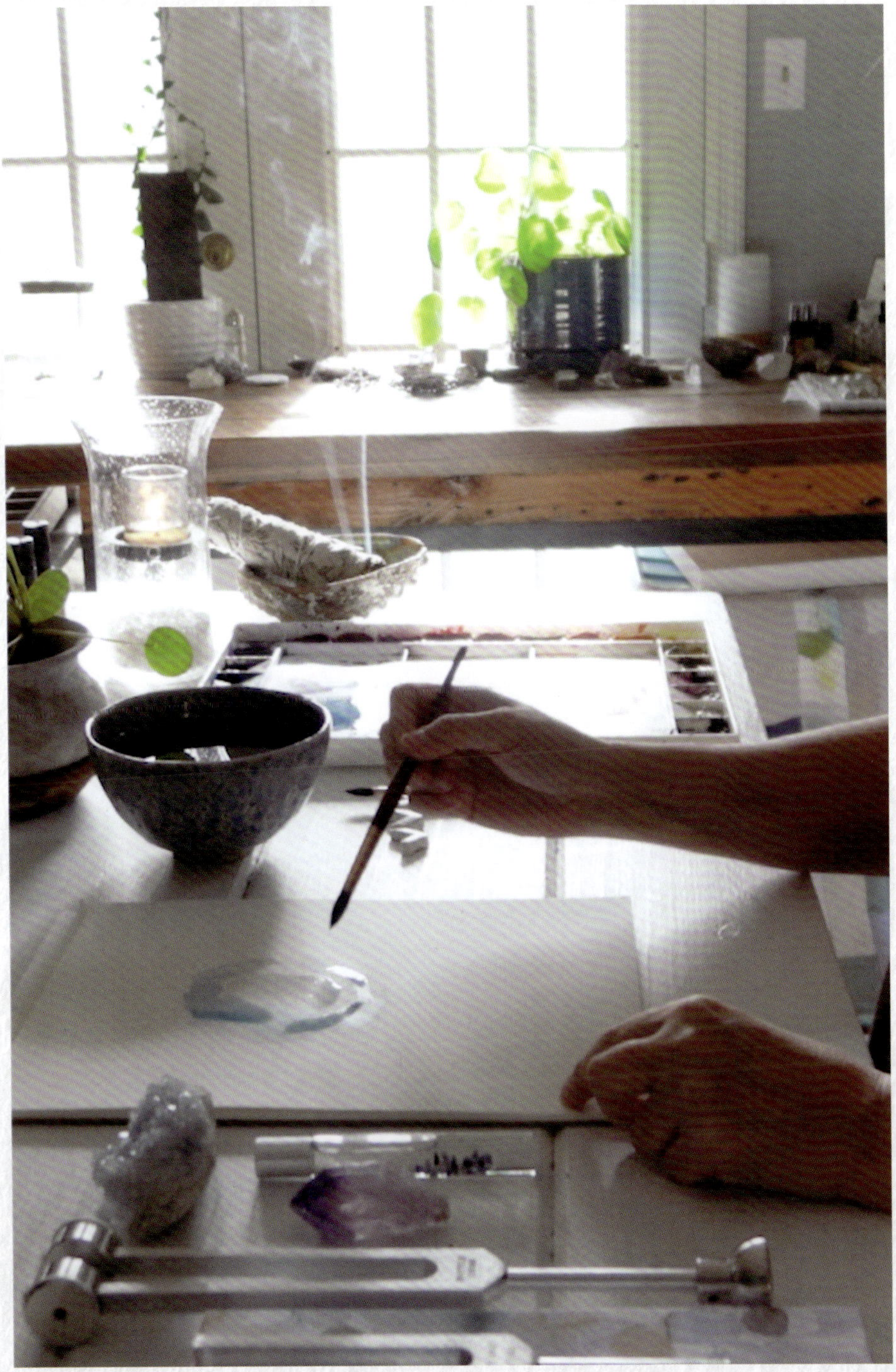

Building a Gentle Personal Practice

The more you practice, you may notice that certain lessons resonate more than others. It is perfectly okay to return to those again and again rather than feeling like you need to move on or try something new.

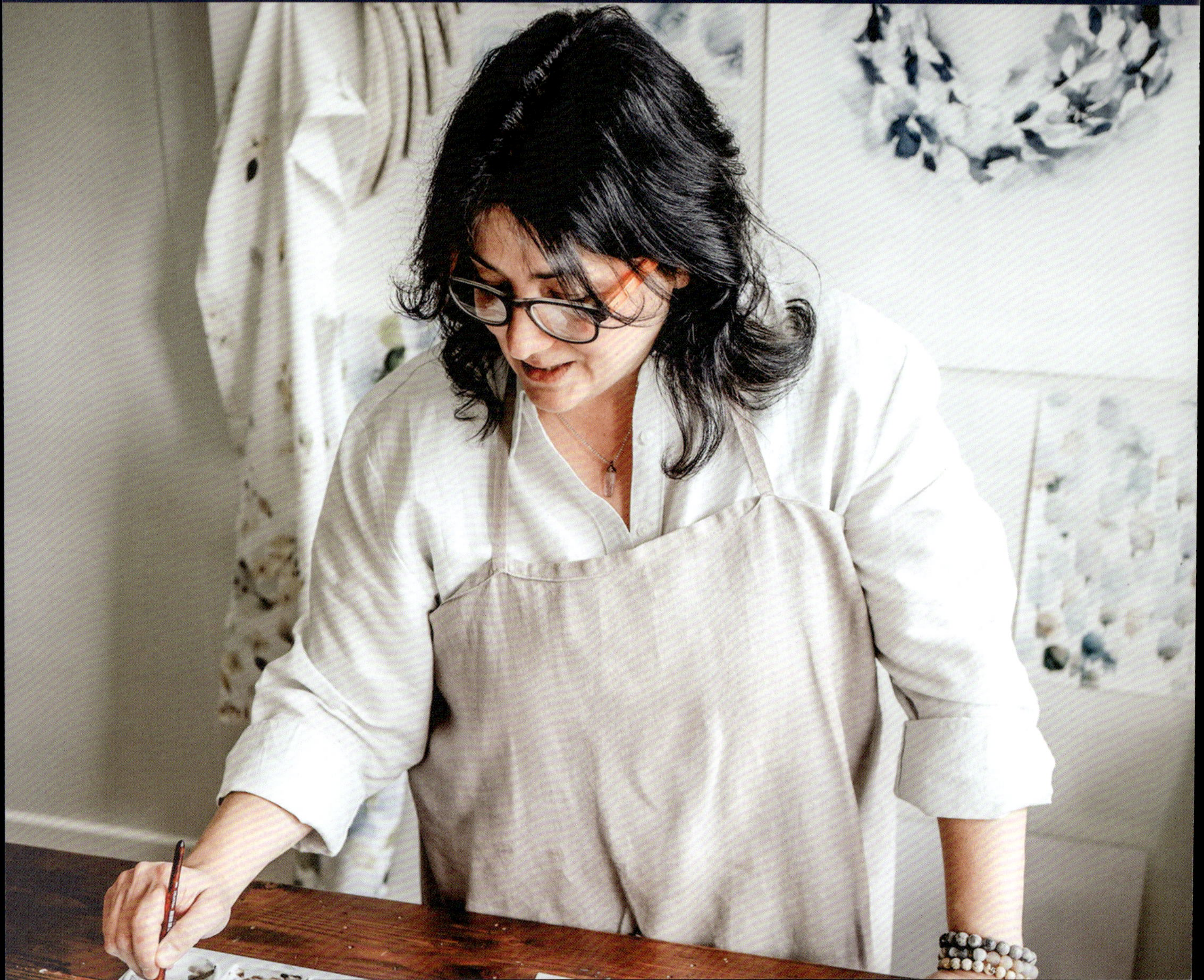

20

This painting practice is not about variety or progress in the traditional sense, but about creating rhythms that feel safe and steady inside your body.

You might return to a calming exercise from "Calm Your Mind" (Chapters 5 through 9) when your thoughts feel busy; choose a grounding exercise from "Connect to Your Body" (Chapters 10 through 14) when you feel tense or disconnected; or spend time with a heart-centered lesson (Chapters 15 through 19) when you are feeling tender and in need of gentleness.

A personal practice does not need to be long or complicated. It only needs to be consistent enough that your nervous system begins to recognize it as a place where it can relax and feel safe.

These small and consistent moments begin to create subtle shifts, and you may start to notice that your nervous system responds differently to the ups and downs of daily life.

Tracking Your Nervous System Over Time

As you work with these lessons, you may begin to notice small changes that are easy to miss if you are only looking for big breakthroughs. You may start to realize that you recover a little more quickly after a stressful moment or that your body feels slightly less tense than it used to. These kinds of shifts are meaningful because healing rarely happens all at once and more often unfolds quietly through small changes that build over time.

One of the most important things to understand about nervous system regulation is that it does not mean your life suddenly becomes calm or free of challenges. Stressful situations will still happen, and hard times will still come up. The difference is that you are slowly learning how to bring supportive tools with you into those moments, so your nervous system begins to experience that even when something is stressful, you are still here, you are still breathing, and you are still safe.

You do not need to track your progress in a formal way or keep detailed records unless that feels right for you. Simply noticing what you observe, with curiosity rather than judgment, is enough.

These small shifts begin to build on each other, quietly strengthening your ability to return to calm and steady yourself when life becomes difficult. That is nervous system regulation.

This practice was born out of a deep need for peace and healing, and it grew from a time in my life when I didn't really know what I was doing. I only knew that I felt a little better when I did it, and at the core, that truly is all that matters.

I hope you continue on with your painting practice, carrying these lessons with you and allowing them to expand in whatever ways feel right to you. The techniques in this book are simple enough to be applied to anything you feel inspired to paint, and you may begin to notice your own curiosity growing as you ask yourself what other kinds of shapes you might explore or how many different kinds of landscapes you could create. Every mandala can tell its own story, and every sacred circle can hold you however you need to be held. The more time you spend painting, the more the practice becomes something personal that grows alongside you.

Allow yourself to play, experiment, and remain curious. Let the practice evolve naturally, and trust that it will become whatever you need it to be.

A Final Invitation

If you carry one thing with you from this book, I hope it is the understanding that healing rarely happens in big dramatic moments. Far more often it unfolds through the quiet practices we return to again and again.

When I first began painting this way, I didn't think of it as nervous system regulation or meditation or healing. I was just looking for a way to relax and create. I knew that I always felt better when I was creating. I could easily get lost in the brushstrokes and find peace in the colors. Everything would quiet down, and for a little while, I felt more at home in my body.

For so long, I was searching for answers to my health challenges, trying to understand why I felt the way I did and how to make things better, and yet some of the most meaningful healing did not come from pushing harder or finding the perfect solution. They came from small moments of care that slowly added up over time.

Sitting down with a brush and a cup of water, watching color spread across the paper, and allowing the gentle movement of my hand to guide my attention back to the present moment gradually created a quiet place I could return to whenever life felt overwhelming. That is the spirit I hope this book leaves with you.

Some days your painting practice may feel deeply calming and restorative, and other days it may simply offer a few minutes of pause in the middle of a busy or stressful day. Both are meaningful, and both are part of the same gentle process of learning how to care for yourself in ways that feel supportive and sustainable.

You are building a relationship with yourself, a relationship rooted in patience, kindness, and the willingness to meet yourself exactly where you are. My heart is there with you, a silent partner in your journey, cheering you on, holding energetic space, and sending peaceful, healing energy to you.